P9-CKS-644

December 2006

Ross & BJ,
May next year bring a shift
left and the attendant bliss.
Sláinte, Craig

The Progressive Patriot

www.**booksattransworld**.co.uk

The Progressive Patriot
A Search for Belonging

BILLY BRAGG

BANTAM PRESS

LONDON · TORONTO · SYDNEY · AUCKLAND · JOHANNESBURG

TRANSWORLD PUBLISHERS
61–63 Uxbridge Road, London W5 5SA
a division of The Random House Group Ltd

RANDOM HOUSE AUSTRALIA (PTY) LTD
20 Alfred Street, Milsons Point, Sydney,
New South Wales 2061, Australia

RANDOM HOUSE NEW ZEALAND LTD
18 Poland Road, Glenfield, Auckland 10, New Zealand

RANDOM HOUSE SOUTH AFRICA (PTY) LTD
Isle of Houghton, Corner of Boundary Road and Carse O'Gowrie,
Houghton 2198, South Africa

Published 2006 by Bantam Press
a division of Transworld Publishers

Copyright © Billy Bragg 2006

The right of Billy Bragg to be identified as the author of this work has been asserted in
accordance with sections 77 and 78 of the Copyright, Designs and Patents Act 1988.

The quotation from *The Lion and the Unicorn* (copyright © George Orwell, 1941) is reproduced by permission of Bill
Hamilton as the Literary Executor of the Estate of the late Sonia Brownell Orwell, Martin Secker & Warburg Ltd.
The quotations from 'The River's Tale' and 'Puck's Song' by Rudyard Kipling are reproduced by permission of
A P Wyatt Ltd on behalf of The National Trust for Places of Historic Interest or Natural Beauty.
A Diary for Timothy: Crown copyright.
'The Boxer' copyright © 1968 Paul Simon, 'I Am A Rock' copyright © 1965 Paul Simon, 'Kathy's Song' copyright © 1965 Paul
Simon, 'Scarborough Fair (Canticle)' copyright © 1966 Paul Simon. Used by permission of the publisher: Paul Simon Music.

A catalogue record for this book is available from the British Library.
ISBN 9780593053430 (from Jan 07)
ISBN 0593053435

All rights reserved. No part of this publication may be reproduced, stored in a retrieval system,
or transmitted in any form or by any means, electronic, mechanical, photocopying, recording,
or otherwise, without the prior permission of the publishers.

Typeset in 11/16pt Sabon by
Falcon Oast Graphic Art Ltd.

Printed and bound in Great Britain by
Mackays of Chatham Ltd, Chatham, Kent

1 3 5 7 9 10 8 6 4 2

Papers used by Transworld Publishers are natural, recyclable products made from wood grown in sustainable
forests. The manufacturing processes conform to the environmental regulations of the country of origin.

To The Clash – the flame you lit is still burning bright.

Patriotism has nothing to do with Conservatism. It is actually the opposite of Conservatism, since it is a devotion to something that is always changing and yet is felt to be mystically the same. It is the bridge between the future and the past.

George Orwell, *The Lion and the Unicorn:*
Socialism and the English Genius

Contents

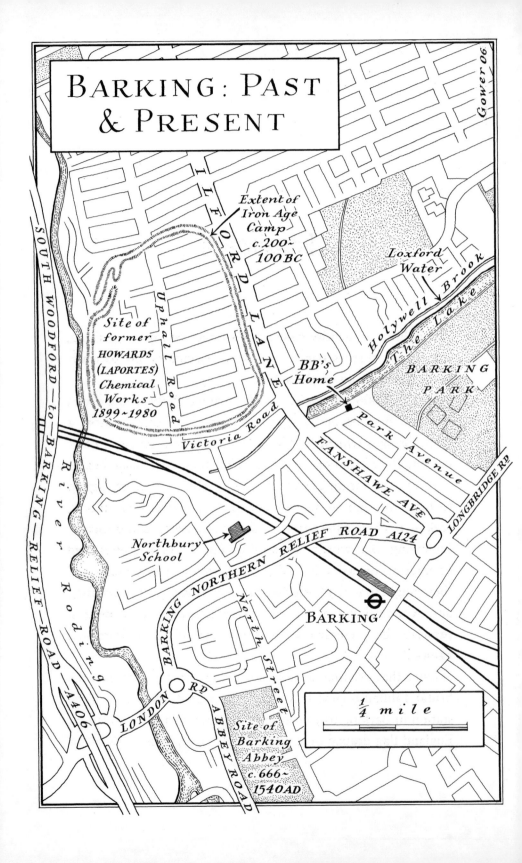

BARKING: PAST & PRESENT

Gower 06

Extent of
Iron Age
Camp
c.200-
100 BC

Loxford
Water

Holywell Brook

The Lake

ILFORD LANE

Uphall Road

Site of
former
HOWARDS
(LAPORTES)
Chemical
Works
1899~1980

BB's
Home

BARKING
PARK

SOUTH WOODFORD—to—BARKING—RELIEF—ROAD

River Roding

Victoria Road

Park Avenue

FANSHAWE AVE

LONGBRIDGE RD

Northbury
School

BARKING NORTHERN RELIEF ROAD A124

BARKING

North Street

BARKING—RELIEF—ROAD—A406

LONDON RD

ABBEY ROAD

Site of
Barking
Abbey
c.666~
1540 AD

¼ mile

Introduction

The politics of identity have always informed my songwriting, but it took three separate yet interconnected events to really focus my thinking on the subject.

In May 2006, the racist British National Party won a dozen seats on Barking and Dagenham Council in east London, a breakthrough which, for the first time, saw a far-right party become the official opposition in a British council chamber.

At the first meeting of the new assembly, the BNP attempted to force through an amendment to the council's constitution, seeking to change the nature of the commitment to anti-racism. Following the words 'Promoting equal opportunities and celebrating diversity by reducing all types of discrimination' they sought to insert 'including against the indigenous majority, and, while valuing everyone's culture, to recognize the need to preserve the pre-eminence of traditional British culture and values'.[1]

Later that evening, an Afghan immigrant who had fled the brutal Taliban regime was repeatedly knifed outside the Tube station in Barking town centre by four white men, who left an England flag draped over him before running off.[2]

The BNP, the self-proclaimed 'foremost patriotic political party in Great Britain', had come to town.

I'd long been suspicious of what passed for patriotism in England, finding it far too narrow and constricting for my tastes. The obsession with hierarchy and authority seemed designed to keep people like me in my place, and I felt sickened by the casual racism and quick-tempered belligerence that simmered beneath its surface.

Most of all, I resented the arbitrary power that patriotism claimed over my soul – the notion that because of my place of birth I should naturally share the same pride and prejudices as everyone else in my tribe.

At its heart, patriotism is a faith, one in which we were all brought up, and although most of us no longer observe it as dutifully as our parents and grandparents did, we remain familiar with its icons and rituals, introduced to us at school and reinforced throughout our culture.

As I grew older, however, I realized that, despite what I had been taught, my country was not the first or the best in the world, neither the greatest nor the mightiest, and certainly not the most just. Developing a more questioning approach to history, I came to regard the icons of patriotism as symbols of oppression, imperial domination and exploitation. The rituals of pomp and circumstance seemed designed to detract attention from the iniquities of the present by constant reference to a more glorious past. But I began to notice that more and more people were slipping out of the cinema before the national anthem was played.

Any residual patriotism I harboured was eventually knocked out of me by the sight of the neo-Nazi National Front marching through the streets in the 1970s, using the Union Jack as a symbol of their bigotry. The image of football hooligans rampaging through foreign cities, chanting my country's name, didn't help either. If these people were patriots, as they claimed to be, then I knew for sure that I wasn't.

During the 1980s, when patriotism became almost an ideology under the Tories, I found a new dissenting faith, internationalist in spirit, collective in principle, committed to social justice and determined to hold those in power to account. It countered the unquestioning loyalty demanded by patriotism with notions of solidarity that transcended nation, religion and race.

My conversion to this egalitarian movement was triggered by an event in my own country, which transformed my casual opposition to the far Right into a fully fledged engagement with left-wing politics. Having grown up in a household where politics was seldom if ever mentioned, the 1984 Miners' Strike provided me with my political education, teaching me to think in an ideological way, encouraging activism and offering me an alternative history of Britain.

At school, I had been taught that our history comprised little more than kings, queens and princes, supported by a cast of aristocratic admirals and generals. However, at rallies and meetings during the Miners' Strike, it was made clear that we were part of a long tradition of struggle in which the people won their rights from a ruling class that had opposed them all the way.

I learned that the freedom which I enjoyed had had to be fought for, from the Peasants' Revolt to the Diggers and the Levellers, from Captain Swing and Ned Ludd to the Chartists and the Suffragettes. For the first time I heard of Tom Paine and the Tolpuddle Martyrs, of the Ragged-Trousered Philanthropists and the Battle of Cable Street. I began to appreciate how my life had been shaped by the Labour land-slide of 1945 and the founding of the Welfare State. Here was our radical tradition and, by standing in solidarity with the miners, I was now part of it.

It felt like coming home.

And yet, there was something about England and what it meant to be English that I just couldn't shake off. During the heady days of punk rock, I had taken 'Route 66', that great hymn to the American highway, and 'translated' it into the English landscape, rewriting the lyrics as a love song to the A13, the biggest road in our neighbourhood, whose dual carriageway ran from London all the way to the kiss-me-quick fantasy land of Southend-on-Sea. If Springsteen could romanticize the industrial landscape of his New Jersey home, I didn't see why I couldn't do the same for estuarine Essex. There was a punk perversity in what I did, but there was also a genuine pride in singing about my own manor.

This sense of place continued to inform my songwriting. Tracks such as 'A New England' helped make my name as a solo performer. My experiences during the Miners' Strike inspired 'Between The Wars', its union banners and cradle-to-the-grave imagery evoking a very English sense of socialism. This thread continued throughout my work. Even my most political album, *The Internationale*, which featured songs from Ireland, Nicaragua and the USA, still had room for William Blake's 'Jerusalem'. Eventually, the Englishness that had always been an undercurrent in my work became explicit on my 2002 album *England, Half English*.

Not everyone in my audience was prepared for me to address such issues head on. I sought to sugar the pill by setting the lyrics of the title song to the tune of an Algerian exile's lament for his homeland. The original Arabic lyric contained the phrase 'Oh my country, oh my country, what a beautiful country you are,' the translation of which I sang at the close of my paean to Englishness.

When I first played the song before an audience, an old friend who shared my liberal beliefs queried the use of those lines, saying, 'You're being ironic, right?'

No, actually. I'm not.

I do love my country, in a similar manner to which I love my son.

My son is a part of me, and I want the best for him; I want him to flourish, to be at ease with himself, to be admired. But I recognize that he is not perfect, and when he makes mistakes I am compelled to speak out and correct him – I can't merely accept and applaud everything he does just because he's my son. Why not? Because I love him and I don't want him to grow up to be a spoiled brat whom others despise – I want him to understand that there are consequences for his actions in the wide world. When he lives up to my expectations, I am immensely proud. And when we're apart, I think of him every day.

If I love my country in the same way, does that make me a patriot? Well, no, not in the traditional sense. Patriots seem unable to accept any criticism, however constructive. They value loyalty above honesty, deference over respect. And yet I can't help but notice that patriots get upset when their country fails to live up to their expectations, just like I do. OK, the things that upset them are completely at odds with those things that trouble me, but at least we have something in common – like me, a patriot is someone who gives a shit about their country.

This has led me to wonder if there are types of patriotism that differ from the traditional model, that are forward-looking, honest, respectful of others. It may seem like an odd concept, but it's not without precedent.

There are clearly two different strains of nationalism. How else can you account for the diametrically opposed policies of the far-right British National Party and the left-of-centre Scottish National Party? While the BNP campaign vociferously for an end to immigration, the SNP are currently calling for an increase in migration to Scotland to help reverse the country's alarming decline in population. The BNP declares on its website that it exists 'to secure a future for the indigenous peoples of these islands in the North Atlantic which have been our homeland for millennia'. The SNP's statement of values on its website could not be more different. It begins: 'No one country and no one human being is worth more or less than any other.'

Which of these two opposing parties are the genuine nationalists – the racist BNP or the progressive SNP? And if it is possible to take a traditionally reactionary force such as nationalism and use it as a vehicle for promoting social justice, as the SNP do, is it possible to utilize patriotism in a similar manner?

Perhaps a more pertinent question is why would anybody want to consider doing something which, for many leftists, amounts to thinking the unthinkable? How does a rehabilitation of patriotism help the progressive cause?

Anyone with an interest in the social/political dialogue cannot have failed to have noticed that over the past decade the politics of identity have risen to the top of the agenda, while Marxist solutions to society's problems have disappeared from sight. It is an unpalatable yet none the less simple truth that you are much more likely to get elected in Britain today by proposing that we leave the EU than by calling for the abolition of capitalism.

Hostility towards immigration has been accompanied by a rediscovery of national identities in the wake of devolution. Margaret Thatcher's success in England during the 1980s had its counterpoint in electoral unpopularity in Scotland and Wales, where she was seen as being 'too British'. Her resultant negative attitude towards England's smaller neighbours had the effect of loosening the ties of union and strengthening the case for devolution.

Within a few years of the Conservatives losing power in 1997, the Labour government had created a Scottish parliament and a Welsh national assembly. Having demanded recognition and got it, the Scots and Welsh settled down to enjoy their new relationship with the British state.

The English appeared to view devolution with equanimity. Sure, there were one or two little niggles: on the 2001 Census in England and Wales, the ethnic options for white people were British, Irish or Other, while in Scottish households a Scottish option was included. The English were being deprived of their right to exist, claimed some, but then so were the Welsh.

Attempts were made to drum up anger about such obscure matters as the West Lothian Question and the Barnett Formula, but these were of interest only to political anoraks in the editorial columns. Nationalism, it seemed, just wasn't one of those things that the English did.

Yet something was stirring. Following the new devolution settlement, a major high-street greetings-card retailer began to mount in-store promotions for St George's Day, dressing its shop windows in red and white and offering a variety of celebratory cards to mark England's national day.

In 2003, the streets of London were flooded with thousands of people waving England's flag, the St George's Cross, in celebration of our victory in the rugby world cup.

The summer of 2004 saw the spontaneous appearance of thousands of English flags, many of them flying from car windows, in support of the national team playing in the European Football Championships.

In 2005, crowds filled Trafalgar Square in central London waving the St George's flag and singing William Blake's 'Jerusalem' – England's unofficial national anthem – following the victory of the English cricket team in a thrilling Ashes series against Australia.

Not everyone is comfortable with these developments. Some baulk at any flag-waving by the English. All those years of allowing racists to hijack our national symbols have done their damage. The belligerent behaviour of a minority of English football fans abroad has also done much to alienate people from their flag. The emergence of the British National Party, which since 2002 has begun to pick up council seats in England, is cited as further proof that this resurgence in flag-waving is a sign of an ugly nationalism taking hold among the English.

Concern about flag-waving is not merely a knee-jerk re-action to celebration of English nationhood. It has to be recognized that, whereas Scottish and Welsh nationalism are articulated by parties whose politics are to the left of New Labour on most issues, nationalism in England has found its voice through the BNP, a self-declared whites-only party with links to the European neo-Nazi movement.

Clearly, the vast majority of people flying the England flag in support of our national team are not racists and deserve to be able to express their national pride without being condemned as bigots. However, when viewed alongside the rising popularity of the BNP, the issues raised by this new sense of assertiveness must be addressed.

For the English, these are uncertain times. Devolution has given new confidence to Scotland and Wales, while casting doubt on the future of the UK and England's primary position within it. At the same time, the European Union has expanded and is seeking new powers to make it a major player on the global stage. Both these developments threaten to diminish Britain's – for which read England's – importance.

Over the past few years, articles have appeared in the national press bemoaning the fact that the majority are prevented from speaking their minds by a liberal media intent on promoting multiculturalism. The cultural sensitivity shown towards minorities within society is not, they claim, afforded to the culture of the majority population. Radio phone-ins on the subject of 'Englishness' are regularly deluged with callers who complain bitterly that they are 'no longer allowed to be English'. When challenged, none are able to say exactly who is banning them from 'being English' or even what such behaviour might entail. None the less, their perception of being discriminated against remains, along with the irritation it clearly causes them.

This sense of disconnection is not confined to Little Englanders alone. The constitutional pressure group Charter88 recently highlighted people's frustration with the way the political system seems to be stifling debate rather than promoting it. It warns that growing numbers of people are beginning to lose their faith in the ability of democracy to make a difference to their lives.[3]

When such a sense of powerlessness creeps over a society, there is a tendency for the majority to seek ways of reasserting their status as the primary group within the nation. The reasons why such an urge might manifest itself in twenty-first-century Britain are complex: the pressures of working in the deregulated job market, where 'flexibility' means living with the constant threat of being fired; the recent record increase in immigration, leading to greater competition for resources; the dizzying pace of change in a globalized economy – all have contributed to a general sense of insecurity that has not been assuaged by affluence.

These feelings are particularly strong amongst the poor – the visible retreat of the state over the past decades has left those without skills or opportunities with the feeling that nobody cares what happens to them. Whatever the causes, history warns us to beware of politicians who seek to exploit such feelings of desertion and disenfranchisement for their own ends.

Fascism, the ideology which seeks to benefit from the anxieties thrown up by the sense that nobody is listening to the majority, was not, in its original form, inherently anti-Semitic. The movement which Mussolini led to power in Italy in 1922 was open to, and supported by, Jew and Gentile alike. Initially a reaction to the threat of communism, Italian fascism was also hostile to the values of liberal democracy, opposed egalitarianism and was fuelled by an ultra-nationalist modernism personified by its leader, Il Duce. It was not until 1938 that Mussolini introduced anti-Semitic legislation in order to strengthen his ties with Hitler.[4]

The rise of Italian fascism should also be viewed in the context of the new balance of power in Europe following the First World War. Italy had gained territory and prestige from the Treaty of Versailles and Mussolini sought to exploit this new status by staking a claim as a European power, enhancing the pride – and thus earning the support – of the majority of Italians.

For Germany, however, Versailles was a deep psychological blow. Prussian militarism had been the driving political force since the country was unified as a nation state in the wake of the Franco-Prussian War of 1870–71. Defeat on the Western Front, followed by the loss of territory and colonial possessions, along with the severe reparations demanded by the victorious Allies, angered many Germans, who saw Versailles as an unjust way of continuing the war by other means. The 'War Guilt' clause in the treaty, which required Germany to accept the blame for causing the war, only added to the sense of national humiliation.

Defeat also resulted in Germany becoming a democracy overnight. The fledgling Weimar government struggled to get the economy back on its feet, but the pressures of living under the conditions of the Treaty of Versailles proved too difficult. When, in 1923, the German government defaulted on reparation payments, French and Belgian troops occupied the industrial Ruhr, which during the difficult post-war years had been the most productive region of Germany.

Resentment at such treatment and at the economic hardship that accompanied hyperinflation did not lead directly to the emergence of Adolf Hitler, but a perception among ordinary Germans that liberal democracy had been imposed upon them, and was thus part of the punishment meted out at Versailles, made them more susceptible to the anti-democratic forces of fascism.

Stripped of their monarchy and empire, their rigidly controlled society opened up to modern ideas of equality and representation, and finding themselves maligned by international opinion, a powerful need arose among the German people to reassert their primacy as the majority group within society. Crucial to this urge to express their sense of superiority was the need to identify an inferior group among the population on whom to vent their frustrations. Hitler simply provided them with a target for this inarticulate rage.

There had been Jewish communities in Germany since Roman times, but their numbers had been swollen in the late nineteenth and early twentieth century by Jewish refugees fleeing the Russian Empire following violent pogroms. These immigrants, crossing into Germany from modern-day Poland and Ukraine, were often destitute and were unable to return home in fear for their lives.

The presence of 'outsiders' can be a cause of friction in times of economic and social insecurity, and in such circumstances populist politicians are able to benefit from stirring up irrational fears among the indigenous population. Under the leadership of Adolf Hitler, German fascism took on a virulently anti-Semitic tone. When the Nazis came to power in 1933, Hitler's guiding principle was the restoration of the superiority of the German people. In order to achieve this, he plunged the whole of humanity into the abyss.

The Nazis were not a specifically German phenomenon, but a terrible illustration of what can happen in any society if the urge of the majority to reassert itself is taken to the extreme. The Rwandan genocide of 1994 is a recent example of such behaviour, when militias from the Hutu majority murdered an estimated one million members of the Tutsi minority and their sympathizers.

Worryingly, there are signs that, across the developed world, anxious majorities are beginning to lash out at the minorities in their midst. In Spain, the government is being urged to stop the 'avalanche' of illegal immigrants who try to enter the EU via the Canary Islands. French MPs recently supported a controversial immigration bill making settlement in France harder for unskilled workers. Holland, a country known for its liberal policies, now has Europe's most stringent immigration requirements for would-be immigrants. Even the USA, a nation built upon immigration, has called for a tightening of its borders in order to discourage migrant workers.

The events of 11 September 2001 have further fuelled fears of 'the other', exacerbating tensions between indigenous and immigrant communities. Muslims particularly have been identified as holding values contrary to those of the host country.

In response to the horrific attacks on London by Islamist suicide bombers on 7 July 2005, calls for a reassertion of British values in a manner which unequivocally proclaimed their innate superiority appeared in the press. Within a year, the BNP had risen to become the main opposition party on Barking and Dagenham Council and immediately set about making their case for the pre-eminence of indigenous culture and values.

The BNP are clearly hoping to take advantage of the insecurities of the majority. The fact that, in some areas, the English are susceptible to their politics of race hate should be cause for alarm. The BNP are bigots whose policies are

designed to stir up division among neighbours. Their arguments are built on lies concocted in order to cynically
manipulate the genuine concerns of ordinary people. Their
presence in an area often leads to a rise in racial assaults.

So how best to counter them? Deny them a platform for their
views? That has been the policy of the anti-fascist movement
for over a decade, yet does not seem to have stemmed the tide.
Should we ban them and arrest their leaders? That would
surely be counter-productive – Adolf Hitler gained greater
credibility among his supporters while he was in jail. A
different approach is required, one that directly addresses the
need of the majority to feel that its culture and heritage are
given due prominence.

For the past thirty years, the Left has been fighting fascism
with one hand tied behind its back. Our egalitarian support for
internationalism has prevented us from properly engaging in
the debate over identity. Reluctant to make any concessions to
reactionary nationalism, we have, by default, created a
vacuum, leaving it to the likes of the BNP and the *Daily Mail*
to decide who does and who doesn't belong here.

Regardless of whether or not we feel comfortable discussing
such things, the coming years will see a growing debate about
the nature of 'Britishness'. The introduction of ID cards will
impose a form of belonging on us all – whether we want one
or not. So far, much of the discussion has centred around the
notion of 'British values'. What these might constitute has not
yet been established. To some, they offer a return to the mores
of the 1950s. Others see them as a vehicle for withdrawal from
the EU. Cynics suggest that our core values amount to little
more than over-indulgence and fecklessness.

Elsewhere, though, a debate has begun which looks beyond

simplistic notions of values towards more solid concepts of citizenship, such as rights and responsibilities. The British have a fine tradition of campaigning for their liberties, particularly the right to be included within the protection of the law, which dates all the way back to Magna Carta. The Left have been the traditional champions of this struggle, a fact which offers us an opportunity to engage in the debate about what it means to be British on our own terms. In order to join this debate, we need to address issues of identity and belonging in the context of equality and rights, using examples from within our national culture.

Critics may carp that our commitment to egalitarianism under-mines our ability to make the case for British values; that our insistence that rights must be universal is a betrayal of the indigenous majority; that we are full of self-loathing for our own heritage and people; that, ultimately, our loyalties lie elsewhere.

These charges need to be countered with arguments from our history; we must tease out stories of the struggles and cam-paigns that won us the rights that we enjoy; we must prove that these episodes mean as much to us as the Battle of Trafalgar does to the traditionalists. They must be constantly reminded that we, too, have our own traditions and are proud of them.

Some would argue that this process has already begun, citing the Durham Miners Gala and the Tolpuddle Martyrs Festival as examples of how we come together to celebrate our collec-tivist heritage. However, if we hope to win the debate about who does or does not belong in our society, we need to go beyond our own territory in order to convince the majority that we have their interests at heart.

We need to challenge the Right's monopoly on patriotism, not by proclaiming our blind loyalty to our country, right or wrong, but by developing a narrative which explains how we all came to be here together in this place, and how successive generations of those who were initially excluded from society came to feel that this was where they belonged.

This book is an attempt to identify that narrative. It does not seek to define such flimsy concepts as 'Britishness' or 'Englishness', nor their supposed mirror image, 'multiculturalism'. Instead, by exploring those things which, after years of feeling alienated by my country, have contributed to my own sense of belonging, it aims to reconcile patriotism with the radical tradition.

1
Apollo in Essex

If you see me performing in concert, the night will invariably end with a ritual declaration of identity: 'My name is Billy Bragg, I'm from Barking, Essex. Thank you very much. Goodnight.' Although it's now over twenty years since I last lived there, I've always been conscious of where I come from – happy when my home town does well, disappointed when we let ourselves down, offended when outsiders make disparaging remarks.

By identifying myself strongly with Essex, I have sought to counter the negative stereotype that was foisted on the county in the 1980s. 'Essex Man' was a term invented to demonize the newly affluent white working class, whose predilection for sovereign rings and right-wing Thatcherism made them into folk devils in the eyes of the predominantly middle-class media. Such people did undoubtedly exist, but they lived all over the South-East, fiercely protective of their family and property, dismissive of the Welfare State, and English to the point of belligerence.

While everyone in the country saw Essex through the

distorted prism of the 'Essex Man' cliché, declaring that I was from Barking was a reaction to growing up in the suburban obscurity of one of London's many satellite towns. In my youth, I longed to come from somewhere glamorous or, better, notorious. As it was, I came from the place most kids come from: Nowheresville.

Identifying myself with my home town – to the extent that I gained the nickname 'The Bard of Barking' – was my way of helping to put the town on the map. After twenty years, however, Barking remained, for most people, little more than another stop along the eastern end of the District Line.

Then, seemingly overnight, the town was catapulted to national prominence. The notoriety that I had longed for as a youth had finally arrived in the shape of the British National Party. The most recent manifestation of the British fascist movement, the BNP was founded in 1982 by former National Front leader, John Tyndall. A devout follower of Adolf Hitler, Tyndall once stated that '*Mein Kampf* is my Bible.'[1] The current leader, Nick Griffin, has sought to obscure the party's Nazi roots in the hope of gaining greater legitimacy, although he felt confident enough to claim recently in the *Mail on Sunday* that the gas chambers at Auschwitz were built after the war.[2]

In the local council elections in May 2006, the BNP surprised everyone when they won a dozen seats on Barking and Dagenham Council. In terms of national politics, this was meaningless – the BNP won only thirty seats across the country, on a night when over three thousand were up for grabs. On a local scale, however, it was a disaster. The BNP had won handfuls of seats before, mostly in the former mill towns of the North-West, but the result in Barking and Dagenham represented a real breakthrough. The Tories and Liberal Democrats had been decimated and, although Labour held on to thirty-nine seats, for the first time a fascist party had become the official opposition in a council chamber. Within twenty-four hours, headlines began to speak of Barking and Dagenham as the race-hate capital of Britain.

I was shocked at the scale of the BNP's gains. I've been actively opposing racism all my adult life – it was the cause that first politicized me – and the BNP are just the latest manifestation of a neo-Nazi strain that I first encountered in the 1970s in the form of the National Front.

Now the fascists had a power base in my home town. And this wasn't some electoral fluke whereby the two main parties had split and the BNP benefited by scraping in through the middle. They had won in every ward in which they had put up candidates – in fact, of the thirteen BNP candidates who stood, only one had failed to be elected. Had they managed to put up a full slate, they may well have won control of the council.

The result was a bombshell. Barking has been under Labour control since the town council was formed in 1931. When the London borough was created by the amalgamation of Barking and neighbouring Dagenham in 1965, Labour Party control continued uninterrupted.

This was Labour's heartland, yet the BNP had been able to take a dozen seats off Labour, and do so with the support of large numbers of traditional Labour voters to boot. The recriminations started immediately as people cast around for something – or someone – to blame. The warning signs had been there: the BNP had won a seat in a council by-election two years before with a massive 52 per cent of the vote. Then, a year later, in the General Election, the fascists had their best result in the country in Barking, almost beating the Tories into second place – a mere thirty votes separated the two.

My sense of disbelief soon gave way to anger that the BNP had targeted my home town, flooding the streets with activists, going from door to door stirring up bigotry, seeking to exploit the genuine concerns of local residents for their own divisive ends. I was disturbed by the ease of their victory. But most of all I was dismayed by the signal that this result would send to the rest of the country. Barking, I feared, would become a by-word for intolerance, a place where incomers were not welcome, an openly racist town in the midst of multicultural London.

My own sense of identity was shaken. Was this the true face of my home town? Like any other area of suburban sprawl, there had always been racial incidents in Barking, especially in the hard and heavy years of the 1970s, but most of the time the different communities had rubbed along together. Now I wasn't so sure. Were these my people? Was this my heritage? I began to ask myself if there was any pride left in being able to declare that I was from Barking, Essex.

When I was born there in 1957, Barking actually was in Essex. A red shield depicting three Saxon swords – the county's coat of arms – adorned the school books of my infant days until, in 1965, the town, along with several others in the south-west corner of the county, became part of the newly created administrative area of Greater London.

Overnight, the old Essex municipal boroughs, most bearing names that appeared in the Domesday Book, lost their distinctive identities. Ilford, Wanstead and Woodford merged to create Redbridge; Romford and Hornchurch became Havering; West Ham and East Ham were amalgamated to form Newham, while Chingford, Leytonstone and Walthamstow disappeared into Waltham Forest. Even Dagenham, site of the Ford Motor factory, economic linchpin of the whole area, found itself incorporated into the only former Essex borough that was allowed to retain its identity: the London Borough of Barking.

What was so special about our town that it should be saved from civic extinction? The answer lay in its history. When these other towns were still villages, Barking was the home of the largest fishing fleet in England. When these villages were hamlets, Barking was a great ecclesiastical centre. When the Domesday Book was written, Barking was the second most highly populated town in Essex. And in the years before Caesar came with his legions and the history of Britain began, when all around was nothing more than bare heath and marshland, an earthwork bank enclosed a settlement larger than any other in south-east England on the spot where Barking would one day stand.

The source of this prominence was the river. Barking sits on the north bank of the Thames, some seven miles east of London Bridge, at a point where the river bends sharply. Ships entering or leaving the nearby Royal Docks would have to negotiate this bend while avoiding other river traffic travelling between the Pool of London and the sea.

During my childhood, the Thames was still busy with commerce, and on those evenings when a thick mist drifted up from the river, sometimes as I lay in bed I would hear the distant blast of a ship's horn as the skipper attempted to round the blind corner at Gallions Reach, the mournful sound carried into town by the strange acoustic properties of the fog.

The Gallions Hotel, built on the north bank of that bend in

the river, opened in the early 1880s to serve passengers for the P&O liners that worked the Far East routes out of the Royal Docks. Rudyard Kipling mentions the place in his first novel, *The Light That Failed*. His work was the only poetry to be found in our house when I was growing up, which explains why he gets quoted in my lyrics as often as Bob Dylan and the Clash.

I first came into contact with Kipling as a cub scout, learning the story of *The Jungle Book* at source, before it was Disneyfied for popular consumption. More to my taste was Kipling's other Indian boy-hero, Kim.

Looked upon now as an anachronistic Boy's Own tale from the days of the British Raj, *Kim* is, none the less, a great adventure story. Yes, most of the book's characters are racial stereotypes speaking a caricature of the English language, and, to modern ears, the things they say sound at best quaint and at worst plain offensive. However, the same charges could be levelled at Mark Twain's *The Adventures of Huckleberry Finn*. The two books were published within seven years of one another and their young protagonists have much in common. Like Huck, Kim O'Hara is a young white boy 'of the very poorest', as Kipling relates. Both children have absent parents and share a dogged determination not to be 'civilized' by the adults they encounter. The title conferred on Kim, 'Little Friend of All the World' would equally suit Huck.

The books are similar in content, too, with narratives that centre around travels undertaken with an 'alien' companion: Kim journeys through British India with a Tibetan lama, while Huck traverses the Old South with a black slave. Twain's liberal use of the term 'nigger' has caused consternation to some, as does the threat of the Irish padre to make a man of

Kim – 'a white man and a good man' – by saving him from the native Indian company in which he delights. Although I found *Huckleberry Finn* a difficult read as a child, I now recognize it as an American masterpiece. *Kim* drew me in immediately, as an adventure story should. Both are classic books for boys.

My father was a great fan of Kipling. Having been born in Barking in the 1920s, Dad hadn't really been much further than the Essex countryside, which, when he was a boy, began just a mile or so from the terraced street where he grew up. An only child, he enjoyed reading and put great store in the 'book learning' that was to be had from encyclopedias and compendiums. He was doing well enough in his final year at secondary school to lead his parents to believe that he might continue his studies, but within a few months of him leaving school, aged fifteen, the Second World War broke out, effectively ending any thoughts of further education.

During the London Blitz, Dad worked as a control-room messenger, helping to keep communications open in the aftermath of air attacks on Barking. He also spent some time in the Home Guard. When he turned eighteen, in 1942, he enlisted in the Royal Armoured Corps, becoming a tank-driver and mechanic.

Sent to India to prepare for the invasion of Japanese-held Malaya planned for the following September, the 43rd Royal Tank Regiment arrived in Hyderabad in August 1945. But no sooner had Dad and his comrades set up camp than the atom bombs were dropped on Hiroshima and Nagasaki and the Japanese surrendered. The war was over. There would be no invasion of Malaya.

However, any thoughts of a swift return to England were dashed by the Viceroy, Field Marshal Wavell. Back home, the newly elected Labour government had decided that Britain should quit India and Wavell was tasked with conducting an orderly withdrawal. It wasn't to be.

In the event, bloody rioting broke out between Hindu and Muslim communities, who both wanted to stake their own claims to post-imperial nationhood. British troops were constantly called out to quell this unrest and the tanks of the 43rd Royal Tank Regiment were able to passively assist in operations as they were equipped with hugely powerful search-lights. These were called CDLs – canal defence lights – and had initially been developed to illuminate targets on the far side of the numerous canals and rivers that the Allies would encounter as they advanced into Germany. Once the war in Europe had ended, the tanks were earmarked for the jungles of Malaya, where their thirteen million candle-power searchlights, which at a thousand yards produced a beam 340 yards wide and 35 yards high, would make it possible to engage the enemy at night. Instead they were deployed to great effect along the Chowringhee Road in Calcutta during the riots in February 1946.

As a result of the ongoing civil unrest, my father found him-self spending the two years from 1945 to 1947 as one of the last soldiers of the British Raj, helping to police the partition of India.

Dad brought a love of Rudyard Kipling home from India with him and Kipling brought India into our living room. Not the high pomp of 'If' or 'Recessional', nor the imperial hubris of 'The White Man's Burden' – what my father enjoyed most was the khaki Kipling of *The Barrack-Room Ballads*.

This was soldiers' poetry with a broad cockney accent, set to the rhythms of an East End music hall, familiar to me from the old songs that my maternal grandmother would play on the piano by ear, leading us all in raucous singing when the family got together at her house for parties.

Kipling was criticized for his use of colloquial language when the collection was published – as was Mark Twain for the prevalence of dialects in *Huckleberry Finn* – but these ballads were not from drawing-rooms or club-rooms but from the barracks, domicile of the ordinary British soldier, known to the late-Victorian public as Tommy Atkins.

Kipling's ear for the vernacular gives the reader a sense that one is sharing a pipe and some porter with a bunch of old sweats, listening to their complaints and reminiscences: how can a man survive on a pension of a 'Shillin' a Day' after all we've seen and done? D'you remember 'em hanging 'Danny Deever' in the morning? Christ, what a show that was! The 'Fuzzy-Wuzzy' – now there was a first-class fightin' man; 'ere's to 'The Widow at Windsor . . . and Missus Victorier's sons, poor beggars!'

My father was fond of quoting the ballads, and from his lips they sounded like nothing less than the voices of our warrior ancestors, handed down by oral tradition. This sense, of old tales told over camp fires long ago, was never stronger than when Kipling spoke of our home town.

Browsing one rainy lunchtime in the school library, I came across a fragment of a poem he had written called 'The River's Tale', which spoke of the prehistory of the London area:

> And Norseman and Negro and Gaul and Greek
> Drank with the Britons in Barking Creek.

This vision of a multicultural past certainly chimed with my contemporary experience, reflecting the diversity of my classmates, whose parents had come to Barking to seek work at the car factory. But the two lines of poetry also struck a deeper chord, hinting at a knowledge of local folklore.

One bright Sunday morning, as we waited for the Woolwich ferry to take us over the Thames, my father had pointed to the high land across the river to the south of Barking. It was along this ridge, he told me, that Julius Caesar marched his five legions in 54 BC, searching for a place to ford the river. When he came to where Shooters Hill Road runs today, Caesar would have had a panoramic view of the London area. Of course, there was no Londinium for him to cast eyes on; it had not yet been built. The largest site of human habitation he would have seen, my father assured me, was the massive settlement of Uphall Camp, rising from the marshes across the river on the banks of Barking Creek.

Reading those lines from 'The River's Tale' set me to wondering whether Kipling had heard that story too. Stephen Pewsey, in his notes accompanying the Godfrey Edition reprint of the 1894 Ordnance Survey of Beckton, mentions that Kipling once stayed at the Gallions Hotel en route to the East. While he waited for the tide to turn, did someone mention the local antiquity still to be seen just a few miles north on the banks of the River Roding, which flows into the Thames at Barking Creek?

Perhaps Kipling had taken a stroll across the levels to the Roding, following its meandering course past Cuckold's Haven, crossing over to the eastern bank by the town quay at the Six Gates crossing. From there, a brief walk to the far end of North Street and a careful crossing of the London, Tilbury and Southend railway line would have brought him out into open fields just south of the prehistoric monument known as Uphall Camp. Back then, its southern ramparts were almost ploughed out, although they were visible enough to become the parish boundary between Barking and Ilford when the latter was created from the former in 1888.

Following the footpath across the camp to the north-east quadrant, Kipling would have found an impressive twelve-foot-high section of surviving earth rampart. Walking to the north-west corner and climbing Lavender Mount, a conical feature now thought to have been a seventeenth-century mill mound, he would have been able to take in the enormous scale of the area once enclosed by the ancient earthworks.

From the top of the Mount, he would also have appreciated the camp's close proximity to the Roding, which formed its western boundary, perhaps realizing that such easy access to Barking Creek and the Thames, two miles to the south, would bring the inhabitants into contact with people from the continent and beyond. Perhaps he had this spot in mind when he wrote 'The River's Tale'?

The site is still marked as an antiquity on some maps and the last vestiges of the earthworks were said to be still visible in the year I was born, but since the early twentieth century the remains of Uphall Camp have slowly disappeared beneath industrial development and housing. In 1899, Howards Chemical Works, covering all the western half of the site, began producing a great diversity of products, including quinine, luminous paint, solvents, munitions and, most famously, aspirin.

By 1900, the eastern half of the camp was covered by several hundred two-up, two-down terraced houses. The Victorian town-planners, unable to say with any accuracy who had actually inhabited the settlement that they were about to obliterate, decided to hedge their bets, naming the first four streets they built Roman Road, Saxon Road, Dane Road and Norman Road respectively.

By the 1980s, the chemical works had closed down and the factory was demolished to make way for more houses. The site was so toxic that highly specialized techniques were needed to clear the area in order to make it safe for habitation. Huge white double-skinned tents were erected, beneath which workers toiled in contamination-proof suits to protect themselves from the noxious residue of over eighty years of chemical processes.

Peculiar and unpleasant smells emanated from the site. Radioactive materials such as thorium were discovered buried in dumps. The level of contamination was so great that it was considered too serious a health hazard to transport the waste through the streets by lorry. Instead, the developers took the extraordinary step of constructing a rail siding on the site, which connected with the main London-to-Southend line which passes near by. In this manner, over 300,000 tons of contaminated material were removed, much of it topsoil. Later, the railway was used to bring in new, clean topsoil from elsewhere.[3]

During this period, archaeologists were given the opportunity to explore the site, although, due to the high levels of contamination, their excavations were limited to a small area that had been the allotment gardens of the factory workers and the eastern bank of the Roding, just beyond the limits of the chemical works. It was thanks to their efforts that the importance of Uphall Camp and its relationship with the river began to emerge.

The River Roding takes its name from a group of villages in central Essex where the river rises. However, *The Victoria County History of Essex* states that 'The Roding was known before the sixteenth century as the Hile (recorded in AD 958), a British name from which that of Ilford is derived.'[4]

British, in this context, means the people who inhabited the area before the Romans came. The Victorian town-planners had got it wrong – Uphall Camp had not been built by Romans, Saxons, Danes or Normans, but by the Ancient Britons. They were the people whom we know today as the Celts and the language they spoke – Brythonic – evolved into modern Welsh. The names that the Celts gave to their settlements have all but disappeared from places subsequently settled by the English-speaking peoples, but we are reminded of their presence in the names of our rivers: Avon, Aire, Derwent, Exe, Ouse, Stour, Severn, Thames, and Trent are, like Hile, believed to be Celtic in origin.[5]

It is possible to gain some insight into the pronunciation of the name Hile by reference to historical documents. The Domesday Book calls Ilford 'Ilefort' in 1086. A medieval document renders it as 'Hileford'. The latest evidence for the name comes from a map dated 1577, where the river is marked as the 'Iuell'.[6] These sources suggest that, despite the fact that it gives us the 'il' of modern Ilford, 'Hile' is a two-syllable word pronounced 'hi-yl'. Modern Welsh, which has evolved from the language of the Ancient Britons, contains a word that is pronounced 'hi-yl': *haul*, the sun.[7]

That this word, or one very similar to it, was being used in antiquity is indicated by the fact that the two other branches of the Brythonic language, Cornish and Breton, which split from Welsh after the Roman occupation, both contain similar words

29

for sun: *howl* in Cornish[8] and *hoel* in Breton.[9] Given this evidence, it is possible to speculate that the ancient Celts knew the Roding in their own language as 'The River of the Sun'.

Although the exact nature of their religious beliefs is far from clear, there is strong archaeological evidence that the Celts venerated rivers. The Iron Age people deposited high-status metalwork objects such as swords and shields into rivers as a ritualistic way of honouring the spirit of the place. The Thames seems to have been a particular focus for this practice, given the number of exotic objects that have been recovered from it over the years.

Could the ancient British name of the Roding connect the river with the worship of a solar deity, and Uphall Camp be a focus for the veneration of a sun god? Pamela Greenwood, who excavated the site in the late 1980s, observes that 'Uphall Camp, still impressive and imposing in the Roman period, and endowed with a spring, may have led people to give it a religious or ritual significance [as] a focus for specific activities.'[10]

The connection between the site and water rituals is further suggested by the old name of Loxford Water, a stream that runs into the Roding beside Uphall Camp. *The Victoria County History of Essex* states that 'The present name, first recorded in 1609, is probably a back-formation from that of the manor of Loxford. In 1456 the lower part of the stream (where it passes the Camp) was called Halywellbrooke.'[11] This name – a corruption of Holy Well Brook – offers evidence of a water cult at the site. There are still many holy wells to be found in Britain, although their veneration tends to have been confined to the 'Celtic fringes' of western Britain. They were traditionally endowed with healing properties.

The presence of a healing spring on a site associated with the worship of the sun may give us a hint as to the name of the settlement. Given that the major Greek, Roman and local gods were interchangeable across the Empire, could it be that the Romans, arriving in AD 43 and learning that the local Celtic people used the site to worship a healing solar god, simply named the place after their equivalent deity, Apollo? If so, then the modern name of Uphall Camp may be a distant echo of the name that the conquering Romans gave to the site – 'Apollo's Camp'.

What is clear is that some time during the second century BC, the local Iron Age population constructed a massive enclosure on the eastern bank of the River of the Sun. Built on a well-drained knoll atop the gravel terraces that border the Thames marshlands, it occupied a strong strategic position overlooking the whole area. With ramparts at least six metres high and external ditches several metres deep and wide, it would have been an impressive sight. Five hundred and fifty metres in length and between 400 and 500 metres wide, with an enclosed area of some 65 acres, its only contemporary rivals in scale would have been the hillforts that sprang up in the south and west of Britain during the Iron Age, though the greatest of these, Maiden Castle in Dorset, is only 43 acres, little more than two thirds the size of Apollo's Camp.[12]

Although only able to excavate a mere 2.5 acres of the site, the archaeologists found evidence of a great deal of activity from the Celtic period. An imported shale bracelet was re-covered, along with three 'potin' coins. These are cast from tin-rich bronze and are believed to be the earliest coins produced in Britain, dating from around the time the camp was built. It is unclear whether they were actually used as currency, although as they were rudimentary imitations of the bronze coinage of the Greek colony of Massallia, present-day Marseilles, their status implies some connection with foreign trade.

Nick Merriman, in *Prehistoric London*, states that the potin coins were 'probably used for more direct transactions, particularly at markets at tribal boundaries'. He goes on to speculate that Uphall was the venue for one of these markets.[13]

Conclusive evidence as to the role of Apollo's Camp remains elusive. Any ancient artefacts that had survived intact beneath Howards chemical works for the past eighty years would have been lost when the topsoil was removed during decontamination. The rest of the camp remains covered by late-Victorian housing. This forces us to base any assumptions about the purpose of the site on its location and whatever evidence may be gleaned from pre-twentieth-century sources.

The most complete map of the site is also the earliest that survives. 'A Plan of an Ancient Entrenchment in Up-Hall Fields in the Parish of Barking' was drawn up by John Noble around 1735. It shows a continuous rampart surrounding a slightly oblong-shaped enclosure, with a second, outer bank on the western flank, running parallel to the Roding. One end of the outer bank is open, suggesting that it may have been flooded to allow small vessels to harbour beneath the ramparts.[14]

That the function of the camp is orientated towards the river seems to be confirmed by the presence of a single entrance, with its own creek, in the top north-western corner of the site, facing the river, adjacent to the outer-bank harbour entrance. In 500 BC, the tidal signal of the Thames was considerably weaker than it is today, with the tide head of the river being somewhere between Westminster and Blackfriars Bridge. As a result, the power of the tide in the tributaries of the Thames would also have been weaker, leaving Apollo's Camp at the very edge of the tidal range – an ideal place to build a harbour.

Although most texts classify the site as an Iron Age hillfort, the lack of evidence of wooden pallisaded defences or, more significantly, a hill, serve to underline the fact that 'hillfort' is a generalized term used to describe most enclosed settlements built during the first millennium BC.

In his masterful study of the period, *Iron Age Communities in Britain*, Barry Cunliffe identifies three distinct types of settlement amongst the 3,300 structures classed as hillforts. More than half of these are small sites of less than three acres which he classifies as defended homesteads. The second type are the true hillforts, large rampart-defended enclosures situated on dominant hilltops, which provided both a communal meeting place and refuge in times of danger. Hillforts represent a level of social organization above that of defended homesteads and probably followed them chronologically. Cunliffe identifies the third phase of these developments as enclosed *oppida*.

Oppidum (plural *oppida*) is a Latin term the Romans gave to their larger towns or administrative centres. When campaigning against the Celts in Gaul, Caesar described their major enclosed settlements as *oppida* and archaeologists subsequently adopted the term. In Iron Age Britain, enclosed *oppida* represent the final stage before the development of open urban settlements – the first towns.

Cunliffe's enclosed *oppida* tend to be larger in scale than their predecessors, the hillforts, and sited in valleys, offering a clue as to the nature of Apollo's Camp. Furthermore, excavations carried out there in the late 1980s found indications of a street pattern amongst the round houses that once stood in the workers' allotments, hinting at urbanization.

Most significantly for Apollo's Camp, Cunliffe states that enclosed *oppida* 'developed in positions chosen specifically for their economic importance in relation to trade routes'.[15]

Ten miles east of Uphall stands the Lakeside Shopping Centre, which, its owners claim, is 'the most comprehensive shopping destination in Europe'. Together with the adjacent retail park, it forms part of Europe's largest shopping area. Situated on an unprepossessing site on the edge of the Thames marshland at West Thurrock in Essex, Lakeside was built with a single purpose: to attract passing trade.

Here, the M25, London's orbital motorway, bringing a never-ending stream of traffic from the north and south, crosses the main east–west route to the capital, the A13 – a fact surely pivotal in convincing the developers to build a massive 'shopping destination' on this spot. Situated just a few miles north of the enormous bridge and tunnel complex at Dartford Crossing, the centre's location puts it within one hour's drive of an estimated eleven million people.

Bearing in mind that the ramparts at Apollo's Camp enclosed some 263,000 square metres – twice the floor space of the Lakeside Centre[16] – could its developers also have had their eye on passing trade? Even before the Romans came to Britain, the Thames was a major trading route, offering access to the interior from the Continent and vice versa.

For a continental trader sailing up the Thames looking for markets at which to trade, the River of the Sun – the modern Roding – would have been the first navigable creek on the northern side of the river, deep enough to allow a seafaring vessel to pass through the wide marshes to the higher ground of the gravel terrace. A settlement with a small harbour built on such a site would have the potential to become a major trading post, with ease of access to and from the Continent.

The Thames – acting like a prehistoric M25 – bringing a constant flow of passing traders; the Hile/Roding doing the job of the A13 – connecting highway and site: a perfect place to create the prime 'shopping destination' for the Iron Age tribes of the northern Thames hinterland. If Apollo's Camp *was* the Celtic Lakeside Centre – and its position in the landscape and functionality of design point to as much – then its scale should tell us something about the site's success as a focus for trade. Something so big could have only justified being built if it was capable of attracting people from far and near. It is simply unique; the largest known Iron Age site of its kind in the region.[17]

The tribes that are traditionally believed to have lived in the north Thames region at the time had their capitals in the centre of their territories: the Trinovantes to the east at Colchester, and the Catuvellauni to the west near St Albans. No evidence of an Iron Age settlement in central London has yet been unearthed. The city seems to have sprung up around the bridge that the Romans built there in the early years of the occupation.

Might the massive enclosed *oppidum* on the banks of the River of the Sun have been the first major settlement in the Thames Valley? Situated on the border between the territory of the Trinovantes and the Catuvellauni, a place also accessible to the Kentish tribes across the river, regularly visited by continental merchant ships, could it have been a place where different cultures met to trade and make merry?

Was Apollo's Camp London before London was built?

This is all speculation, of course, as much a flight of the imagination as Kipling's 'Norseman, Negro, Gaul and

Greek'. Yet Kipling knew his history and based his poem on archaeological facts, combining them with a strong sense of the place, letting his imagination join the dots. He was a master at connecting with the *genus loci*, never more so than in *Puck of Pook's Hill*, a children's book published in 1906.

Kipling could see Perch Hill from the windows of his home in Sussex and, renamed 'Pook's Hill', he used it as the backdrop for a series of short stories which recount the history of England, from Roman times to the year 1215, through imagined events on the Sussex Weald and beyond.

And, under Kipling's pen, Old England turns out to be quite a diverse place: Norseman, Negro, Gaul and Greek all merit a mention in passing, while the narrative unfolds against a back-drop of constant immigration: Romans, Picts, Vikings, Saxons and Normans all wade ashore on Pevensey Beach, one after the other, to claim their corner of our island.

In the final chapter, which concerns the events that led to the signing of Magna Carta in 1215, Kipling cast as his hero Kadmiel, a Jewish moneylender from Moorish Spain, from whom the barons are desperate to borrow money in order to finance their opposition to King John. If they only had sufficient funds, they could finally hope to force him to agree to their demands.

Kadmiel is a totally fictitious character, but Kipling has him withhold funds from the barons until they agree to alter the fortieth clause of the Great Charter. Where the barons had written 'To no free man will we sell, refuse or delay right or justice', Kadmiel stipulates that the clause be changed to read 'to none will we sell, refuse or delay right or justice', ensuring that the liberties of Magna Carta apply not just to the noble-men but to everyone.

Kipling's son and daughter were the models for Dan and Una, the two children who accidentally summon Puck, 'the oldest Old Thing in England', by performing *A Midsummer Night's Dream* three times on Midsummer's Eve beneath his – 'Pooks' – hill.

It's a book that I loved reading as a child, particularly the opening poem in which Puck, that most native of all imps, calls the children's attention to the crop marks that 'show and fade' on the Downs:

> Trackway and Camp and City lost
> Salt Marsh where now is corn –
> Old Wars, old Peace, old Arts that cease
> And so was England born!

My father also had this gift, the ability to see history in hills, often stopping the car on journeys to the coast or countryside to point out the site of some battle or a lost road across the fields. Although possessing a similar sense of place to Kipling, he made it clear that you didn't have to go to rural Sussex to connect with Puck's England. We too had our own folklore, poking through the paving stones at the dark end of our street.

Once, my father told me, at the far end of Victoria Road, where the houses abruptly come to a dead end, cut off by the railway viaduct that crosses the Roding beside Apollo's Camp, people used to say that you could see traces of a fairy ring in the dark marks in the meadow. Nonsense, of course, said Dad. There are no fairies in Barking. What they were seeing, he assured me, were the post-holes of a long-gone wooden structure – probably a Celtic roundhouse.

As a ten-year-old, I had a morning paper round that never

took me more than half a mile from our house. Firstly, I'd deliver to the little clump of prefabs that stood on the site of what is now the Barking Mosque, then I'd continue on along Ilford Lane as far as the Plough public house. The last and longest part of my round took me all the way down Victoria Road, where the terrace of bay-fronted houses traces the line of the southern ramparts of Apollo's Camp.

On winter mornings before dawn, at the far end of the street by the railway viaduct, when mist rising from the Roding dulled the street-lamps' glow, I would sometimes become aware of the past looking down at me from the old camp. The feeling was so strong that it would send me scurrying back to the light and warmth of the paper shop, careful not to look over my shoulder.

There was a dark, satanic presence at the end of Victoria Road, a monstrous thing that devoured two thousand years of history. However, it was not the glowing fires of dozens of Iron Age roundhouses that I glimpsed through the haze, but the Christmas-tree illuminations of the chemical factory, shrouded in its own foul cloud of emissions.

A map of Barking town centre published in *The Victoria County History of Essex* in 1966 shows the land on either side of the Roding covered with factories, many of which had been there since the turn of the century. Barking's proximity to the river made it ideal for bringing raw materials in from abroad, and with the arrival of the railway in the 1850s it was equally attractive for the distribution of finished products.

Victorian London grew at a phenomenal rate, and as more of the city was taken up with housing, public-health legislation was passed to control pollution in urban areas. When a new gasworks was needed to supply the metropolis with light and warmth, the marshland at Barking was deemed a suitable site.

The Beckton gasworks opened in 1870 and was in its day the largest industrial complex in the world, with ships docking at its jetties day and night to deliver coke for the manufacture of town gas. Over a thousand Barking men were employed there, from a population of just under seven thousand.

At Creekmouth, the Barking Guano Works produced fertilizer extracted from imported bird droppings. For much of the late nineteenth century, the guano trade was Peru's most important source of revenue. European ships queued to fill their holds with bird droppings, which had accumulated, in places to a reported thickness of three hundred feet, in the shag colonies on the Chincha Islands near the southern port of Pisco.[18]

Around the time that a chemical factory was being constructed on the site of Apollo's Camp, the old jute mill along the Roding became a rubber factory. A match works opened soon after.

Barking's future as an industrial centre was sealed in 1924 when the Ford Motor Company bought some land on the marshes near Dagenham Dock and, between 1929 and 1931, built what was to become the largest manufacturing plant in the whole of southern England. At its peak, Ford employed over thirty thousand people in vehicle construction, with at least half that number again working in local ancillary companies supplying parts and specialist equipment.

When I was growing up in Barking in the sixties, everyone's dad seemed to work at the car plant or the docks. Then, around the time I was delivering newspapers on chilly mornings down Victoria Road, things began to unravel. One by one, the docks closed down as containerization shifted the work to

Tilbury and Rotterdam. In the seventies, as North Sea gas came on tap, the Beckton gasworks closed. The heavy industries along the Roding went into decline. Slowly, the area came to rely on motor manufacturing as its main source of employment.

Barking's relationship with Ford mirrored that found in the mining, ship-building and steel towns of the North. And when the decline in manufacturing came, the borough was just as vulnerable. In the past thirty years, employment at Ford has dwindled from thirty thousand to under three thousand. The plant only makes diesel engines these days – vehicle production has been moved elsewhere.

Even with the loss of so many jobs, 18 per cent of the workforce in Barking and Dagenham are still involved in manufacturing – compared with an average of 7 per cent for the rest of London. That figure puts the borough on a par with cities like Sheffield, Newcastle and Middlesbrough.[19] The town has suffered other losses. The big department stores have moved away, either to massive, out-of-town shopping malls such as Lakeside, or to other, more prosperous high streets. The old sense of neighbourliness has withered too, as former council tenants have bought the houses they grew up in, sold them at a profit and moved on.

The idea of having a job for life, of qualifying from technical college with an engineering degree and going to work at one of the specialist companies supplying Ford – the highest aspiration for secondary-school boys when I was a lad – has all but disappeared, along with the sense of security that our parents built their dreams upon.

A source of much friction in recent years has been the provision of social housing in the borough. Traditionally, residents of Barking and Dagenham have had high expectations of getting decent accommodation from the council. One of the largest programmes of council-house building took place in the borough during the 1920s and 1930s, when over twenty-five thousand houses were built on what became known as the Becontree Estate.

Here, slum-dwellers relocated from London's East End were rehoused in what was then the largest municipal housing estate in Europe. Their children were in turn allocated council houses for themselves, likewise their grandchildren. However, during the 1980s, many council houses were sold off to their tenants. The Tories' Right to Buy had the effect of bringing home ownership to many for the first time, helping them to realize their aspirations. The awful sting in the tail was that the same legislation forbade councils from using the revenue to build more social housing.

Barking and Dagenham Council managed to hold on to some of their housing stock, but the boom in London house prices of the past decade has not reached the borough, where the value of property is the lowest in the whole of Greater London – half the city-wide average. This has led to a steady influx of people into the borough, predominantly immigrants working in low-paid jobs, seeking the cheapest accommodation, often living many together in one house in order to keep down their cost of living. As a result, between 1991 and 2001 the number of people living in Barking born outside the British Isles leapt from just 3.5 per cent to 13.4 per cent, an increase greater than in any other town in the UK over the same period.[20]

And while immigration has transformed London into a vibrant, diverse metropolis, the shift from homogeneity to multiculturalism has been sudden and startling for some. In the 2001 Census, 85.2 per cent of people in Barking and

Dagenham described themselves as 'white', the sixth-highest proportion of the population, compared with the thirty-three other Greater London boroughs. Yet while this figure appears to be high, it masks a huge demographic shift.[21]

For those seeking simplistic reasons for the town's decline, this sudden influx offered an easy answer: the unforgiving economics of globalization, this invisible engine of irresistible change that had wreaked havoc with their lives, was somehow made manifest by the newcomers in their midst.

Given these facts, it was perhaps merely a matter of time before those who aim to impose a racial hierarchy on society should crawl out from their bierkellers and begin to prey on the people of Barking.

Evidence of the gravel knoll on which Apollo's Camp was built in the second century BC is still visible to those with a keen eye for the landscape. It can be plainly seen at the southern end of Uphall Road, where the tarmac rises ten feet in a mere two hundred yards from the junction with Victoria Road. Other than that, the new houses built on the old Howards site give no hint that there was ever a chemical works there, never mind a massive and unique prehistoric monument. Lavender Road snakes through the estate, but any connection with the Lavender Mount and the ramparts of Uphall Camp has been smothered by the flowery titles of the roads that adjoin it: Hyacinth Close; Dahlia Gardens; Foxglove Crescent; Tulip Drive. Perhaps someone hoped that these streets, by the very fragrance of their names, might eradicate memories of the sour stench of the chemical factory.

The lower Roding Valley is now dominated by the South Woodford to Barking relief road, which follows the course of the river from the foot of the M11 down to the A13 near

Cuckold's Haven. As this recently built stretch of the A406 passes by the site of the camp, it rises up to clear the viaduct which carries trains across the River Roding – a body of water once revered by local people as the River of the Sun, now almost constantly in the shade of this elevated section of the North Circular Road.

And so Apollo's Camp slumbers beneath the dull roar of a dual carriageway flyover, three lanes in each direction; despite the constant flow of humanity, very few passers-by have any sense of the history that lies below.

2

The People of the Hyphen

I eschew the built-in dictionary that came with my laptop computer. Just a few clicks of the mouse and the correct spelling of 'eschew' will magically appear, ready-made for me to use. I won't have a moment to ponder on the word above it in my paper dictionary: 'escheat – the reversion of property to the State or, in feudal law, to a lord, on the owner's dying without legal heirs'. I am reminded to update my will. The word above 'escheat' is even more gravid with mortality: 'eschatology – the part of theology concerned with death and final destiny'. The fact that my spell-checker has nothing even to compare with such words only serves to underline my point.

'In clear A to Z form', the cover of my hardback thesaurus boldly proclaims. None of that Roget's lark here then, where the word you seek is hidden within some obscure linguistic genealogy on wan pages crammed with grey words that struggle to breathe. Non merci, Monsieur Roget. *The Concise Thesaurus* does what it says on the tin. Head words in bold type, homonyms treated as separate head words, all manner of senses of synonyms, and sometimes even antonyms. Best of all, it provides 'tables' – lists of words that, while not strictly synonyms, are associated in some way. What a joyful distraction they are.

Page 337 has a list of eighty-eight types of grasses, sedges and rushes, including 'bent', 'fog', 'spelt' and the charmingly named 'timothy grass'. My dictionary is on hand to inform me that timothy grass is a fodder grass named after Timothy Hanson, who introduced it in Carolina *c.* 1720.

Page 642 of the thesaurus lists the fifty-one branches of psychology. Much fun can be had with the phobias that cover two whole pages like a rash. Some lists are utterly mystifying, such as the twenty-one types of inflorescence, amongst them 'involucre', 'peduncle', 'raceme' and 'spadix'. Whilst recognizing that such a list may be a crossword compiler's dream, I have to admit that I don't actually know what inflorescence is.

My favourite list appears on page 649: the Attributes of Quarks and Antiquarks, which are as follows: beauty, blue, green, red, bottom, charm, down, minus-blue, minus-green, minus-red, up, top, strangeness, and, lastly, truth. It is perhaps to be expected of a theoretical elementary particle which owes its name to a phrase uttered in *Finnegan's Wake* that it could be said to exhibit truth as an attribute.

It was while I was searching one day for the synonyms of 'perception' that my eye strayed to a list of Peoples of the World, Ancient and Modern. They were spread over a page and a half, 360 of them, each one proclaiming the existence of a distinctive ethnicity. The Moabites, who fought against Elisha and Jehosaphat in the Second Book of Kings, were there. The Hottentots, famous for their 'clicking' consonants, are listed, as are the 'wily' Pathans. Some, like the Friulians, sound as if they come from an episode of *Doctor Who* rather than an autonomous region of north-east Italy. Others, such as the Scythians, left no written record of themselves and are known only through the writings of others.

One group stood out from the others on the list: the Anglo-Saxons were the only people to have a hyphen in their name.

Hyphenated identities are all the rage these days, particularly in the USA, but these modern constructs are descriptive of a shared heritage. The first part of the term describes the country or continent of origin or ancestry, followed by the country of residence or birth, for instance Irish-American.

The term Anglo-Saxon carries no such connotations. The former is no longer a distinct racial group, the latter is not a country. Anglo-Saxon is a singular identity and one of great antiquity.

My Oxford dictionary gives several definitions:

1. Of the English Saxons (as distinct from the Old Saxons of the Continent).
2. Of the English people as a whole before the Norman Conquest.
3. Of English descent.

Taken together, these three definitions provide the briefest of outlines as to how 'Anglo-Saxon' came to be the ethnic identity of the English.

'Of the English Saxons (as distinct from the Old Saxons of the Continent)' is a reference to our ancient origins. History tells us that the Saxons were among a number of different tribes who came to settle in Britain from northern Germany in the years following the end of the Roman occupation.

The Romans divided the peoples that they encountered in

Western Europe into two distinct groupings, divided by the physical barrier of the River Rhine: the Celtic peoples lived to the west of the river, in modern Belgium, France, Britain and Ireland, while the Germanic tribes lived to the east, in what is now Holland, Denmark, Germany and beyond.

The process by which the Roman province of Celtic Britannia was transformed into a Germanic country called England had its origins on the steppes of Central Asia. Nomadic tribes of pastoralists, perhaps driven by environmental change, left their traditional territories and swept into south-eastern Europe in AD 370. Known as the Huns and fighting as highly mobile mounted archers, they spread terror amongst the settled agricultural communities.

Amongst the many peoples forced to leave their lands to escape this onslaught were the Visigoths, who fled their home in present-day Romania to seek sanctuary within the Roman Empire. Reluctantly, the Romans let them in, treating them so badly that eventually they rebelled, marching on Rome itself. With the Visigoths threatening northern Italy, the legions of the Britannia garrison were recalled to Rome. They were never to return.

Without this military presence in southern Britain, there was no one to keep the road network in good repair. With no legions to pay, there was no longer any need for coins to be struck. Trade began to dwindle and contact with the Empire began to falter as the Celtic Britons were left to fend for themselves. The colonial infrastructure, which had taken four hundred years to build, crumbled in a generation.

At this point, around AD 410, a period of British history begins for which there is little contemporary record of events – what used to be known as the Dark Ages. Now historians prefer less evocative terms such as 'post-Roman', 'sub-Roman' or 'early medieval', which I believe fail to convey the mystery and drama of these times of great change and turmoil, so forgive me if I continue to refer to the period between AD 400 and 700 as the Dark Ages.

The first candle to illuminate this darkness was lit by a monk named Bede living in Jarrow, Northumbria, who produced his *History of the English People* in AD 731. Before the development of archaeology as a science based on the analysis of material evidence, Bede was the prime source for those seeking to explain how the English came to Britain. Bede's book was copied after his death and widely distributed throughout medieval Europe, being first translated into Anglo-Saxon during the reign of Alfred the Great. The *History of the English People* came to be accepted as the definitive version of events following the end of the Roman occupation of Britain.

Bede describes how:

On the departure of the Romans, the Picts and the Irish, learning that they did not mean to return, were quick to return themselves, bolder than ever.[1]

In 423, Bede recounts, the 'wretched Britons' wrote to the Roman Consul describing their predicament and asking for help:

The barbarians drive us into the sea, and the sea drives us back to the barbarians. Between these, two deadly alternatives confront us, drowning or slaughter.[2]

In the next chapter, Bede tells how, after great hardship, the Britons successfully won back control of their country:

Meanwhile the famine which left a lasting memory of its horrors to posterity distressed the British more and more. Many were compelled to surrender to the invaders; others, trusting in God's help, continued their resistance. Making frequent sallies from the mountains and the caves and forests, they began at length to inflict severe losses on the enemy who had plundered their country for so many years.

Thereupon, the Irish pirates departed to their homes unabashed, intending to return after a short interval, while the Picts remained inactive in the northern parts of the island, save for occasional raids and forays to plunder the Britons.[3]

However, by 449 the barbarians had returned. Vortigern, leader of the Britons, decided to seek help in repelling the Irish and Pictish invaders.

What follows, Bede's account of how the Germanic seafarers came to settle in Britain, has become the origin myth of the English people:

In this time, the Angles or Saxons came to Britain at the invitation of King Vortigern in three longships, and were granted lands in the eastern part of the island on condition they protected the country: nevertheless, their real intention was to subdue it. They engaged the enemy advancing from the north, and having defeated them, sent back news of their success to their homeland, adding that the country was fertile and the Britons cowardly. Whereupon a larger fleet quickly came over with a great body of warriors, which, when joined to the original forces, constituted an invincible army.

These newcomers were from the three most formidable races of Germania, the Saxons, Angles and Jutes. From the Jutes are descended the people of Kent, and the Isle of Wight and those in the province of the West Saxons opposite the Isle of Wight who are called Jutes to this day.

From the Saxons – that is, the country now known as the land of the Old Saxons – came the East, South and West Saxons. And from the Angles – that is, the country known as Angulus, which lies between the province of the Jutes and the Saxons and is said to remain unpopulated to this day – are descended the East and Middle Angles, the Mercians, all the Northumbrian stock and the other English peoples. Their first chieftains were Hengist and Horsa.[4]

The durability of this version of events should not be under-estimated. *Life in the United Kingdom*, published in 2002 by the Home Office to help new immigrants understand modern British society, repeats Bede's claim that the English are descended from the Saxons, Angles and Jutes, who invaded the country and pushed the Celtic Britons back to the western fringes.[5]

Every country has its own archetypal story which serves to explain how it came to exist, even those whose historical origins are well known. Take the United States of America, for example: inhabited for tens of thousands of years by indigenous peoples, visited by the Vikings during the Dark Ages, colonized in the early seventeenth century by the Spanish, French and Dutch, and settled since by peoples from all over the world, the complex origins of the USA have been simplified by historians into a single event in December 1620.

The arrival at Plymouth, Massachusetts of the Pilgrim Fathers was not even the first attempt by the English to colonize America. However, there was something about the nature of the Massachusetts Bay settlers that encouraged subsequent generations of Americans to identify strongly with them. They were English speaking, hard working, morally conservative and, above all, a God-fearing people. Since they were admired for these qualities by nineteenth-century American historians, the story of the Pilgrim Fathers was chosen to explain why the USA emerged as an English-speaking, Protestant, capitalist state.

Given that he was writing some three hundred years after the events he sought to describe, Bede's explanation of how the English came to Britain was a similar exercise in selective historiography. His primary purpose in writing the first history of the English people was to illustrate that Roman Christianity, which he represented, was capable of replacing the power of the Roman Empire as a unifying political entity. The Germanic tribes may have belonged to separate ethnic groups and lived in different kingdoms within Britain, but the Church could forge them into a single people in the sight of God – firmly, Bede hoped, within the orbit of the Church of Rome.

To that end, he needed to sell to his audience, the ruling classes of the Germanic tribes in Britain, the glorious notion of a *gens Anglorum* – an English people. However, such was the ethnic diversity of eighth-century England that Bede was unwilling, for reasons of political expediency, to construct a narrative in which a single tribe or clan could claim to be the founding fathers of the nation. To ensure that his audience would not only understand his version of events but, more importantly, identify with the narrative, Bede was forced to provide a role in his origin myth for each of the dominant ethnic groups of his day.[6] In what may be the earliest example of political correctness, he made sure that the leaders of the Saxons, Angles and Jutes, 'the three most formidable races' as he reverently calls them, were able to see their ancestors represented in the saga, each with equal significance.

Thanks to Bede, the very earliest concepts of what it means to be English are founded on immigration, multi-ethnic diversity and inclusion.

The second dictionary definition of Anglo-Saxon, 'of the English people as a whole before the Norman Conquest', denotes the term which historians traditionally use when referring to the period after the Roman occupation and before the Battle of Hastings. However, 'Anglo-Saxon England' is a sweeping generalization which hides a richly diverse period of our history.

The historian Procopius, writing from Byzantium around AD 550, describes the island of Brittia as being inhabited by three nations: the Britons, the Angles and a race he calls the *Frisiones*.[7] The Frisians were a Germanic tribe which inhabited the north coast of Holland and Germany, where today a string of islands bear their name. Of all the continental Germanic races, the Frisians lived closest to Britain and it is assumed that the Angles, Saxons and Jutes came to Britain via Frisia, which lay on the overland route from their home territories. To this day, Frisian remains the closest of all the Germanic languages to English, offering evidence to support Procopius's claim that they were among the sea-borne invaders of Dark Age Britain.

There is strong evidence of a Frankish presence in Kent. The Franks were a powerful confederation of Germanic tribes who conquered Gaul in the early sixth century, and cross-Channel trade with Francia was very important to the Anglo-Saxon economy. Links with the East Saxons are suggested by the fact that Earconwald, the bishop of London, who in AD 666 founded an abbey at Barking, had a Frankish name.[8]

The multicultural nature of the society that Bede was living in is further illustrated by an artefact fashioned in Northumbria some time between 650 and 750. The Franks Casket – which takes its name from Sir Augustus Franks, the benefactor who donated it to the museum – is a small whale-bone box which may have contained sacred relics. Its four sides are carved with scenes from Christian, Roman, Jewish and Germanic culture, each surrounded by a Scandinavian runic inscription. The front panel is divided between a depiction of the Adoration of the Magi and a scene from the story of Weland, the Anglo-Saxon smith god. The back shows the Jews fighting to defend their temple at Jerusalem from the Romans. On the right-hand panel, a horse-headed man is seated on a mound, while three hooded figures converse in the corner, a scene assumed to be of pagan significance. The left-hand panel depicts Romulus and Remus, legendary founders of Rome, being suckled by the she-wolf. This juxtaposition of Roman, Middle Eastern, Christian and pagan imagery in a single artefact suggests that the casket was made for someone who gave equal significance to each of these scenes.

There are even traces of Islamic influence in Anglo-Saxon England. British coins from this period are often derived from earlier designs or foreign prototypes, as local rulers sought to equate their status with that of the Roman emperors of the past or the continental powers of the day.

When Offa, king of the Mercians, decided to impress his neighbours by minting a gold coinage in AD 774, he chose to equate himself not with the glory of Rome or with his contemporaries across the Channel, the powerful Merovingian kings. Instead, he ordered his craftsmen to strike a coin that was an exact copy of the golden dinar of the Abbasid caliph, al-Mansur. They went so far as to replicate the flowing lines of Arabic script proclaiming, 'There is no God but Allah', between which they simply inserted the words OFFA REX.

Prior to the rise of Wessex, from whose kings the English monarchy claim their descent, Offa was the most successful of the Anglo-Saxon kings, eventually ruling all of England south of the Humber. His decision to identify himself with al-Mansur suggests that other Anglo-Saxon kings would have been respectful of the power and status of the Islamic caliphate.

Further diversity was provided in the ninth and tenth centuries by Danish raiders who settled in East Anglia and Yorkshire. So great were their numbers that King Alfred was forced to divide England between the Anglo-Saxons and the Danes. By the time of the Norman Conquest, England was arguably more Anglo-Danish than Anglo-Saxon: of the half-dozen kings before William, four of them had been Danes.

1066 remains the most significant date in English history because it was the last time that the country was brought to submission by hostile forces. Some present-day English nationalists claim that 1066 marks the point at which England ceased to be truly English, when our laws and customs began to be corrupted by outsiders. There are even those who go so far as to argue that in order to be truly English you must be able to trace your ancestry back to the pre-Conquest population.

In 2004, a charity called the Steadfast Trust sought donations for the benefit of the indigenous population of England, whom they referred to as the Ethnic-English, defining these as 'the descendants of, and [those] who share as their common ancestors, the pre-1066 population of England'. However, for those seeking solace from notions of racial purity in Anglo-Saxon England, history paints a different picture. In the thousand years that separated the Roman invasion from the Norman Conquest, there had been successive waves of immigration.

The Romans were first, bringing thousands of legionaries with them from continental Europe, Asia and Africa. When a Roman soldier retired, he was given land to farm wherever his legion was stationed at the time. For 350 years, this practice added to the ethnic make-up of the country, as retired legionaries set up home in Britain and took local wives.

When Rome withdrew, the Picts and Irish came in such numbers that the first thing the Angles, Saxons and Jutes had to do on arrival was help the Romano-Britons to push these interlopers back to the fringes of Britain. In the years that followed, Frisians, Franks, Danes, Norwegians and Baltic Vikings arrived as traders or raiders, settling in large numbers along the east coast of England.

Such is the diversity from which England emerged. No wonder we alone, among all the races of the world, possess a hybrid ethnicity. The hyphen in Anglo-Saxon is symbolic of our ancient multicultural traditions.

So much for the events of the first millennium AD. The final dictionary definition for Anglo-Saxon, 'of English descent', brings us right up to date, posing questions about what it means to be English today.

What are the qualifications for being English? Officially, there aren't any. On my passport, my nationality is stated as 'British'. For legal purposes, that is what I am. If I wish to, I can change my nationality, to French or Chinese or Tongan; but not, however, to English.

If I choose to call myself English, that's fine. I won't need a new passport, nor will I have to change my nationality. I don't have to register with anyone or make a formal declaration. All I have to do is think of myself as belonging to England. Being English is a state of mind.

It follows that anyone born in England can be English if they so choose. The only time you'll need official documents to prove that you are English is if you are chosen to represent the country at sport. The England rugby, cricket and football teams provide us with one of our few opportunities to come together in celebration of our English identity. They also do a pretty good job of reflecting our society, reminding us who we are.

In recent years we have seen the cricket team captained by Nasser Hussein, watched England field a football team with more black players than white, and seen our rugby team become world champions with the help of mixed-race players such as Jason Robinson. All were English enough to represent their country at the highest level, but not all of them would claim to be of *English descent*. Some have roots in Africa, while others trace their ancestry back to places such as India, Wales, Scotland or Ireland. International sporting rules give them the choice of representing the country of their birth or that of their parents or grandparents. Happily for us, they chose to play for England.

The notion that you can be English without being ethnically English is not a particularly modern concept. Immigration has ensured that, throughout our history, there have been Englishmen and women whose beliefs or appearance marked them out as being descended from somewhere else. Content to share their nationality while recognizing others' differing ethnicities, the English eventually sought out an ethnic identity of their own.

Throughout the seventeenth century, the English parliament struggled to define the national identity. The problem had begun when James Stuart became King of England on the death of Elizabeth I. The Stuarts were Scottish Catholics, while the English saw themselves as a Protestant nation whose independence was constantly under threat from Catholic France and Spain.

The Catholic kings of Europe were absolute monarchs, governing as they pleased. In contrast, England had developed a system of government by consent, a tradition which stretched all the way back to Magna Carta. As a result, the English had a strong antipathy towards the use of arbitrary power by monarchs.

The Stuarts were fatally attracted to the idea of absolute monarchy, provoking several confrontations with Parliament, seeking to place themselves above the law. To resolve this problem, Parliament was forced to take a series of unprecedented steps. All proved to be constitutional dead-ends.

In 1642, the high-handedness of Charles I led to a civil war which ended in defeat for the Stuarts. Parliament hoped to negotiate a new settlement, but Charles's insistence on the Divine Right of Kings to rule as they pleased led to stalemate. What could Parliament do? He was the king, after all.

Determined to uphold the right of rule by consent, Parliament put the king on trial for treason, accusing him of acting against the interests of his people by starting the Civil War. Charles was found guilty and executed, and the monarchy was abolished, creating an English Protestant republic. However, this solution failed and in 1660 the Restoration brought the Stuarts back, albeit on Parliament's terms. Charles II was able to gain the confidence of his people by curbing his

Catholicism. However, his brother, James II, was not so circumspect, imposing Catholicism on a reluctant nation. As a result, the Stuart Restoration failed when Parliament imported a Protestant king from Holland. The arrival of William of Orange duly caused James to flee to France with his family.

That seemed to have solved the problem, but when William died without having any children, all hopes of a Protestant dynasty came to rest on his sister-in-law, Queen Anne. When her only child died in 1700, Parliament found itself back in the same old fix. Next in line for the throne was another Stuart.

Parliament couldn't afford to take any more chances. In 1701, they abandoned any pretence of following the ancient tradition of hereditary principle and passed a law which forbade any Catholic from becoming monarch. The Protestant Georg Ludwig von Braunschweig-Luneberg, Elector of Hanover, a German duke, was the beneficiary, becoming king in 1714, ahead of fifty-eight Catholics, each of whom had a better claim to the throne.

Furious at this sleight of hand, the Stuarts instigated abortive uprisings in Scotland with the aim of returning a Catholic to the throne. The Protestant succession was far from secure. In 1745, the Jacobite army, led by Charles Edward Stuart, Bonnie Prince Charlie, came within 120 miles of London before being forced to return north of the border.

Concerned for the popularity of the Hanoverian kings, their supporters began to draw comparisons between the Anglo-Saxons and the new royal family. Hanover was strongly identified with the Protestant cause, so evidence of England's Germanic roots explained, by implication, her preference for a Protestant king. The fact that the Irish and the Scots clung to their Catholicism, it was suggested, was attributable to the fact that they were not Anglo-Saxons, but Celts, whose traditional Catholic loyalties were well known.

This attempt to reflect the politics of eighteenth-century Britain by recourse to the racial identities of the Dark Ages sparked a revival of both Celtic and Anglo-Saxon studies, as each side began to explore their own traditions.

The Anglo-Saxon Chronicles, compiled by Alfred the Great in the late ninth century, were translated into modern English for the first time during the reign of George III, whose mother, Augusta von Sachsen-Gotha, was, as her name suggests, a genuine Saxon. A new-found enthusiasm for all things Anglo-Saxon was unleashed in 1840 when George III's granddaughter, Queen Victoria, married a real live Saxon prince, Albert von Sachsen-Coburg.

A cult of Anglo-Saxonism swept through academia. Books were written comparing Albert to Alfred the Great. Bede's *History of the English Peoples* was rediscovered by historians and the story of the Angles, Saxons and Jutes began to be taught to successive generations of British schoolchildren.

This nationalist fervour was by no means confined to England. The rise of the nation state had inspired other European powers to rummage through their own pasts in search of a dominant ethnic identity. By the end of the nineteenth century, this process was complete. The French declared themselves to be Gallic; the Germans, Teutonic; the English plumped for Anglo-Saxon: a pre-Conquest term that described their post-Reformation identity within the multiethnic construct that was the United Kingdom of Great Britain and Ireland.

3

A Tradition of Dissent

We can change our nationality, but none of us can change our ancestry. However, the recent growth in online genealogy has allowed us to learn more about the people from whom we are descended. The availability of records on the internet has contributed to a democratization of the past, allowing anyone to research their own family tree and discover facts about their ancestors that add new facets to their identity.

My interest in finding out who I was descended from began with a school calligraphy project in 1970, when I was twelve. The first family tree that I constructed consisted of those relatives my father knew, as far back as his own grandfather. Sitting me down with a large sheet of paper, Dad patiently talked me through three generations of Braggs, helping me to draw up a basic genealogy.

My only other source of information was a great-aunt, my grandfather's last surviving sibling, who was then well into her eighties. Aunt Hannah lived two streets away from us, occupying the upper floor of a Victorian terraced house like ours. She was a widow, childless, and we were her only relatives who lived locally.

To visit her flat was to step back in time. She had no TV or radio, as her home was not connected to the electric mains. Cooking was done on a big, black, coal-fired range that sat in the fireplace and her few rooms were lit by wall-mounted gas lamps, which were turned on and off by means of a tap on the fitting.

As she couldn't get out very much, I was often despatched to do her weekly shopping at the Co-op. While she searched for her fish coupons in the back room, I would sit alone in her parlour, listening to the steady hiss of the gas lamps, studying the faces in the old photographs on her wall. I knew these people were related to me – I could even see the family re-semblance – but who were they? Where had they come from? What lives had they led? I felt that if I could only find out, it might help answer some of the questions of my existence, not least how I had come to be born in this place called Barking.

Although Aunt Hannah's memory for dates wasn't too good, the people in the photographs were still familiar to her and she was able put faces to the names that Dad had given me. My family tree was coming together like a jigsaw puzzle: I had names and faces, what I needed next were dates and places.

Through much of the nineteenth century, the centre of Barking was the town quay, where, in 1832, 140 large vessels were based, crewed by over five hundred men. As London's closest fishing port, Barking's small inshore vessels, called smacks, could, on certain tides, sail up to Billingsgate market to deliver the freshest seafood in the city. Barking was home to the Short Blue fleet, which, during the course of the nineteenth century, would grow to be the largest commercial fishing fleet in the land. Ice collected in winter from the marshes and stored in icehouses at Creekmouth was ferried out to the fishing fleet to ensure that the catch stayed fresh.

In 1865, the railways reached Yarmouth, meaning that fish caught in the Great Silver Pits of the North Sea could be brought to London quicker by rail than by sail. Barking's days as a fishing port were over. The Short Blue relocated to Gorleston on the Norfolk coast and Barking's commercial centre moved from the quay to the railway station.

Originally built on what was in the 1850s the eastern edge of town, the station was extensively rebuilt in 1889. When Barking became an Urban District Council in 1894, plans were laid out for housing and a large municipal park in fields further east. Barking New Town was to consist of rows of two-storey, bay-windowed, terraced houses, slightly larger than cottages. Over five hundred were built between 1895 and 1905, the last on the eastern fringe of the development, where the back yards of the houses on the eastern side of Park Avenue overlooked the ornate gardens and boating lake of Barking Park.

My dad's maternal grandfather, George Austin, moved into Park Avenue shortly after it was built and our family has lived there ever since. By the time I was born, Barking New Town was among the oldest housing stock in the borough, and was no longer on the eastern fringes, but in the centre of a town that boasted a population of over seventy-two thousand.

Living in one place for several generations allowed for the accumulation of many layers of family history. The most important artefacts were gathered together in an old portable desk said to have been owned by my great-grandfather, Frederick Bragg. The desk is a fine piece of late-Victorian craftsmanship, a darkly varnished wooden strongbox with brass fittings which opens to reveal a slanting green baize desk-top, some twenty inches wide by twenty-two inches long, complete with two inkwells and a receptacle for pens and nibs.

That it belonged to Frederick Bragg seems to be borne out by the presence, among its contents, of several handwritten calling cards for the Anchor and Hope, the beerhouse that he kept on the west bank of the quay at Barking around the turn of the century. Among the items collected here are a small Bible, some school attendance medals for the early 1900s, a pocket watch and a collection of memorial cards. Edged with black and bearing ornate biblical quotations, these were issued by undertakers for bereaved families to send to acquaintances, notifying them of the time and place of a funeral. Giving the age of the deceased, as well as the date of death, these little cards, infused with mourning and grief, allowed me to add dates to the names and faces in my family tree. Bearing the words 'Rock of Ages, cleft for me', one of the cards announces the passing, in April 1903, of Frederick himself.

Alongside an advert for 'Whitbreads Bottled Beers: London Stout, London Cooper, Indian Pale Ale, All in Splendid Condition – 2/6 per dozen', The *Barking Advertiser* of 18 April 1903 reported:

Death of a Barking Licence Holder: The death occurred on Saturday evening last, at his residence, of Mr Frederick Bragg, the landlord of the Anchor and Hope beerhouse. Mr Bragg held the licence for about six years, and was well known to Barking townspeople, as for many years he had previously been engaged at Beckton Gas Works during his last years of service as a rope-runner.

When the Gas Light and Coke Company opened their Beckton gasworks on 150 acres of windswept Essex marshland near Gallions Reach in 1870, it was the biggest employer in the world. Thousands of men stoked furnaces in intense heat, working twelve-, sometimes eighteen-hour shifts, day and night, seven days a week, providing heat and light for the growing metropolis.

As demand was much greater during the winter, many workers were laid off as summer approached, leaving them to seek casual labour in the nearby London Docks. Following large-scale lay-offs in March 1889, the gasworkers organized a protest meeting at which they formed the first of the new industrial trade unions, the National Union of Gasworkers and General Labourers. Their immediate demand was for an eight-hour day.

Unlike the craft unions that had preceded them, the industrial unions represented a less well-paid workforce and so were unable to charge the high fees that were necessary to see members through hard times. Rather than act as a safety net for their members, they were proactive, willing to take action in order to achieve their aims. Led by Will Thorne, who had been trying to organize the gasworkers since he began working at Beckton in 1884, there was 100 per cent support for the union within the plant.

The employers, realizing that they could not hope to maintain gas supplies without skilled workers, gave in without a fight, conceding that there would henceforth be three shifts every twenty-four hours instead of two, with no reduction in pay. The eight-hour day was born.

Almost immediately, the dockers in the nearby West India Docks, many of whom had themselves been employed at

Beckton during the winter months, were inspired by the gasworkers' victory to demand a basic wage of sixpence an hour. The strike for the 'docker's tanner' lasted for a month and gained wider publicity throughout the world than any previous dispute.

As a result, victory, when it came, gave great confidence to the forces of social change. The industrial action of 1889 ushered in the era of 'new unionism', which in turn led to a new political movement which culminated in the formation of the Labour Party a decade later. The campaign for the eight-hour day at Beckton gasworks, the first success of the modern trade-union movement, would have huge repercussions for the lives of the working people of Britain.

My great-grandfather, Frederick Bragg, worked at the Beckton Gasworks from around 1880 until 1897, throughout the new unionism period. Yet the gains he and his colleagues secured were under constant threat. By the early 1900s, the wave of unionism that had been inspired by the successes of 1889 had faded away. As trade fell off, so the employers reverted to old practices and union membership went into decline. In early 1910, the Dock, Wharf, Riverside and General Worker's Union, which had come into being as a result of the 1889 strike, called for the formation of one big union within the London Docks. In March 1911, the National Transport Workers' Federation was formed as a result of the amalgamation of seventeen unions active within the docks.[1] The impetus for this amalgamation had been provided by the setting up, in 1909, of a new body to oversee the working of the various Thameside docks – the Port of London Authority. Now union leaders could sit down with their employers and hammer out problems in a spirit of cooperation.

The new union, buoyed by strong economic growth and low unemployment at the waterside, launched a campaign for a wage increase to eightpence an hour for day work and a shilling an hour for overtime – the first increases in the industry since the strike for the 'docker's tanner' had achieved the sixpence-an-hour rate some twenty years earlier. As well as a uniform rate of pay for all workers within the docks, the Federation sought the full recognition of all port transport unions in London. This was the only way that they could hope to regularize the hiring of casual labour. Hands were hired as and when required to unload ships by a much-loathed process known as the 'call-on'. Men, often desperate for work, were herded together, while a foreman walked up and down selecting the strongest-looking among them for a day's work. The employers insisted on recruiting the men inside the dock gates, where the foreman could make sure that any 'trouble-makers' – union sympathizers – were denied employment. The unions demanded that men be taken on outside the dock gates, where union officials could ensure that every man hired had a union card.

An agreement was reached over the issue of payments, but the employers refused to give ground on hiring practices and, although their leaders recommended acceptance, the dock workers rejected the Port Authority's offer. On 2 August 1911, the majority of men in the Royal and Surrey Docks absented themselves from work. Their leaders pleaded with them to accept the offer of higher wages, but the continued practice of hiring within the dock gates had infuriated the men and they demanded an all-out strike to resolve the issue.

The docks came to a standstill. The Port Authority refused to budge, and on 11 August, Ben Tillet, the dockers' leader, called the permanent labourers out. These were the men who were not subject to the 'call-on', skilled professionals who had the security of being employed by the Port Authority.

The permanent men clearly had the most to lose – the guarantee of work and the promise of a pension after years of service. Until now, they had stayed largely out of the fray, allowing at least a few ships a day to be unloaded. When they too came out on strike, nothing moved in the docks whatsoever. Cargo rotted, profits were lost. Within twenty-four hours of the permanent men coming out, the Port of London Authority had reached five separate agreements with the unions and the Federation declared the strike over.

The *Shipping Gazette* of 12 August 1911 reported:

At one time yesterday it looked as though the struggle would be prolonged. The strike committee had taken upon itself to call the permanent men employed by the Port of London Authority to leave their work . . . the Port Authority distinctly intimated that it did not intend to re-open matters, and the strike leaders yesterday threatened that there would be no peace in the port until they did. Fortunately they have thought better of it. The Port Authority has gained its point while at the same time its general manager promises to use his good offices to reinstate those men who have quitted his employment [supported the strike] whether under a mistaken sense of duty or otherwise.[2]

The following Monday, the majority of men reported for work, expecting there to be no recriminations for their actions. However, the Port Authority, feeling betrayed by its professional workforce, issued dismissal notices dated 11 August to some three thousand of their permanent labourers, including my great-grandfather, George Austin.

Among the documents and photos collected in the old portable desk is a letter addressed to 'G. Austin, Permanent Labourer' from the Port of London Authority:

> Having absented yourself from work today without leave, the
> Port of London Authority hereby notify you that you are
> dismissed from their service for misconduct.

The text is mimeographed on to the page, with my great-grandfather's name and the word 'Permanent' written in by hand. George Austin, having worked in the London Docks since the late 1880s, was summarily dismissed for taking an active part in the strike.

Again the docks ground to a halt, this time in support of the permanent men. Industrial action spread to the Liverpool Docks, and by the end of the week a national rail strike had been declared. Food distribution was hit and supplies began to run out in London. The government became involved, threatening to send in the Army to break the strike.

Over the weekend of 18–19 August, talks were held at the Home Office and the issue of union recognition was at last settled. Under pressure from the government, the employers conceded that men should be 'called-on' outside the dock gates. The following Monday, the majority of men resumed work, my great-grandfather among them. The action of the permanent labourers on 11 August had tipped the scales and been pivotal in ending the humiliation of the 'call-on' which their casual colleagues were forced to endure each day.

Some time after the 1911 dock strike, George Austin moved

with his family to his in-laws' house in Park Avenue, Barking. He was still working as a dock labourer when his elder daughter, May, married my grandfather, William Bragg, in 1918.

I assume that, as Frederick Bragg's only surviving son, William inherited the portable desk from his father. Certainly William's hand can be detected on the items deposited there. The photographs and calling cards are of his parents and siblings; the letter from the PLA is addressed to his father-in-law; the Bible and school-attendance medals belong to his wife, my grandmother; the school books and papers are those of their only child, my father. Grandad is the link. This is his collection. It begins around the time of his birth in 1893 and comes to an end with his death in 1953.

Most precious of all of the desk's contents is the diary that William kept in a small black notebook, beginning in January 1911 when he was seventeen years old. The first entry records what came to be known as the Siege of Sydney Street:

Jan. 3rd Tuesday. Terrible outrage in the East End (connected with the Houndsditch Murder) When Winstone [sic] Churchill gave orders for a maximum gun and 3 R.A. guns, also the Scots Guards 'called' out and ordered to fire on assassins. Assassins burned to death.

He makes several entries a month, mostly brief records of national events – the launch of the Thames dreadnought *The Thunderer* at Dagenham docks, the Cup Final between Newcastle and Bradford City, the Kaiser dining at Buckingham Palace. Occasionally details of his own life appear. Referring to himself in the third person as 'Sonnie', we learn that on 3 March 1911, 'Sonnie started today on the machine at FG

Andrews' (he was by trade a metal-worker). He joins the crowds at the Coronation in June 1911 and sticks a brand-new green halfpenny stamp showing King George V at the top of the page to celebrate.

Few entries are longer than three lines and he makes no comment on the events that he is recording. However, the first hint of where his sensibilities might lie appears in July 1911, when he makes a note of the major political figures of the day. Under the heading 'Parliament (1911)' he lists just four members of the Liberal government:

Mr Asquith: Premier.
Mr Lloyd George: Chancellor.
Mr W. Churchill: Home Sec.
Mr J. Burns: B of Trade.

Significantly, he chooses to place John Burns alongside these three titans of the Liberal Party. Burns was a lifelong socialist who had come to prominence during the 1889 dock strike. In 1892 he was elected as an MP for the Independent Labour Party, and subsequently accepted cabinet office in the 1906 Liberal government. As the first working man to become a minister, Burns would have been the most prominent trade unionist of his day. His appearance here, alongside such political heavyweights as Lloyd George and Churchill, is, I believe, significant, suggesting that my grandfather felt that Burns and the ideas that he represented were of some importance.

This is borne out by my grandfather's record of the events of the following month. The outbreak of the 1911 dock strike, in which his future father-in-law George Austin would take part, causes William to pen an entry which takes up a whole page.

On 9 August he details the number of dockers, carmen, lightermen, coalporters, stevedores, tug-boat engineers and casual labourers in the London docks that are on strike, some 125,000 in total. He goes on to mention the support of Liverpool railwaymen, porters at Billingsgate and Smithfield markets, and also a number of arrests.

Then, as if an afterthought: 'Veto debate in the Lords'.

The 1911 Parliament Act was passed the next day, asserting for the first time the supremacy of the elected House of Commons over the hereditary House of Lords by removing the latter's power of veto over government bills.

My grandfather, just turned eighteen, is showing a healthy interest in the politics of his day. He notes approvingly the 1913 National Insurance Act. 'Maternity benefits commence 30 shillings for a birth.' Later he records, 'Full benefits obtained out of the National Insurance Act.'

The sinking of the *Titanic* merits a brief entry and he mentions seeing 'a flying exhibition by the noted aviator Mr B. C. Hack in the Barking Park'.

An entry describing his own twenty-first birthday on 19 June 1914 – 'Grand Party from 7 o'clock till Sunday night' – is followed a week later by grimmer news: 'Assassination of the Austrian heir to the throne, the Archduke Francis Ferdinand and his morganatic wife the Duchess of Hohenberg.'

He only has time to note the victory of Carpentier of France over America's Gunboat Smith in the world boxing championship before his attention turns again to the 'serious trouble between Servia and Austria trying to make a European War. Servia fire first shots'. The next entry simply reads, 'Tues. July 28th War Declared'.

William swaps from pencil to purple pen as the war between

Austria and what we now call Serbia escalates. The awful momentum of the events which overtook Europe that summer is evident even in these brief entries:

Thursday July 30th Partial mobilisation of Russian Army. Belgrade bombardment.

Friday July 31st Martial law declared in Germany. General mobilisation in Holland. London stock Exchanged closed until further notice. Bank rate raised to 8% highest since 1873.

Saturday Aug 1st Germany declares war.

Sunday Aug 2nd Cabinet sit. German Army invades France.

There is no entry for Monday 3 August. Like many others across Europe, my grandfather pauses to reflect on these events. Then, the inevitable:

Tuesday Aug 4th (11 o'clock) Great Britain at war with Germany. Midnight ride with Frank to Buckingham Palace.

Frank Green was William's best friend and together they cycled through the streets of the East End, into the City where the bells were ringing, to join the thronging crowds in a spontaneous outburst of patriotic fervour outside Buckingham Palace. Pressed between the diary's pages, no more than 2cm by 4cm, is a souvenir of that midnight ride: a fabric Union Jack on which is written in ink the word 'WAR'.

William Bragg had just turned twenty-one and the world that he had known was about to disappear for ever.

Initially the diary carries on as before. The events of 1914 produce as many pages as those years which precede it. 1915 is equally detailed. William remains at home in Barking, but the war gets ever closer. London is bombed and he sees a Zeppelin 'brought down all aflame by our airman Lt. Robinson of Hornchurch'. Towards the end of 1915, the entries become less frequent. Documents left between the pages help fill in the gaps.

A blue folded form, its edges holed with age, bears the heading 'Certified Copy of Attestation'. William writes his name, address and occupation – printer – and answers the 'questions to be put to the recruit before enlistment'. No, he is not married; yes, he is willing to be vaccinated; and yes, he is willing to enlist in the 28th Middlesex Regiment. The form is signed and witnessed.

However, the rest is left incomplete. Stamped in purple ink across the top of the form are the words 'Not Accepted. Medically Unfit. Finsbury Barracks 27 Nov 1915'.

Photographs of my grandfather often show him standing awkwardly, one shoulder higher than the other, the result of a difficult birth which his twin brother did not survive. It was this disability which led to him being declared unfit for military service.

Although unable to serve, he did work for the war effort. A certificate kept in the diary states that in 1917 he was doing protected work as a metal smelter at the Atlas Metal Alloys Company, making aircraft parts for the newly formed RAF. Further evidence of his contribution to the war effort is found in a letter pressed between the diary's pages. From General Alexander to Atlas Metal Alloys, it is dated 10 April 1918:

Secretary of State for Air and Air Council ask me to convey to your firm, your staff, and workers, their sincere thanks and appreciation of your able efforts during the past six months, which have enabled the Royal Air Force in the Field to receive such satisfactory supply of Aircraft Equipment, and to make good their losses so well through the unexampled fighting of last month.

Was it the pressure of his job that stopped William from keeping his diary after November 1915, or was it perhaps the realization that he would not be taking a direct part in the fighting? Whatever the reason, 1916 barely covers four pages, while the following year merits only one entry. In February 1918, after seven years and over one hundred pages, the diary peters out, the last entry noting the Bolshevik Government's acceptance of peace terms with the Germans.

Perhaps other interests were taking up his time. Two months later, on 27 April 1918, he married my grandmother, May Kathleen Austin, at St Margaret's Church in Barking.

These people were very real to me when I was growing up. There were photographs of my father as a child with George Austin, the permanent labourer from the London Docks; there were even photos of Dad with the two siblings of Great-Grandfather Bragg that he had told me about, Alfred and Elizabeth. In a picture taken some time in the mid-1930s, my father, maybe ten years old, sits between his great-uncle and great-aunt, the former born in 1859, the latter in 1864, while behind them, his malformed shoulders clearly visible, stands my grandfather, William Bragg.

Only my great-grandfather, Frederick Bragg, seemed unimaginably distant. There were no photographs of him with his children or grandchildren. In fact, only two photos of him survive. One, taken at Threadwell's studio in Stratford, East London, perhaps in the 1880s, shows a fresh-faced man with a chinstrap beard, wearing a frock coat and a stern look. The other comes from a locket and is the size and shape of an old penny. On closer inspection, it appears to be a photograph of a photograph – some shadow is observable on the right and top of the image. It shows Frederick, apparently somewhat older, in full beard, cap, waistcoat and shirt-sleeves, raising his right fist against a policeman, just visible on the right of the frame, who has grabbed my great-grandfather's left hand.

It must have been taken before 1903, when Frederick died – an action shot from a time when most photographs were posed. However, there is no sign of the humour that should be present if two friends were joking in front of the camera. Frederick's face is expressionless. The policeman, though, has the demeanour of restraint about him. If it was posed, why bother to re-create an altercation with the law? Could it be a genuine police photograph taken as a record of some criminal activity?

I can remember talking about this picture with Aunt Hannah. We noted the presence of the policeman – she even told me his name, which, as I recall, was PC Kinner. To my intense frustration, I don't remember asking her what was happening in the picture. I am left now to speculate.

The fact that my great-grandfather is the oldest person in our family that I have a pictorial record of only adds to the enigma of this image. Frederick Bragg was born in Kirby, just outside Walton-on-the-Naze in Essex, in March 1856, son of William Bragg, husbandman, and Elizabeth Hudson. These details, which come from his birth certificate, marked for many years the extent of my knowledge of the family.

Aunt Hannah died, aged eighty-four, in 1972, and after my father's death four years later, my interest in genealogy waned. I was glad that I had asked all those questions of Aunt Hannah and Dad, but apart from leaving me with the ability to identify people in old family photographs, what had my research told me about my identity? That I was from Essex, my father was from Essex, his father was from Essex, and his father was from Essex, all the way back to our common ancestor, William Bragg, who was probably from Essex too.

If my dad's people were thin on the ground, my mother's family seemed to be everywhere. Whenever we went shopping along Ilford High Road or to Romford Market, it seemed that we were apt to encounter another of her relatives. Mum's immediate family were very close and we saw her four sisters and brother and their children regularly. These auxiliary relatives that we bumped into while shopping were drawn from the ranks of her twenty-eight uncles and aunts and their families, whom we seldom visited.

My maternal grandmother, Daisy, had a dozen siblings and came from an East End family, the Simmonds, who all had wonderful Victorian names like Art, Perce, Len, Dolly, Nell and, of course, Victoria. My maternal grandfather was one of sixteen surviving children of an Italian immigrant couple who had been married in the Italian Church in Clerkenwell, central London, in 1906.

Some time around the turn of the century, my great-grandfather, Alphonso D'Urso, arrived in London from Italy and, like all new arrivals, he sought out people from his own community to help him make a start in this new country, finding work as an ice-cream vendor and marrying Trofimena Guidotti, a girl from his home village. My grandfather, Aneilli, was their first child, born in the heart of London's East End in March 1907.

In common with many enterprising immigrant families, my great-grandparents opened a corner shop, selling fruit and veg on Cable Street. While Trofimena worked behind the counter, Alphonso, who never learned to speak English, produced his own ice-cream which he sold from a barrow on Tower Hill, switching to roast chestnuts in winter.

My mother and her family lived a short walk from the shop, in the Glamis Road Buildings. Life in the East End of the 1930s was not always easy for immigrant families. Mum's elder sister recalls seeing Oswald Mosley addressing crowds with his fascist Blackshirts near the Troxy Cinema in the Commercial Road. As children, they were sometimes warned by their parents that if they were not indoors before it got dark, the Blackshirts would come and take them away.

In June 1939, the family moved to Hitherfield Road in Dagenham, one of the twenty-five thousand families relocated by London County Council to the massive Becontree Estate. After the war, my parents met at an ice-skating rink in Forest Gate and were married in 1953. Over the years, Mum's siblings married and moved away from East London, to the leafier parts of Essex and beyond. Nothing remained of her Italian heritage during my childhood, not even her Catholic faith, which would only re-emerge after my father died.

In just a few generations, the D'Urso family had become totally assimilated. None of the people we met at Romford market showed any trace of their Mediterranean roots, other than that exotic surname. So complete was this transformation that no one was able to remember whereabouts in Italy Alphonso had come from – not even his own children. Some thought it was Turin in the north; others claimed it was near Naples in the south.

My mum's younger sisters, knowing of my interest in genealogy, kept asking me to find out, but I had no idea where to begin. Then, in 2000, one of my cousins noticed a familiar surname on a customer-service form in the garage where he worked. Anyone named D'Urso or Guidotti tends to be related to us in some way or another. Sure enough, this customer was a distant cousin, and it transpired that he had recently been to Italy and had discovered where the family had originated from.

Just south of the Bay of Naples, the Amalfi Coast is dominated by the Lattari Mountains, which run all the way down to the Tyrrhenian sea. The slopes are so steep and in-hospitable that a single road cut from the cliffs, hundreds of feet above sea level, connects villages that until the nineteenth century were only accessible by boat. Alphonso D'Urso was born here, in the village of Minori, in 1882. The family lived in a house on the via Petrito, one of the winding narrow streets, little more than passages, which snake up the side of the valley in which Minori sits. Eventually, the streets give way to the lemon groves that cover the hillsides. It was here that Alphonso and his family worked.

In 2001, while gigging in nearby Naples, I took a day trip there in search of my Amalfitano roots. The views from the via Petrito are spectacular, with the town of Ravello perched atop the mountains to the west and the Bay of Salerno stretching away to the distance. The lemons hanging from the trees are so much more, well, 'lemony' than the thin-skinned, waxy specimens we see in our supermarkets. Generations of my ancestors doubtless worshipped at the twelfth-century basilica of St Trofimena, which contains the relics of the saint herself, patron and protector of the Amalfitano people. And there are still D'Ursos to be found in the bars, drinking the local speciality, limoncello liqueur.

Within a few months of that visit, my mother received a letter from one of her distant cousins on the Simmonds side of the family, asking for details for their family tree. We exchanged letters and I subsequently received a thirty-page illustrated dossier outlining the history of seven generations of the Simmonds family, going all the way back to 1720.

Impressed by this sudden upsurge of genealogical inform-ation and now with a family of my own, I felt it was time to explore the Bragg family tree once again. Consulting the notes I'd made twenty-five years earlier, I was able to acquire the birth certificates for my great-grandfather's brother and sister, from which I learned that both had been born in the Essex village of Thorrington.

The Essex Record Office at Chelmsford holds microfiche copies of church registry records and there I found them: my great-grandfather, Frederick, his brother and sister and five other siblings, most of them born in Thorrington, to William Bragg and Elizabeth Hudson, between 1843 and 1867. Their wedding certificate named William's father as George Bragg, labourer. I had finally managed to add a new generation to our family tree.

Yet the trail immediately ran cold. While there were many members of the Hudson family mentioned in the Thorrington parish registers, prior to his marriage there was no record of William Bragg, nor of his father, George. Perhaps another twenty-five years would have to pass before I was able to add another generation to the tree.

However, I now had access to a tool which was unavailable

back in 1975 – the internet. In the past few years, British Census returns for the latter half of the nineteenth century have been made available for research via the National Archive website. They can tell you where your ancestors were on a certain night, and name family members, their age, profession and, crucially, their place of birth.

The 1861 Census revealed that William Bragg was living with his wife and four children at Great Bentley, in Essex, that he was a forty-year-old agricultural labourer, and that he was born in a place called Rattlestone, near Bury St Edmunds.

The village was actually called Rattlesden, and on checking its 1861 Census returns, I found to my surprise that William's father, George Bragg, my great-great-great-grandfather, born in 1776, was living there at the time, still working as an agricultural labourer at the age of eighty-four.

But who were these people? What were their lives like? Was it possible to glean anything more about them than the dry details of the Census?

Visiting Rattlesden, I learned from a churchwarden that there had been Braggs in the village until recently, and that they had been members of the Baptist chapel rather than the Church of England. Correspondence with the village pastor revealed that George Bragg had been instrumental in the chapel's foundation in 1813.[3]

The English Baptists trace their roots back to the Protestant dissenting sects of the seventeenth century, known collectively as the Independents, who were united by a belief in congregational administration of religious and church matters without any ecclesiastical or political interference. The divisions that emerged within Protestantism in the hundred years that followed the English Reformation were not founded on great religious differences; what divided them was their response to the imposition of authority.

The Church of England was formed to free the English from the arbitrary power of the Pope. The Presbyterian strain developed within the Anglican Church in opposition to the power of bishops, insisting on the authority of ministers and elders. The Independents went even further, placing authority in the hands of the congregation itself. This insistence on equality before God, combined with a healthy opposition to arbitrary power, would ultimately lead to demands for democratic reform.

The Independents began to find common ground with the Presbyterians in opposition to King Charles I, who insisted on appointing 'Arminian' bishops to the Church of England – Protestant clerics whose rituals echoed those of Catholicism. Angered by this behaviour, the Presbyterian majority in the English Parliament drew up a resolution condemning Arminianism.

As a result of such moves to limit his powers, Charles dissolved Parliament in 1629, vowing never to summon another. For eleven years, England was subject to personal rule as Charles, ignoring the long-standing tradition of rule by consent, sought to emulate the Divine Right of Kings exercised by the Catholic monarchies of France and Spain. He raised taxes and tried to bring all the different Protestant sects under the control of the Church of England, of which he was supreme head.

When Scottish Presbyterians resisted the imposition of the Anglican prayer book, Charles raised an army against them, only to be soundly defeated in what became known as the Bishops' Wars. In the aftermath, the Scots occupied the north-east of England and refused to withdraw until the king had summoned Parliament.

Charles capitulated and the Parliament of 1640 set about curtailing the ability of the monarch to rule without consent. The time between parliaments was limited to three years. The right of the king to dissolve Parliament at will was removed. Further Acts were passed which removed the right of bishops to sit in the House of Lords. The aim was to limit the royal prerogatives – those rights, privileges and powers which the monarch could exercise without the approval of Parliament.

Things reached a head with the Militia Bill, with which Parliament sought to take control of the armed forces. Realizing that without an army to command he could no longer control events, Charles rejected the Bill. Three days later, he left London for York, there to gather his supporters and prepare to fight his own subjects in defence of the Divine Right of Kings.

When the Civil War broke out in August 1642, the Independents, Oliver Cromwell among them, sided with the Presbyterians in Parliament. However, while the latter hoped to negotiate with the king to create a reformed monarchy, the Independents wanted the king to be defeated and held to account.

Such political aspirations were articulated by the Levellers, a radical group who sought to put political flesh on the dissenters' beliefs. The Levellers called for greater religious toleration, an extended franchise, rights guaranteed in a written constitution and a government answerable to the people rather than to the king.

The Baptist faith was particularly active among the rank and file of the New Model Army, drawn mostly from the eastern counties of England, with many regiments having their own Baptist minister. By the end of the war, the New Model Army was the most democratic institution in the land, with promotion based on merit not status, and representation of the lower ranks to the commanding officers through elected 'agitators'.

When Charles was captured, Presbyterians in Parliament sought to negotiate his return to the throne on conciliatory terms. His outright rejection of their proposals sealed his fate. The Presbyterians were purged from Parliament and the Independents, backed by the army, took the only course that could guarantee an end to the conflict. They put the king on trial for treason, on the principle that every citizen, no matter how mighty, should be held accountable for his actions. The promise of Magna Carta, that no one in England is above the law, guided their hand.

Charles was found guilty and was executed in January 1649, ushering in an English republic. The hopes of the Independents were not realized, however, and when the monarchy was restored eleven years later, the Baptists paid dearly for their support of what veterans of the New Model Army referred to as 'the Good Old Cause'.

The Cavalier majority in the Restoration Parliament passed a law compelling conformity to the Church of England and its bishops. Further Acts forbade religious meetings outside the control of the Anglican Church and banned dissenting ministers from large towns. These restrictions forced the Baptists to meet in buildings such as barns or sometimes in the open air, where they listened to itinerant preachers who were dismissed by the Church of England establishment as 'illiterate peasants' and 'mechanics'. Despite this persecution, the Baptists continued to make the connection between religious and civil liberty throughout the eighteenth century. The Leveller ideals of the 1640s still shaped their thinking. In 1793, a Baptist publication attacked the unfair distribution of constituencies, arguing for the sovereignty of the people, annual parliaments, universal suffrage and vote by secret ballot, all key demands of the Chartist Movement which would emerge in the 1830s.[4]

Baptist support was strongest in rural areas, where small-holders and agricultural labourers constituted much of the membership. Each Baptist congregation was a 'free and voluntary society' where members were encouraged to contribute to the meeting.

This rejection of hierarchy represented a threat to the established order, undermining not only the authority of the Anglican clergy in the village, but also the position of the local landowner. By refusing to sit behind the squire in church every Sunday, the Baptists in Rattlesden marked themselves out as people who believed in equality and freedom of conscience.

In the years that followed the French Revolution, the establishment grew ever more suspicious of the dissenting churches. Parliament passed laws designed to curb 'the insidious effects of popular preaching', and some itinerant Baptist preachers found themselves in danger of being thrown in jail by those who feared that they had come to stir up trouble in the area.

An attempt in 1811 to force dissenting congregations to seek licences from the local magistrate – usually the squire – back-fired and led to the repeal of those Acts of Parliament which forced non-conformists to hold their meetings in secular buildings or else in the fields.

The Rattlesden Baptists had been meeting in a barn prior to 1813, when the congregation – George Bragg and his wife Ann among them – were able to meet openly in the chapel they had built for themselves in the village. Their descendants were still worshipping there as late as 1980.

The format of the Baptist congregation, in which all are encouraged to contribute, finds an echo today in the meetings of the local parish council, where the power of the squire has been superseded by the democratic right of everyone to have a say in the decision-making process. My great-great-great-grandfather's belief in toleration and freedom of conscience, ideas that marginalized him in his own community, have since become central to our national sense of who we are.

The healthy disregard for deference that the British people manifested in the latter half of the twentieth century was not a side effect of modern society. It was the flowering of a dissenting tradition which was finally able to express itself with the arrival of universal suffrage and the right to a free education.

This process of democratization has now extended further. The internet allows us to explore our own family trees, giving us a deeper understanding not just of who we are, but of the progress that ordinary people have made since the nineteenth century. Coming face to face with death in the workhouse or the appalling rates of infant and child mortality a hundred years ago is both a sharp antidote to nostalgic notions of the 'good old days' and a stark reminder of why we now enjoy the benefits of a welfare state.

My personal identity, in all its contemporary complexity, is informed by my knowledge of the people that I am descended from. The lives that they lived illuminate not only my family history, but the social history of our country. The story of how my ancestors worked the land in East Anglia and elsewhere until their children moved away in search of a better life is a constant theme, one that explains not only how my Italian ancestors came to be here, but also why the Angles, Saxons and Jutes left their homelands to find new pastures in Britannia.

Although my passport may declare that I am British, I feel that I am primarily English, as were three-quarters of my ancestors. It is an identity that I feel able to declare without having to surrender any of my Amalfitano heritage. I am, after all, of predominantly English descent.

Does that make me, ethnically, an Anglo-Saxon? I think it does, albeit one with a bottle of limoncello cooling in the fridge.

4

Voices from Across the Ocean

The car ferry to Walcheren Island only takes twenty minutes, a journey so brief that passengers are encouraged to stay in their vehicles while the captain steers a course across the grey waters of the River Schelde into Flushing. I once made the crossing as a twelve-year-old on a school trip to the Low Countries. Though I have no memories of the day we spent on Walcheren or of any of the other Dutch towns and cities we visited, the ferry crossing stays with me.

It was Wednesday, 13 May 1970. I can be sure of the date because I still have the mimeographed folder that the school gave us, part itinerary, part guidebook: *The Northbury School Journey 1970*. I'd first been abroad with the school in 1967 when I was a junior there. Now it was my younger brother's turn to take the trip and, as my parents were both going along to help out, I went too, despite the fact that I had left for secondary school the previous summer.

The folder gives details of the places we visited: Knokke in Belgium; Delft, home of the famous blue pottery; the bulb fields of Haarlem; back to the Belgian cities of Ghent and

Bruges, before returning home on the boat-train. All I recall, though, is the ferry crossing and the feelings that it unleashed. Even then, only the moment itself is clear in my memory; the events that led up to it are sketchy, at best.

I am sitting in the back row of the school coach with several boys of my age who have also made the trip. We are out of earshot of teachers and parents. Bored by the flat landscape, we have spent much of the morning kneeling on our seats looking out of the back window, waving to passing motorists. We drive on to the car deck of the ferry and park. Another coach pulls up alongside us. It is full of girls who are about our age.

The girls wave to us. We wave to them. They smile at us. We smile at them. They flirt with us. We act the goat, attempting to conceal our excitement that these girls are paying any attention to us.

We write messages on the paper napkins that we've been collecting at various restaurants and cafés, holding them up to the window. Where are you from? Where are you going? What are your names? I still have one that asks 'Are you English (Anglais)?' tucked into the pocket of the school journey folder.

They don't respond with messages of their own, but it is clear that they like us – perhaps even 'fancy' us. We are utterly beguiled by their behaviour. If only we could get off the coach and meet them . . .

But suddenly we are across the river. The ferry unloads and the girls are gone. Our sense of enchantment is shattered and we struggle to contain the feelings that our brief encounter has unleashed. However, at twelve years old, none of us has the language to deal with such powerful emotions and a pensive silence descends on the back of the coach. None of us wants to let on how moved we have been by what happened. Fearing I might blurt out something embarrassing, I move away to find a seat by myself and spend the rest of the journey with my head pressed against the window, gazing into the middle distance.

The unfairness of it all weighed down on me. They liked us, those girls, and we liked them. A bond was forged back there and now we'd never see them again. I was deeply upset, yet I didn't feel that I could express how I felt – to do so would be to admit that . . . *I liked girls.* Turning my face to the window, I realized that I was alone. I couldn't talk to my mates; I couldn't run to my teacher; my parents wouldn't understand. Where could I turn to for comfort?

And then this happens: from above my head, a descending guitar line comes tumbling out from a tiny speaker.

I am just a poor boy, though my story's seldom told . . .

Some Dutch radio station is providing the perfect soundtrack to my mood. The music draws me in. When the singer is joined by a harmony vocal my heart lifts and I know instinctively that this song is about me. As the song builds to a string-drenched crescendo, it is as if someone somewhere has turned on a tap in my emotions. My eyes fill with tears and I am overwhelmed by the poignancy of my situation, a bitter-sweet feeling that both troubles and comforts me.

There wasn't a great deal of music in our house as I was growing up. We didn't own a record player, so any music I heard came from the radio. My parents' main form of recreation was ballroom dancing, and, consequently, they had little interest in the pop music of the day. However, in October 1967, when the BBC launched Radio One, a channel dedicated to pop music, Tony Blackburn's breakfast programme soon became an integral part of my morning routine.

As my interest in pop music grew, my parents responded by giving me a reel-to-reel tape recorder for Christmas 1969. The Fidelity Braemar was a sturdy portable domestic tape machine, with manual controls which, when shoved into 'play' or 'fast forward', gave a resounding clunk, like the gear stick on the works van that Dad sometimes brought home at weekends.

As soon as the machine was out of its box, I began taping songs from the radio. 'I Saw Mummy Kissing Santa Claus' by Freddy 'Parrot Face' Davies was among the first to be recorded, along with Nina and Frederick's 'Little Donkey' – it was Christmas morning, after all. Thankfully, as the day wore on, my tastes became a little more discerning, 'It Mek' by Desmond Dekker being the last thing I committed to tape on that dizzy first day.

The Fidelity came with an audio input, marked 'radio gram', for recording directly from an outside source, but as we only had a transistor radio, all my recordings were done with the cheap microphone that came with the machine. Any noise that was audible in the room while I was taping would also be recorded for posterity. Doors slamming, dogs barking and a siren wailing can be heard during 'Where Do You Go To, My Lovely?', but Peter Sarstedt sings on, seemingly unperturbed by these interruptions.

I quickly caught the home-taping bug and by the time I went to Holland on that school trip, six months later, I had amassed several tapes' worth of tunes. Yet none of them was capable of touching me like that song did in the aftermath of the ferry trip across the Westerschelde.

The memory of the girls on the coach stayed with me for

several days, eventually becoming submerged beneath the hundred other new experiences that followed fast behind it as the tour progressed. If I thought of them at all, it was only in passing.

Back in England, memories of the school trip had begun to fade when, one morning, I happened to hear the song again over the radio. It was as if the singers were intoning the words of a magic spell – the morning seemed to slide to a halt and for a moment I was transported back to that day on the ferry.

But it was not the girls that my emotions were swooping towards, although they played an important part in the experience; it was the sense of loss, the sorrow of something unfulfilled that welled up inside me. I felt I was back in that place, looking out over the flat Dutch coastline, feeling utterly alone on a coach full of people.

Now, however, it was a good feeling, an exquisitely painful poignancy that I wanted to hold on to. The strings rose up and again I thought I might cry, but the song ended, the room came back into focus and I gathered up my thoughts and headed off to school, unable to shake off a deep longing once more for those girls, for that bitter-sweet ache, but above all for that song.

'The Boxer' by Simon and Garfunkel had been released as a single a whole year before I'd heard it on that Dutch radio station as we drove across Walcheren Island. It was taken from their bestselling album *Bridge Over Troubled Water*, which reached the number-one spot in February 1970. As I wasn't paying a great deal of attention to the personalities of the singers and bands in the charts at the time, I knew little about the duo, apart from the fact that their music was a route to some kind of ecstasy, a catalyst for emotions more intense than

I had ever known before. I felt as if I had stumbled into a different reality, in which the sound of a certain song could transport me to another place. But this secret world was not accessed through the back of a musty wardrobe; it was everywhere, able to emerge suddenly from any nearby radio and tear a hole in the fabric of the everyday, ambushing my emotions every time I heard that song.

Home from school, I set up my equipment, donned my headphones and tried to tune into any place that 'The Boxer' might be coming from. My search brought gems such as Creedence's 'Bad Moon Rising' and 'Mr Tambourine Man' by the Byrds into my collection. I came tantalizingly close, managing to capture 'Bridge Over Troubled Water', Simon and Garfunkel's most recent hit. Yet of the elusive 'The Boxer' there was no sign.

Sometimes, however, you can be looking so hard that you don't see what is right under your nose.

Paul lived on Park Avenue, just around the corner from our house. We had been friends in the same class at Northbury School since the Infants and now travelled together on the bus every day to and from our new secondary school. He had a stereogram and access to a pile of records, most of which belonged to his sixteen-year-old sister, Lesley. Before long, I was taking my tape recorder to Paul's house, where we'd plunder Lesley's record collection for top tracks to use in the spoof radio shows that we'd record on my machine, aping the mannerisms of the DJs we heard on Radio One.

I also took the opportunity to record the cream of Lesley's long players – albums by The Temptations, the Four Tops, Diana Ross and the Supremes and the classic *Tamla Motown Chartbusters Vol. 3*. Given Lesley's impeccable taste and the massive popularity of Simon and Garfunkel that summer, it was only a matter of time before she added *Bridge Over Troubled Water* to her collection.

Paul's father ran his own painting and decorating business and their house had one of the first knock-through lounges in our street. All the other houses on Park Avenue had pokey little front and back rooms. Simply removing the dividing wall created a whole new interior to the house. However, it had one flaw: you couldn't play records on the stereogram if somebody was watching the telly.

Instead, we set my tape machine up in the sun lounge at the bottom of Paul's garden, as far away as possible from any audible disturbance. Borrowing his sister's portable record player, I placed the mic close to the little speaker on the Dansette, put the album on and pushed the levers on my tape machine into record.

As the first plangent piano chords of the title track filled the room, Paul and I sat in reverent silence, religiously following the lyrics on the back of the sleeve, while the album made warm, vinyleous sounds that perfectly matched the dappled shade of the summer's evening.

The mic did occasionally pick up the sound of birds singing in the garden, which troubled me at the time, but, listening back, they seemed to add to the overall ambience of the recording. I got so used to hearing them on my tape that when I eventually bought the album myself years later, it was the birdsong that I missed.

The only real intrusion occurred when the voice of Paul's father broke in over the intercom to tell him that *Reach for the Sky*, a stirring film of the life of World War Two pilot Douglas Bader, had just started on TV and that we should come into the house and watch it. Paul must have asked to be reminded, determined not to miss this classic war film. Yet neither he nor I responded. For the first time in our lives, the new heroes of youth culture had superseded the heroes of the Battle of Britain.

Soon I had the whole of the album on tape, just after 'Back Home' by the England 1970 World Cup Squad. In the weeks that followed, I immersed myself in what had been a previously unattainable holy grail, totally unaware that I was listening to one of the most popular records of the pop era.

Bridge Over Troubled Water was inescapable in 1970, topping the British album charts a staggering five times. It began its run by knocking perhaps one of the greatest pop records ever made off the number-one spot – *Tamla Motown Chartbusters Vol. 3*. It stayed at number one for thirteen weeks, eventually being replaced by *Let It Be*, the Beatles' final album. But the Fab Four were only able to hold the Dynamic Duo at bay for three weeks before *Bridge* returned to the top spot for another month. It took no less than Bob Dylan himself to interrupt their run, but his *Self Portrait* spent only a week at number one before Simon and Garfunkel returned. As summer turned to autumn, the Moody Blues carefully passed the coveted number-one spot to Creedence Clearwater Revival, only for the Rolling Stones to fumble the catch in early October and allow *Bridge Over Troubled Water* back to the top. Pink Floyd's *Atom Heart Mother* scaled the peak for a brief moment, but it took the combined efforts of *Led Zeppelin 3* and *Tamla Motown Chartbusters Vol. 4* finally to end Simon and Garfunkel's reign at the top. *Bridge Over Troubled Water* still holds the record for the longest stay in the album charts – a staggering 303 weeks.

At the age of twelve, I was unaware of this huge popularity. None of my peers were listening to Simon and Garfunkel, so, in terms of playground bragging rights, they belonged to me personally. I could be found at the lunchtime disco in the gym, dancing along with everybody else to the cranked-up riff of Norman Greenbaum's 'Spirit In The Sky', or unselfconsciously singing along to the chorus of 'Young, Gifted And Black' by Bob and Marcia. But the school disco was no place for introspection.

Simon and Garfunkel called for a more reflective mood – their music needed to be explored in the privacy and solitude of your own room, where the songs could take you to places you had never been, in the company of such great characters as Baby Driver, the Only Living Boy In New York and Frank Lloyd Wright. They all came alive in my imagination, drawing my gaze to the bright horizon that was 1970s America. I followed the Boxer through the streets of New York as he sought some comfort there and I hit the road, coast to coast, with the poor guy who was just trying to keep the customer satisfied. And at the end of it all, as the applause on the live cut of 'Bye Bye Love' faded away, I saw myself among all the other characters – the shy songwriter who has waited all his life to be asked to play in the achingly beautiful 'Song For The Asking'.

I had recently written a poem called 'This Child' for English homework, and after my teacher had established that it was all my own work and not copied from some obscure poetry anthology, I was invited to read it out on local radio, something which no one I knew had ever been asked to do.

Perhaps I should have demurred, afraid that I might seem bookish reading my poem, scared of sticking out from the crowd. Instead, I took the invitation as a vindication of my dream to become a singer-songwriter and escape from the life that seemed to await me. At the moment, it was a pretty abstract dream. It would be another four years before I learned to play the guitar, but that didn't stop me writing songs, filling notebooks with page after page of lyrics while keeping the tunes in my head. Listening to *Bridge Over Troubled Water* fuelled this dream, putting me at odds with the plans that everyone seemed to have for my future. How could I explain this to my parents? They were a loving couple who lavished attention on me, but their idea of being really moved by a piece of music was a brisk quickstep across the dance floor.

However, their devotion to ballroom dancing gave me the space to indulge in passions of my own. They attended many a Saturday-night social, leaving me to baby-sit my younger brother, and while he watched TV in the living room, I sat in my bedroom, listening to my Simon and Garfunkel tape, using their music to build a safe place where I could hide from the outside world.

But this invisible den was not a place into which I could invite my peers. Sure, we shared things that were beyond our parents' understanding – Marvel comics, reggae music, flares – but sitting around discussing the delights of pushing oneself to the brink of tears while listening to Simon and Garfunkel was, I feared, just too existential for my mates. They might think I was soft.

When that summer ended and we went back to school, everything had changed. Our old secondary modern had merged with a local grammar school as part of the Labour government's plan to create a system of comprehensive education that was based on ability rather than selection. If Harold Wilson had his way, I would be one of the last kids to disappoint their parents by failing the eleven plus.

Our new school was called Barking Abbey Comprehensive, named after the local Benedictine nunnery, founded by the East Saxons in AD 666 on the banks of the Hile, a mile or so down-river from the site of Apollo's Camp. Around the time that Alfred the Great was uniting the English, the abbey was sacked by Viking raiders, whose flat-bottomed long-ships could glide effortlessly up Barking Creek.

Re-establishing itself on the eastern bank of the river, the abbey became a centre of great scholarship, the abbess being amongst the most powerful women in the land. The Venerable Bede consulted with the nuns at Barking when writing his *History of the English People*. By the time of the Norman Conquest, the town was thriving in the shadow of the abbey, which would eventually grow to be one of the great religious foundations of medieval England.

In 1540, the abbey was demolished when Henry VIII dissolved the monasteries, and the town, which had once rivalled Colchester as the largest in Essex, lost its influence. Excavations in 1911 revealed the foundations of a massive church 330 feet long, which, in medieval times, would have towered over the flat landscape of marsh and meadow that bordered the Thames. All that remains to be seen now are the foundations of the great abbey, laid bare below the Saxon church of St Margaret, across the road from Carpet Warehouse and PC World.

Amalgamation with the grammar school brought us into contact with sixth-formers for the first time, a wholly new species who seemed to occupy a position in the school that was somewhere between pupils and teachers. Excused school uniform and with their own common room, they seemed immensely grown up to those of us in the second year.

Once a week, the sixth-formers were expected to conduct morning assembly. After prayers and a hymn, the headmaster would hand over to three or four students, chosen by the head of the English department, who would proceed to enlighten us with some meaningful thoughts.

Unbeknown to me at the time, my new-found heroes were hugely popular amongst teenage girls of a certain introverted sensibility – just the sort who might stay on for the sixth form. Simon and Garfunkel's sweetly melodic harmonies were much less threatening than the angry whine of Bob Dylan. And Paul Simon wrote ambitiously literate songs of alienation which suggested that the answer to all your problems was to shut yourself away from the world, preferably with some poetry or a good book. With their clean-cut, college-boy look, which appealed to teachers and parents, Simon and Garfunkel were ideal candidates for an appearance in sixth-form assembly.

That day duly arrived. Four seventeen-year-old girls – none of them, incidentally, elder sisters of my friends – announced that they were going to play us a song by Simon and Garfunkel. However, the music they chose took me completely by surprise. Instead of some paean to the seedy side of New York City or a song addressing the isolation of the individual in contemporary American life – the kind of thing that I had come to associate with their work – what we heard was very old. And very English.

Are you going to Scarborough Fair? . . .

The words rise up from the cedar-wood stereogram that sits

centre-stage; beyond the vocals, four gentle chimes ring, like distant church bells heard on the wind:

Parsley, sage, rosemary and thyme.

My mind starts racing back to a time before I was born, long before my century, to a time far yet near, to a place I can see but cannot find, that I know but cannot name.

Remember me to one who lives there,
She once was a true love of mine.

A harpsichord joins the voices, giving the music an aura of great antiquity. In response, a counter-melody begins to interweave itself into the original tune, winding around the aural space like an intricate Celtic pattern. As the voices rise to fill the school hall, I seem to hear, within the melodies, echoes of the choir at the great abbey of the marshes and creeks, singing their daily devotions amongst the people of medieval Barking.

For the first time, I feel a connection that goes beyond nationality. This is who I am. This is where I come from.

Of course, I already knew that I was English: I had been born in England to English parents; I lived in England and spoke the English language; give me a multiple-choice questionnaire about identity and I would tick the box marked 'English' every time. Such things I took for granted.

I had felt the great sense of joy and celebration when England won the World Cup in 1966, but that immortal moment was just that – a moment. Those feelings had been in response to that one event, which would come to be contradicted by other results, other failures. What I felt now was deeper, stronger – a sense of an England that was there when the foundations of Barking Abbey were laid and was still here now. This notion of England did not reside only in some rural idyll, some vision of a green and pleasant land. Even a town like ours, within the urban sprawl of East London, had its history. The Reformation had reduced the abbey to rubble, but the stones had found new homes in the walls of nearby houses, themselves in turn demolished and the stones re-used to build our town. What I didn't know then was that my feelings were no doubt greatly enhanced by the fact that the song was in the Dorian mode, the melancholy musical scale of medieval plainchant, making the connection with Barking Abbey even more explicit.

Again, I found myself ambushed by Simon and Garfunkel. Again they had awakened something deep within me, a sense of being informed not merely by place, but also by time. How had they conjured up this change in me? How could two nice, middle-class, Jewish boys from the Forest Hills suburb of New York, performing with Bob Dylan's backing band in the CBS studios in Manhattan, have unearthed such ageless sensibilities in my young heart?

'Scarborough Fair' is thought to be of Northumbrian origin and is known by a number of titles, among them 'The Cambric Shirt', 'An Acre of Land', 'Strawberry Lane', 'The Lover's Tasks', 'The Six Questions' and 'Whittingham Fair'. The words 'Parsley, sage, rosemary and thyme' are replaced in some variants of the song by other phrases: 'Every leaf grows many a time'; other plants: 'Sing ivy leaf, sweet william and thyme'; or pure nonsense: 'Hickalack, tickalack, farmalack-a-day'. The one constant motif is the reference to 'a true love of mine', although the status of that lover – future or past – varies.[1]

'Scarborough Fair' is a classic example of a riddle song, common in traditional balladry, in which a series of impossible tasks is required as proof of true love. The singer sends an intermediary with demands for his former/would-be lover. He asks for a cambric shirt to be made 'without any seam nor needlework'. ('Cambric' was a word which first appeared in the fourteenth century to describe the thin white linen produced in the French town of Cambrai.) He asks for an acre of land 'between the salt water and the sea strand' – that is, between the place where the waves end and the beach begins. He then demands that the crop grown in this acre be reaped 'with a sickle of leather'.

As sung by Simon and Garfunkel, it is not clear why these tasks are being set. However, one version of the song, from Yorkshire, suggests that it began as a ballad of rejection. A young man sets a series of conditions for his former true love. He calls for the cambric shirt to be washed in a well 'where water ne'er sprung, nor drop of rain fell'. He then tells her to 'hang it on yonder stone, where moss never grew since Adam was born'. His last message to her is that once she has done these tasks, then 'she can come unto me and married we'll be'. The implication is, of course, that it is his wish that they never will marry.

Far from being distraught, she responds by setting him conditions of her own. She asks for the acre of land, suggests that he 'sow it with one peppercorn' and then reap the resultant crop with the aforementioned useless leather sickle – although, showing a feminine eye for presentation, she asks that he 'bind it up with a peacock's feather'. If he remains in any doubt as to how she feels about being spurned, her attitude is made clear in the final verse:

> And when he has done and finished his work
> He can come to me for his cambric shirt.

You don't want to marry me? Fine. Go stuff yourself.

Folklorists hold that the herbs mentioned in the refrain have magical significance and, when worn together, the power to ward off the evil eye. This implies that one of the original protagonists may have been a malign supernatural being, out to steal an unsuspecting soul. That would seem to confirm the belief that the lyrics of 'Scarborough Fair' have evolved from an older song called 'The Elfin Knight', printed broadsides of which date back to the early 1600s.[2]

'Scarborough Fair' dispenses with the supernatural lover, and in the version sung by Simon and Garfunkel, the woman's response has disappeared too. They still chant the names of the magical herbs, but the song has become one of a young man's rejection. And this is no 'Dear Joan' letter. The fact that he asks someone else to convey his conditions to her points to a very public renunciation.

Although you may still occasionally encounter the phrase 'to plight one's troth' as an archaic means of describing an engagement to marry, both 'plight', in this sense, and 'troth' have fallen from use. The former is an Old English word meaning 'pledge', while the latter pertains to 'true' in its original sense, a synonym for 'faithful', as in 'She once was a true love of mine'.

Has this young man been betrothed, and is he now seeking to break the engagement? By setting his lover these impossible conditions if she wishes to be his true love, is he seeking to walk away with his honour intact? Or is he the spurned lover, saying to the girl who 'once was' his true love that he is so hurt that he would not even consider taking her back unless she can complete tasks that no mortal could hope to perform?

If Simon and Garfunkel's 'Scarborough Fair' is indeed a song of rejection, then it struck a deep chord with me. Turning thirteen as 1970 slid into 1971, I was reeling under the pressure of expectations placed on me by parents and teachers, and challenges laid down by friends and enemies at school. I withdrew into my own space, the upstairs box room at the front of the house which barely had room for my bed, my books and my tape recorder. Desperate to gain control of my situation, I began attempting to impose my own order on a threatening world.

My first act was to construct a top twenty of my favourite songs in February 1971. This window to my soul contained no less than fourteen tracks by the artists known to me then as 'Simon and Garfunkle'. The Jackson Five got a look-in at number twelve and McGuiness Flint's 'When I'm Dead And Gone' just nipped in at nineteen. Every track from *Bridge Over Troubled Water* was there, with 'The Boxer' at number three, in recognition of the emotions that it had unleashed on Walcheren Island the year before. 'Marrakesh Express' by Crosby, Stills and Nash was my number-two choice, its promise of exotic destinations helping to fuel my dreams of escape.

At number one sat 'Scarborough Fair', a song which had become central to my sense of self, although I had not yet managed to capture it on my tape recorder. But surely it could only be a matter of time before quizzing my classmates about their elder sisters' record collections paid off?

Joe was a close friend of mine who lived on an estate built by the council in the 1930s. All the roads were named after heroes of the Labour movement: Kier Hardie Way led to Bevan Avenue. A small close was dedicated to the leader of the 1911 Dock Strike, Ben Tillet. Labour Party stalwart George Lansbury had an avenue named for him, as did Margaret Bondfield, who in 1929 was the first woman to become a Cabinet minister. These were not merely important figures from Labour Party history – they were men and women whose actions had led to the improvement of the lives of the ordinary working people. Labour had always delivered for the people of Barking, and as a result, the town had been solidly Labour for as long as anyone could remember.

Joe's house was a bus ride and a walk away, forcing me to lug my seven-kilogram tape recorder on to the number 62 bus and then all the way down Bevan Avenue, but it was worth it. His elder sister, Ruth, had an extensive collection of albums, including two by Simon and Garfunkel – *Sounds of Silence*, their breakthrough LP from 1966, and *The Graduate*, the soundtrack to the Mike Nicholls film starring Dustin Hoffman.

Sounds of Silence was Simon and Garfunkel's first fully realized album and contained some beautiful love songs. The real focus, however, was a brace of songs addressing alienation – the classic title track itself, the poignant 'Most Peculiar Man', 'Richard Cory' and the stirring song that closed the album, 'I Am A Rock'. I don't know what effect this song had on the elder sisters of my school friends, but it gave me great comfort and cause for hope in a world that seemed utterly uninterested in the likes of me. Pushed along by stabs of Hammond organ, and the kind of high guitar lines that had graced records by the Byrds, the lyrics traced the outline of my recent withdrawal, justifying my actions in 4/4 time.

'I've built walls, a fortress deep and mighty', they sing.

Me too! I cried, although the only things deep and mighty about my predicament were the depth of my sense of injustice at my situation and the mighty feeling that I deserved better. The harsh realities of being a fourteen-year-old boy were proving difficult to deal with. I wasn't brash enough to keep the bullies away and my attempts at making an impression with the girls were lamentable. My confidence and ability to concentrate suffered. As a result, my self-respect was in tatters, and yet these lyrics seemed to hold that my retreat from the daunting pressures of the outside world was somehow dignified, heroic almost.

'I have my books and my poetry to protect me' is sung with an almost ecstatic defiance, as if to imply that the hours I had spent with my head buried in the works of Ray Bradbury and Alan Garner would give me the skills required to avoid the flying fists of fourth-form bully boys. I drew succour from this song, finding strength and clarity in its breathtakingly absolutist sentiments. 'I Am A Rock' became my mantra and helped turn my self-pity into rage, shielding me from the insecurities of adolescence like an angrily slammed door.

However, for all my bluster, the track which immediately grabbed my attention on first hearing it was the tender 'Kathy's Song', its introspective lyrics made all the more personal by being the only song on the album which Paul Simon sings alone. It is as if the artist has taken the listener behind the scenery of Simon and Garfunkel – number-one hit singles and all – in order to vouchsafe something important. Know this, he says, there is no comfort for me here:

> I gaze beyond the rain-drenched streets
> To England, where my heart lies.

Those two lines burnt themselves into my consciousness.

As I looked to America for inspiration, and to Simon and Garfunkel in particular, my hero proceeded to take me aside in a moment of quiet reflection and tell me that he would rather be in England.

Listening to the album, I heard something of the English folk songs we sang at junior school. 'April, Come She Will' has a ten-line lyric that could have been taken from an eighteenth-century sampler. And there is something very familiar about the harpsichord-driven 'Leaves That Are Green', with its memorable opening lines reminiscent of the nonsense songs of Carroll or Lear.

Having recorded the whole of the *Sounds of Silence* LP, I had only enough room left on my tape for one song from *The Graduate* soundtrack album. And so it was that I finally captured 'Scarborough Fair/Canticle', the song that had haunted me since I heard it in that school assembly. Listening closely to its lyrics, I now realize that the song has anti-war overtones. Wrapped around the old folk song, Paul Simon had written a counter melody, the 'Canticle' of the title. The lyrics are hard to make out at first, something about a clarion call. In the verse, the phrase 'polishes a gun' leaps out from behind the main vocal. In the penultimate verse, as the song reaches its climax, the lyrics of 'Scarborough Fair' finally succumb to the weight of the counter melody, which comes to the fore to deliver the lines:

> Generals order their soldiers to kill
> And to fight for a cause they've long ago forgotten.

Played on radios all over America when the song was in the top twenty in April 1968, this lyric could only have been interpreted in one way – as a comment on the Vietnam War. Simon's condemnation of the long-forgotten cause could not have been released at a more timely moment, just as Americans were beginning to wake up to the barbarity being committed in their name in Indo-China. On 6 March 1968, as the song climbed the charts, a company of American soldiers entered the village of My Lai, rounded up all the villagers, including the young and old, ordered them into a ditch and shot them all dead. An investigation into this atrocity later estimated that between 450 and 500 people had been murdered at My Lai, none of them combatants.

Utilizing the beautiful melody of an English folk song, Paul Simon had smuggled an anti-war message into the homes of Middle America.

5

To England, Where My Heart Lies

The generation born in the 1940s experienced rock 'n' roll as a revolutionary force. It changed their world by breaking down the racial segregation of American culture, while annoying the hell out of their parents. By the end of the fifties, however, the flame had flickered and dimmed. Elvis was in the army, Chuck Berry was in jail, Little Richard had found God and Buddy Holly had found an immortality of sorts, killed in a plane crash aged twenty-two.

Having absorbed the initial shock of rock 'n' roll, the music industry set about creating teen idols who would not look out of place alongside Perry Como and Connie Francis. Fabian took over from Elvis, Bobby Vee replaced Buddy Holly and Conway Twitty became a household name, much as Chuck Berry had done just a few years before. The new guys had the look but none of the attitude. And teenage music without attitude is just pop.

Quietly at first, but gradually gaining momentum, kids began seeking out music that was the antithesis of the manufactured pop which had neutered the forces that rock 'n' roll had unleashed. Pop music was new and shiny, so they sought out music that was old and tarnished; pop was manufactured, so they learned to prize authenticity; pop was ubiquitous, so they delighted in the obscure; above all, pop music was full of throwaway sentiments, and so songs that spoke of real emotions and deeply held convictions were especially prized.

The first sign that something was going on was when The Kingston Trio hit the top ten with 'Tom Dooley' in October 1958. This traditional ballad had been collected in North Carolina twenty years before, from a man whose grandmother knew the protagonist, Tom Dula, a desperado and Civil War veteran who murdered one Laura Foster and was hanged for his crime in 1868.[1]

Yet the version that climbed to the top of the charts lacked the gory details of the original, and The Kingston Trio looked much too polite to have harmed anyone. 'Tom Dooley' was seen as a novelty hit, but just as its lyrics hid a deeper meaning, the song's appearance in the charts signified a cultural shift.

Whenever popular music becomes stale and predictable, clues to a new direction can sometimes be found in old record shops. Music that has fallen out of fashion, yet retains its potency, can lie dormant in the dusty racks at the back of the store for years, waiting to be rediscovered by a new generation of listeners. In the early sixties, it was folk music from the twenties and thirties that fed a new audience hungry for authenticity. Woody Guthrie's 'Dust Bowl Ballads', which had sold only a few hundred copies when it first appeared in 1940, suddenly became much sought after, as did the recordings made by Huddie Ledbetter – Lead Belly – when he was serving time for murder in the Angola State Penitentiary in Louisiana in 1933.

Hippest of all these records was *The Anthology of American Folk Music*, whose eighty-four tracks, spread over three volumes and twelve sides, were the mother lode for those seeking authentic material. Released by Folkways Records in 1952, the anthology was a compilation of old 78 rpm records released between 1927 and 1932, brought together by Harry Smith, a cultural anthropologist and beat philosophizer who lived on the West Coast.

For anyone interested in learning how rock 'n' roll was born, Harry Smith provided a genealogy. Here were the rural blues, with their roots in the West African griot tradition, living in sin with hillbilly songs whose lyrics could be traced back to the broadsheet ballads of Jacobean England.

To listen to the anthology was to take part in a séance in which revenant voices crackle and moan. Blind Lemon Jefferson pleads that his grave be kept clean. The apparition of Ernest V. Stoneman wonders when you are coming to see him. Holy men cry, 'Oh Death, where is thy sting?' Slow and mournful ballads are sung to double-time banjo, as if the Devil were on the performer's tail.

These voices seemed to emerge from where the street lights ended, beyond the comforting glow of modern America. 'In the pines, in the pines, where the sun never shines', as one of the old songs has it, was a place unfamiliar to most urban American record-buyers, a primal place that the twentieth century had not yet made its own.

The shiny new pop acts that replaced the original rock 'n' rollers could not have seemed further from this old-timey music. Yet one of the most successful bubblegum acts had roots in the dark piney woods.

The Everly Brothers were as manufactured as any pop act

when they burst into the top ten in March 1957 with 'Bye Bye Love'. The two teenagers had been singing with their parents since childhood on radio shows from Iowa to Tennessee. With country-music roots, they were Nashville's attempt to make a buck out of the teen market. Between 1957 and 1960, they scored eleven top-twenty hits, specializing in close two-part harmonies on ballads of teenage trauma such as 'Wake Up, Little Susie' and 'Take A Message To Mary'.

In 1958, the Everly Brothers recorded an album that stunned their teenage fan base. *Songs Our Daddy Taught Us* was a collection of material that would not have seemed out of place on *The Anthology of American Folk Music*. Ike Everly had been a coal miner in Mullenburg County, Kentucky, and the songs he had taught his boys were ballads from the hillbilly tradition.

'Hillbilly' was the name given to the poor southern whites who migrated to the northern industrial cities in the early twentieth century, looking for work. They came from the hills that stretched all the way from south-western Pennsylvania down into northern Alabama: the Great Smoky Mountains, the Alleghenys, the Blue Ridge Mountains and the Cumberlands. Collectively these ranges were known as the Appalachian Mountains.

Geographical isolation, coupled with extreme poverty, ensured that Appalachian culture remained much as it had been when the area was first settled in the mid-eighteenth century by people of English, Scottish, Irish and Dutch-German stock. Hillbilly music was characterized by fiddles and banjos, played at a blistering pace to accompany step-dancing styles which had evolved from British and Irish originals.

The hillbillies also loved maudlin ballads that evoked

feelings of great pathos, often concluding with a strong moralistic message. As befitted such songs of lamentation, a high-pitched singing style was favoured, which had its roots in the keening wail of the Scots/Irish tradition.

This form found its apotheosis in the close-harmony singing of the brother duets. The Monroe Brothers, the Delmore Brothers, the Callahan Brothers and Bill and Earl Bolick, who for entirely understandable reasons performed under the name of the Blue Sky Boys, gave credence to the belief that those of the same blood could harmonize with the greatest purity. Their sound was characterized by pure, high-pitched, two-part harmonies, with one voice carrying the melody whilst the other sang a third or a fifth above.

Most successful of all the brother duets were the Louvin Brothers, from Sand Mountain, Alabama, who released an album in 1956 that became a classic of the genre. *Tragic Songs Of Life* mixed popular songs from the 1930s with old Appalachian ballads; it featured the guitar of the Everly Brothers' mentor, Chet Atkins, and provided a blueprint, both in style and material, for *Songs Our Daddy Taught Us*.

Like the Louvins before them, some of the songs that the Everlys chose to record were only twenty years old. 'Lightning Express' had been recorded by the Blue Sky Boys, 'Silver Haired Daddy Of Mine' by Gene Autry. Others, though, were much older. 'The Roving Gambler' began life in Ireland as 'The Roving Journeyman'. 'Who's Gonna Shoe Your Pretty Little Feet?' is descended from a Scottish song, 'The Lass Of Roch Royal'. 'Barbara Allen', a haunting tale of love and death, is among the most widely disseminated of English ballads and is mentioned by Samuel Pepys in a diary entry dated 2 January 1666.

The fact that these songs are recorded with the barest production, just an acoustic guitar laying down the rhythm, adds to the sense of eeriness that pervades these tales of morbidity and loss. It is as if those two nice Everly boys have suddenly become hollow-eyed wraiths, their smiles turned grim by the gruesome content of the songs, their harmonies, once so sweet, now full of unsettling cadences.

The gothic timbre in their voices is best heard in the brooding 'Down In The Willow Garden', a version of the classic English murder ballad 'The Oxford Girl'. The protagonist, fearful of impending marriage or perhaps unplanned parenthood – his motives are never made clear – murders his innocent fiancée and throws her body into the river, returning home only to be apprehended and hanged.

The song can be traced back to an eighteenth-century English broadside entitled 'The Berkshire Tragedy Or The Wittam Miller'. It crossed the Atlantic with the early settlers, whose descendants rewrote it again and again as 'Rose Connally', 'Pretty Polly', 'The Jealous Lover Of Low Green Valley', 'Banks Of The Ohio' and 'The Lexington Murder'. One well-known version, 'The Knoxville Girl', was the most popular song in the Louvin Brothers' repertoire.

When the Everly Brothers sing 'Down In The Willow Garden', you can hear a deep remorse in their voices. Yet they sing with a high, aching purity as if, having mutilated their sweetheart's body, they are gently, lovingly, laying out the poor girl's corpse.

That Don and Phil Everly had an influence on Simon and Garfunkel is well known – a version of their first hit, 'Bye Bye Love', was featured on *Bridge Over Troubled Water*, and Simon and Garfunkel's first record together, a minor regional hit in 1957 under the name of Tom and Jerry, was an Everly Brothers sound-alike single called 'Hey Schoolgirl'. Yet throughout their career, the point of reference that Simon and Garfunkel return to again and again is *Songs Our Daddy Taught Us*. Tracks from the album regularly appeared in their live set: 'Silver Haired Daddy Of Mine' features on the bootleg recording of their November 1969 show at Miami University, and *One Night In Paris*, a sublime bootleg of their May 1970 gig in the French capital, contains both 'Silver Haired Daddy' and 'Lightning Express'.

Art Garfunkel recorded 'Down In The Willow Garden' and 'Barbara Allen' for his first solo album, *Angel Clare*, and when *Sounds of Silence* was reissued in 2001 as part of the Columbia Legacy series, two of its bonus tracks were Simon and Garfunkel's own versions of 'Barbara Allen' and 'Roving Gambler'.

Songs Our Daddy Taught Us pointed the way forwards for Tom and Jerry after they failed to set the world alight with their follow-up to 'Hey Schoolgirl' in 1959. Paul Simon continued writing and recording bubblegum pop under the name Paul Landis, with little success. He heard something of the pure, high voicings of the Everlys in Joan Baez, a folk singer who herself owed a debt to Jean Ritchie, a singer from the Appalachian tradition.[2]

Simon took to hanging out in Washington Square in downtown Manhattan, where on Sunday afternoons crowds of young people gathered to sing bluegrass, blues, work songs, beat poetry, protest songs, spirituals and, of course, old ballads from the British Isles. It was from this milieu, centred around the folk clubs of Greenwich Village, that Bob Dylan emerged in 1962.

Born Robert Zimmerman in Hibbing, Minnesota, Dylan, like Simon, came from a middle-class Jewish family. He too had been inspired by Elvis Presley, only to be betrayed by Frankie Avalon. Attending college in Minneapolis, he had read Woody Guthrie's *Bound for Glory*, dropped out and headed to New York to find his hero. Realizing that no authentic hillbilly singer could be called Zimmerman, Dylan transformed himself, arriving in New York with a repertoire of songs taken from *The Anthology of American Folk Music*.

His eponymous debut album had much in common with *Songs Our Daddy Taught Us*, in that it contained mostly traditional Appalachian ballads such as 'Man Of Constant Sorrow', or tunes that had been recorded twenty years earlier like Curtis Jones's 'Highway 51'. The two songs on the album that Dylan had written himself – 'Song To Woody' and 'Talkin' New York' – were highly derivative of his hero's style.

Released in March 1962, the album garnered good reviews, but failed to register outside of the folk community, selling fewer than five thousand copies in its first year. Almost immediately, he began work on a follow-up, initially entitled *Bob Dylan's Blues*. Early sessions mostly comprised old blues songs, few of which made it on to the finished record.

Returning to the studio in July 1962, Dylan began laying down tracks: 'Ramblin' Gamblin' Willie', 'Rocks And Gravel', 'Down The Highway', 'Bob Dylan's Blues', 'Corrina Corrina', 'Talkin' John Birch', 'Honey Just Allow Me One More Chance', and 'Blowin' In The Wind' – all except the latter firmly rooted in the blues tradition.[3]

A topical reworking of the old Negro spiritual song 'No More Auction Block For Me', 'Blowin' In The Wind' was a simplistic, repetitive song full of questions, similar in style to the folk standard 'Where Have All The Flowers Gone'. This song would typecast Dylan as the archetypal 'protest singer', spokesman for his generation and left-wing commentator.

Returning to the studio in late October, Dylan seemed to have run out of ideas, with 'Don't Think Twice, It's Alright' the only light on the horizon. Although undoubtedly a great song, it was little different from other confessional love songs coming out of Greenwich Village at the time, quite comfortable sitting alongside Tom Paxton's 'Last Thing On My Mind' or Tim Hardin's 'Reason To Believe' in the repertoire of any respectable busker.

In December, Dylan returned to the studio for the seventh time that year in an attempt to finish the album, recording a run-of-the-mill topical song, 'Oxford Town', and a nonsensical talking blues number, 'I Shall Be Free'. If that was all the material he had for the second album, it was hardly going to set the world alight. However, at the very end of the session, Dylan came up with a song like nothing else he had ever written.

Taking the old English ballad 'Lord Randall', with its opening lines of 'Where have you been, Lord Randall, my son, where have you been my handsome young man?', Dylan had rewritten the words in the light of the Cuban Missile Crisis, which had brought the USA and the Soviet Union to the brink of nuclear war just a month or so before.

'A Hard Rain's A-Gonna Fall' was clearly a topical song, yet its apocalyptic imagery seemed to come from the Book of Revelation via the visions of William Blake and the poetry of Rimbaud. The lyrics also owed something to the Beat poets, but whereas they were concerned with the modern, Dylan seemed to have reached back into the past for inspiration. With this song, Dylan broke free from the restrictions of the folk/blues idiom which proscribed most of the music heard in the coffee houses of Greenwich Village. He also opened up a generational divide. Whereas the simple message of 'Blowin' In The Wind' was instantly memorable and accessible to all, 'A Hard Rain's A-Gonna Fall' seemed impenetrable to the older generation, who felt threatened by the song's unsettling vision of a post-apocalyptic world.

The lyrics lead the listener through a series of disturbing images, each warning what might come to pass should the hard rain fall upon us. It's a journey that takes us to territory into which no singer-songwriter, until that moment, had ever strayed. With the skill of an alchemist, Dylan had brought a new element to his songwriting by fusing together older forms of music. Hungry for more material with which to refine this new process, he headed off to England a week later.

For someone raised in the American mid-west, Dylan seems to have had a strong affinity with the traditions and mythology of England. In his autobiography, *Chronicles: Vol. 1*, he recalls the poet Archibald MacLeish asking him who his boyhood heroes were. Dylan responds by naming two of the central figures of English folklore: Robin Hood and St George the dragon-slayer.[4] Perhaps it was this that drew him to England in search of inspiration.

On arriving in London, he spent every evening in one or other of the many folk clubs that had sprung up in the aftermath of the skiffle boom. All those kids who had learned to play acoustic guitar from Lonnie Donegan needed somewhere to perform and the Troubadour, Bunjies Coffee House and Les Cousins all specialized in the traditional folk music of the British Isles. A great revival was under way.

During his stay, Dylan met Martin Carthy, a twenty-one-year-old Londoner who had bought 'Heartbreak Hotel', 'Rock Around The Clock' and Donegan's 'Rock Island Line' on the same day in 1956. Although drawn to the energy of rock 'n' roll, Carthy was confronted with the sheer impossibility of buying an electric guitar in fifties Britain, so skiffle won out and he settled for an acoustic instrument.

When the skiffle craze petered out, Carthy was among those who stayed acoustic and found their way to the folk clubs. By the time he met Dylan, Carthy had developed a style of guitar-playing and singing that made him the foremost interpreter of traditional ballads of his generation. Carthy taught Dylan the nineteenth-century ballad 'Lord Franklin' and the lovelorn 'Scarborough Fair'.

The trip to England seemed to have a rejuvenating effect on Dylan's songwriting, and on his return to the studio the following April, he cut a bunch of classic songs that were all framed in the English ballad tradition: 'Masters Of War' borrowed the tune of an old song called 'Nottamun Town'; 'Lord Franklin' had become 'Bob Dylan's Dream'; and 'Girl From The North Country' was clearly a re-write of Carthy's 'Scarborough Fair'. Once several of the mediocre blues songs he had recorded had been replaced by these refitted English ballads, the album was retitled *The Freewheelin' Bob Dylan*, and on its release in May 1963 it sold enough copies to earn a gold disc.

Dylan had drunk deeply from the well of English tradition and had returned as the greatest songwriter of his generation.

The folk boom which flourished in the wake of Dylan's success had a profound effect on the songwriting of Paul Simon. His first effort in the folk idiom, 'He Was My Brother', was a song inspired by the Civil Rights movement. Yet when Simon stood up to sing his topical songs in the New York folk clubs, he found little encouragement. A middle-class college boy from Forest Hills trying to sing about racism down south sounded awfully contrived to the bohemians of Greenwich Village.

If he was to gain credibility, Simon would have to do what almost all of his contemporaries had done: reinvent himself. With that in mind, in late 1963 he travelled to England, where he found an audience willing to take his songs at face value. Growing in confidence, he returned to New York in early 1964 and talked himself into a recording contract with Tom Wilson, Bob Dylan's producer at CBS.

Art Garfunkel was hastily summoned and the album that the duo recorded, *Wednesday Morning 3AM*, contained mostly earnest covers of topical songs of the day, with a handful of Simon originals thrown in. The stand-out track was a song that Simon had honed to perfection in the English folk clubs – 'The Sound Of Silence'.

On the release of the album, Simon and Garfunkel made their debut on the New York folk scene, yet were still unable to find an appreciative audience. When the record sold a mere three thousand copies, Art Garfunkel drifted back to college. Paul Simon returned to England.

There he sought out Martin Carthy, from whom Bob Dylan had learned the traditional ballads. Simon picked up 'Scarborough Fair' from Carthy and began writing songs in the English folk idiom. 'April, Come She Will' sounds as if it might have been collected from a Sussex shepherd in 1908, while 'The Leaves That Are Green' has a melody that could have come from Samuel Pepys's diary via the autoharp of Jean Ritchie.

Travelling around the folk clubs of Britain, Simon felt he was finally doing something in the spirit of Woody Guthrie, something that would give him the outsider status he longed for. Clearly aware of the persona he was creating for himself, he wrote the self-mythologizing 'Homeward Bound' while waiting for the milk train after a gig in Lancashire.

The attentive audiences Simon found in England gave him the confidence to develop his own style. 'I Am A Rock', 'Richard Cory', 'Blessed' and 'A Most Peculiar Man' – trademark 'outsider' songs that would eventually appear on the *Sounds of Silence* album – all date from Paul Simon's time in England, as does the hauntingly beautiful 'Kathy's Song'.

On his first visit to England in late 1963, Simon had been taken under the wing of Dave McCausland, who ran a folk club at the Railway Hotel in Brentwood, Essex, on the outskirts of East London. The night after arriving in England, Simon played his first gig there. Taking tickets on the door was the eighteen-year-old Kathleen Mary Chitty.

Kathy worked as a secretary and lived with her parents in nearby Hornchurch, Essex. She was quietly spoken and shy, and she and Simon were drawn to each other. She became both his lover and muse, inspiring his most fruitful period of songwriting.

In June 1965, believing his partnership with Art Garfunkel to have ended with the failure of *Wednesday Morning 3AM*, Simon recorded a solo album in London, showcasing many of the songs he had written during his English sojourn. The cover of *The Paul Simon Songbook* shows him sitting cross-legged on a cobblestone street, studiously scrutinizing a child's doll he is holding. Kathy sits with him, dressed in jeans and V-neck sweater, her long dark hair framing her childlike face. Her eyes are lowered as she, too, studies the doll. In her hand she holds a small figure on a horse. This is the only glimpse we get of her, the dark lady of the ballads. Behind them, the cobblestone street shines wet with rain, echoing the rain-drenched imagery of 'Kathy's Song'.

It's hard to grasp now, given the feelings that song evoked in me when I first heard it, but it seems that the England in which Paul Simon's heart lay was not some green and pleasant arcadia, but a place just a few stops along the District Line from where I lived.

For much of 1965, Simon was living in a flat in Dellow House, just off Cable Street in London's East End. The quickest, cheapest route to Kathy's house in Hornchurch, some twenty miles to the east, would have been by train. Stepney East would have been his nearest station and from there he would have only had to change once – at Barking.

How often, I wonder, during the time he spent in England, did Paul Simon stand on the platform of Barking station, waiting for the train to take him to his Kathy? As it pulled out, did he ever gaze down at the kids in the playground of Northbury Junior School? Or was he looking the other way, along the length of Tanner Street and down Park Avenue, towards the tall poplars that stood sentry at the park gates?

In the shade of those poplars, I stayed loyal to Simon and Garfunkel. My top twenty of July 1971 was full of new entries – Dave and Ansell Collins, Cat Stevens, Smokey Robinson and the Miracles – but the top of the charts remained much the same. 'The Boxer' is still at number three, although Crosby, Stills and Nash have been replaced at number two by the Delfonics' youth-club smoocher 'La La Means I Love You'.

'Scarborough Fair' kept its number-one spot, declaring to the world that England was where my heart lay too.

A year passed before I felt the need to re-order my chart. By July 1972, 'Kathy's Song' had come straight in at number seven, one of four Simon and Garfunkel songs in a top ten propped up by Slade. Above the Black Country glam gurners sat reggae star Jimmy Cliff, then it is all singer-songwriters: Tony Hazard, whose song 'Woman In The West' stays with me to this day, despite the fact that I only heard it a couple of times on the radio; Gordon Lightfoot is in there with 'In The Early Morning Rain', as is Don McLean, whose double whammy of 'American Pie' and 'Vincent' had turned my head, but not to the extent that 'The Boxer' could be dislodged from its number-three position. And at number one, constant, unassailable: 'Scarborough Fair'.

Shortly after I compiled that most recent chart, I talked myself into a Saturday job in a shop opposite Barking station. Guy Norris Ltd had originally been a hardware store, but some time in the 1960s the basement had been converted into a record store, the biggest in town. In the windows of the double-fronted shop, hardware and vinyl vied with each other for custom – the sacred and the profane. One window glorified the latest macho power tools and garden furniture, the other offered the transgressive delights of *The Rise and Fall of Ziggy Stardust and the Spiders from Mars* and *Tighten Up Vol. 4*.

As the Saturday boy in the hardware store, I spent my time selling nails by the pound and helping total strangers choose new wallpaper for their living rooms. My wages I mostly spent in the basement.

Within weeks of starting, I had purchased my first long-playing album – *Simon and Garfunkel's Greatest Hits*. For once I had to make do with someone else's compilation. Of the songs that I was not familiar with, 'America' immediately stood out. From the moment it fades in, the two voices softly humming together, to its calliope organ fade-out, I was captivated by the imagery of this song, the two lovers lost in search of America.

It conjured up the feelings I'd had on first hearing 'Bridge Over Troubled Water', of the Boxer and Baby Driver adrift in the vast land of lost content that was post-war America. I wanted so much to be there with them, on that Greyhound bus travelling down the New Jersey turnpike.

And yet . . . what is the name of the girl who sleeps in his arms as the moon rolls over an open field? Kathy. Kathy Chitty from Hornchurch, Essex. Paul Simon may have walked off to look for America, but his heart still lies in England.

That summer of 1972, I worked weekdays at the hardware store covering for staff members on holiday. I took my lunch breaks down in the record basement, eating my sandwiches in one of the small cubicles where customers listened to records before deciding whether or not to buy. As I had half an hour for lunch, I'd ask the staff to put an album on for me. I heard a lot of great music that way. 'Every Picture Tells A Story' by Rod Stewart, albums by the Sutherland Brothers, Jackson Browne, Laura Nyro.

And then one day I asked them to put on *Bob Dylan's Greatest Hits*. Come the end of the week, I took that album home. The effect this record had on me can be illustrated by the fact that within a month I had swapped my copy of *The Jackson Five's Greatest Hits* with a school friend for his father's original copy of Dylan's 1964 album *The Times They Are A-Changing*. In doing so, I was relinquishing the polished pop production of Tamla Motown for the rootsiest music I'd ever heard.

The stark setting of the songs on *The Times They Are A-Changing* and the harshness of Dylan's voice served only to highlight the power of the lyrics. A sense of righteous anger that I had not felt since first hearing 'I Am A Rock' welled up inside me. But these were not songs of personal isolation, determined to shut out the world. Dylan's reportage coldly gave you the facts – of the lonesome death of Hattie Carroll and the shooting of Medgar Evers, of Hollis Brown, driven to kill his family in despair – but it also asked questions. His expression in the photo on the album cover is that of a man waiting for an answer: what are you going to do about all this?

The title track of the album was a clarion call. Now is the time to put down your books and emerge from the safety of your room and set about changing the world for the better. And as no Kathy had emerged to be my muse, I decided to shoulder my share of the world's troubles and follow Dylan.

He took me on a journey through the music that had inspired him, to Woody Guthrie and beyond, through the membrane of memory that divides the authored lyric from the folk song, acquainting my ear with the blues while sending me through the hollows and hills of Appalachia to hitch a ride on the old hillbilly ballads, back across the ocean to the traditional music of my own country. Dylan brought it all back home for me. Inspired by his lead, I immersed myself in English folk music, borrowing album after album from the folk section of the newly opened Barking Central Library: industrial ballads sung by Bert Lloyd and Ewan McColl; Shirley Collins's plaintive voice, framed by her sister Dolly's haunting pipe organ; the Watersons, like a force of nature, with their roaring harmonies.

Eventually, following the clues that Dylan had laid, I came across Martin Carthy's version of 'Scarborough Fair', the one which Paul Simon had learned back in 1964. Those two Jewish guys from New York had opened my mind to the beauty and power of my own native culture and now I was discovering it for myself, finding songs that once again put me in touch with my own timeless sense of belonging.

The circle was complete.

A few years ago, I was discussing with the author and broadcaster Patrick Wright a series of programmes about the River Thames that he was in the process of making. We exchanged letters on the subject of the estuary and the untold stories that line the Essex and Kent shorelines. He regretted that he had been unable to substantiate the rumour that local boxing legend Billy Walker had been Paul Simon's inspiration for 'The Boxer'. Walker, who with his brother George ran the first boxing training camp in Britain at Corringham on the Essex side of the estuary, was one of the most popular sporting figures of the 1960s. A good-looking man, his curly blond hair and easy-going nature led to him being initially dubbed the Golden Boy, but after a series of hard-fought victories in the heavyweight division, Billy Walker became known as the Blond Bomber. Between 1962 and 1969, he racked up an impressive record of wins, but international success eluded him. His biggest fight came in November 1967, when he challenged Henry Cooper for his British and Empire heavyweight titles at Wembley Pool. The winner would get the chance to fight the world champion, Muhammad Ali. Cooper stopped Billy with a cut to the eye in the sixth round. Within eighteen months, Walker had retired.

Might the Blond Bomber have been the original inspiration for the song that had awakened me all those years before on the island of Walcheren? Tantalizingly, in *The Songs of Paul Simon*, a songbook published in 1973, there are reproductions of two pages of lyrics hastily scrawled on airline notepaper that represent the genesis of 'The Boxer'. In the top left-hand corner, written in the same handwriting as the lyrics, are the words 'Billy Walker'.

I passed this fact on to Patrick Wright as evidence of some connection between Walker and the song. The trail that he had been following was based on a rumour that had circulated around the East End when 'The Boxer' hit the charts in 1969. As Patrick recounted it in a letter to me:

> Walker was opening endless fetes and galas in Kent and Essex
> at the time when Simon was living in and around Dagenham,
> and it used to be said that it was the sight of BW cutting the
> ribbons at some or other such event that set Simon running.

Could Billy Walker have been The Boxer?

I saw him once, when he appeared in the Barking Carnival some time in the mid-sixties. I walked with my family to the top of Park Avenue to watch the parade go by and there he was, guest of honour, in an open-topped Rolls Royce, smiling and waving to the crowd as the procession moved along Longbridge Road before turning into Barking Park, where the annual fair was waiting to be declared open.

And I wonder now if among the crowds on that day there was a young singer-songwriter from New York, watching the parade with his girlfriend from up the road in Hornchurch. Did they join us in the throng that pushed through the park gates to see Billy Walker crown the Carnival Queen? Did Paul Simon walk through Barking fair with his lovely Kathy before slipping off to play a late-night set in some West End coffee house, the seed of a brand-new song germinating in his head?

6

Singing the History

While Paul Simon was busy learning his craft during the sixties folk boom, ideas generated by the original Folk Revival, inspired by Cecil Sharp at the turn of the century, were just reaching me. At Northbury Junior School, attempts were made to teach us English country dancing.

Did no one realize the psychological damage that could be inflicted by forcing pre-teenage boys to hold hands with girls and skip in formation around an assembly hall? Or recognize that little could be learned during lessons that were prone to moments of violent over-enthusiasm interspersed with fits of giggling?

If the aim was to connect us with our native traditions, country dancing had the opposite effect, inculcating me with a cultural aversion to morris dancing which, to be honest, I still struggle to suppress. Rather more successful were the music lessons where we learned songs about colourful figures from Britain's past.

We heard of the beauty of 'The Lass Of Richmond Hill' and witnessed the death of the heartless 'Barbara Allen'. We learned of anti-heroes like 'The Lincolnshire Poacher', 'Rare Turpin Hero' and 'The Raggle-Taggle Gypsies'. We sang sea shanties and nonsense songs with lyrics which seemed full of dark pagan meaning. Who were the lily-white boys and the six proud walkers in 'Green Grow The Rushes-O'? What was the significance of the symbols at your door and the April rainers? And why were the people so wretched to poor 'John Barleycorn'?

And while we sang of archetypes and folk devils, we were also aware that, sometimes, we were singing of history too. 'Song Of The Western Men' related the story of how Bishop Trelawney of Bristol was imprisoned by James II. 'Boney Was A Warrior' concerned the Napoleonic threat. 'Heart Of Oak', with its opening lines, 'Come, cheer up me lads, 'tis to glory we steer/ To add something more to this glorious year,' celebrated the events of 1759, the 'year of victories' that saw British forces triumph against the French at Quebec and in Quiberon Bay. And a particular favourite of the whole class was 'The British Grenadiers', with its 'tow, row, row, row, ro-w, row' chorus.

What these songs had in common, apart from their militaristic content, was that they all came from a particular period of our history – from the Glorious Revolution to Trafalgar and Waterloo – when the English and Scottish parliaments were united to form Great Britain. Yet the *Sing Together!* songbook, from which we learned these tunes, was not some late-nineteenth-century remnant, but a brand-new collection of songs published for schools by Oxford University Press in 1967. By singing them, we were imbibing inspiring tales of the national heroes of our past along with the twelve times table and free school milk.

These songs had the effect of identifying us as British while simultaneously introducing us to our natural opponents, the French. We were staunch monarchists, whose love for our country was rivalled only by our loyalty to our sovereign, while they were untrustworthy republicans who hated everything we stood for. Whereas our liberties were guaranteed by the continuity of the old order, France represented change, disorder and the alien ideals of *liberté, egalité* and *fraternité*.

The songs we learned in junior school were more influential in the formation of our national consciousness than our history lessons were. For while the conduct of the British Empire was coming under scrutiny in the classrooms of the mid-1960s, there is no room for reflection in 'Rule Britannia'.

We were introduced to the traditional version of British history, which had been handed down to us from time immemorial: a gloriously unfolding pageant, in which the aristocracy, guided by divine providence, was able to accommodate the necessary evolution of a constitution unparalleled in world history, whose unique nature gave us alone the right to extend our way of doing things to various less fortunate peoples scattered far and wide across the globe.

The truth, however, was that this particular version of events had been concocted just over a century earlier by a historian bent on using history to make a political point. Although we were unaware of it at the time, those songs that we sang so lustily were our beginner's guide to what academics refer to as 'The Whig Interpretation of History'.

The Whigs were one of the early political factions in Parliament. A powerful group of Protestant aristocrats, they gained ascendancy by engineering the removal of the Catholic King James II in favour of the Protestant William of Orange in 1688, a move designed to ensure that England remained a

Protestant country. When William failed to provide an heir, the Whig Parliament swiftly passed a law, still in force today, which forbids any Catholic from becoming monarch. As a result the Hanoverian George I became king in 1714, despite being only fifty-ninth in line for the throne.

This constitutional sleight of hand allowed the Whigs to remain in government for much of the eighteenth century. However, in the wake of the success of both the American and French Revolutions, there were calls for radical reform.

Continued pressure for change forced the Whigs to introduce a Reform Bill in 1832, which they claimed would sweep away the corrupt practice of buying seats in the Commons and widen the franchise. However, a property qualification was placed on the ballot, which ensured that only males of the metropolitan middle class, who had a vested interest in the maintenance of the status quo, were given the vote. The labouring classes, whose agitation had ignited the reformist cause in the first place, came out empty-handed. The beneficent Whig aristocracy remained in control.

Four years later, frustrated at the lack of genuine reform, the first independent working-class movement in the world emerged in England. The Chartists took their name from a list of constitutional reforms which they formulated and promoted, designed to overcome the limited democracy created by the 1832 Reform Act which had linked wealth with political representation.

The People's Charter demanded that all men should have the right to vote; that voting should be by secret ballot; that all electoral districts should be of equal size; that the property qualifications for MPs should be abolished; that all MPs should be paid and that Parliament should be annually elected.

When the Charter was presented to Parliament in 1839, MPs refused to discuss it. The Chartists organized a second petition in 1842, signed by three and a half million men, none of whom had the right to vote. This too was ignored.

As demands for reform grew, the Whigs turned to history to justify their primary position in society. In Charles Babington Macaulay, whose five-volume *History of England* was published in 1848, the same year as the Communist Manifesto, they found their greatest propagandist.

Concentrating on the period from the Glorious Revolution to the Battle of Waterloo, Macaulay sought to highlight the benefits of the Whig ascendancy. So that no one should doubt his intentions, he prefaced his book with his 'declaration of purpose':

I shall relate how the new settlement [which brought William of Orange to the throne in 1688 and the Whigs to power] was, during many troubled years, successfully defended against foreign and domestic enemies; how, under that settlement, the authority of law and the security of property were found to be compatible with a liberty of discussion and of individual action never before known; how, from the auspicious union of order and freedom, sprang a prosperity of which the annals of human affairs had furnished no example; how our country, from a state of ignominious vassalage, rapidly rose to the place of umpire among European powers; how her opulence and her martial glory grew together; how, by wise and resolute good faith, was gradually established a public credit fruitful of marvels which to the statesmen of any former age would have seemed incredible; how a gigantic commerce gave birth to a maritime power, compared with which every other maritime power, ancient or modern, sinks into insignificance; how Scotland, after ages of enmity, was at length united to England, not merely by legal bonds, but by indissoluble ties of interest and affection; how, in America, the British colonies rapidly became far mightier and wealthier than the realms which Cortes and Pizarro had added to the dominions of Charles the Fifth; how in Asia, British adventurers founded an empire not less splendid and more durable than that of Alexander.

Unsurprisingly, Macaulay's book found a ready audience amongst those whose job it was to administer the British Empire. Here, dressed up as history, was the justification for dominion over land and sea, the reason why God had entrusted to the English the great task of bringing prosperity and good governance to less enlightened peoples of the world.

For historians, Macaulay provided the framework from which to hang the rich tapestry of our island story. In the late nineteenth century, scores of popular-history books repeated Macaulay's version of events and made it available to the newly literate masses for the first time.

The hierarchical nature of Macaulay's narrative was ideally suited to fostering a sense of identity. It was history that under-lined the moral superiority of the winners against the venal motives of the losers. It flagrantly glossed over the failings of its heroes, while highlighting the faults of its villains. It en-couraged the idea that 'abroad' was a nasty place where everyone was envious of what England had achieved. While every country is, to some extent, prone to burnish its own story at the expense of others, the existence of the British Empire seemed to confirm that our way of doing things, the traditional British way, was far superior to any other.

Macaulay produced unashamedly patriotic history, which was then fashioned into an article of faith, a creed that children were taught, an idea that politicians learned to exploit and a notion of national superiority which the mob fell back on when it needed justification for its prejudices. Propagated in class-rooms across the Empire, it was not open to debate – anyone rash enough to question it was condemned as a dangerous radical or a traitor. It was on the rock of this immutable past that traditional British values were constructed.

And so we were still singing about this stuff in junior school in the late sixties. The men who taught me music and history back then were nearing retirement. Short, balding, be-spectacled Mr Rowe and large, round, avuncular Mr Butterworth had probably begun teaching some time in the late 1920s, when the Whig Interpretation of History was being repackaged by a nephew of Lord Macaulay, George Macaulay Trevelyan, whose bestselling *History of England* was published in 1926.

My teachers had lived through the years when that other great historian, Winston Churchill, was masterfully utilizing Whig history as a means of galvanizing resistance to the threat of Nazism. They would have witnessed the brief reappearance of the Whig tradition in the person of Alec Douglas Home, who was prime minister from 1963 to 1964. Before taking up the leadership of the Conservative Party, he had sat in the House of Lords as the 14th Earl Home. A friend said of him, 'in his heart of hearts, Alec believed that the work of govern-ment should be carried on by the members of twelve upper-class families'.[1] Yet within the space of their careers, my schoolmasters would also have seen the British Empire, which had taken over three hundred years to reach its peak, dwindle away to a few territories and dependencies on the fringes of continents over which Britain once held sway. Macaulay's vision of England as 'the umpire of European powers' became untenable when we were actively seeking permission to join the Common Market. American domination of NATO would have provided a further reminder that Britannia no longer ruled the waves.

Around this period, the Whig Interpretation of History began to reveal its flaws. Having perpetuated the idea that English history was, in Macaulay's words, 'eminently the history of physical, of moral and of intellectual improvement', Whig history proved to be incapable of withstanding the painful realities of post-war Britain. While tales of the national heroes of our past had been something to aspire to during the dark days of war, in peacetime they served only to burden us with imperial pretensions that we could no longer live up to.

Like someone who has inherited a big draughty house but can't afford its upkeep, successive British governments struggled to maintain international prestige. In the fifties, that meant owning independent nuclear weapons. When Britain's first hydrogen bomb was tested in 1954, there was little patriotic celebration. The stark realities of all-out nuclear war, which, unlike the Blitz, offered no hope of survival, were simply too horrific to contemplate. By the end of the decade, the Campaign for Nuclear Disarmament had mobilized opposition to the Bomb, and on the Aldermaston marches organized by CND, those too young to have fought in the War found their voice, speaking out in principled opposition to the British state.

Many young people took part in these demonstrations. Wider educational access had allowed many to be the first in their family to enjoy the benefits of further education. They were passionate and articulate, acutely aware of the threat to their future that the Bomb posed. Most of all, they were angry at those who calmly contemplated the annihilation of humanity. Their parents, who had for so long preached responsibility as the greatest of virtues, were, it seemed, now acting irresponsibly with their children's future. Families were divided over the issue of the Bomb. Generations began to take sides.

The end of conscription had produced the first young men for a generation who were not given a short back and sides and taught to take orders from their superiors. And as the post-war economy picked up, young people began to have more money to spend on things that helped them to forget about the drabness of their 1940s childhoods. Newly affluent and determined to be different from their stuffy parents, they began to rebel against the traditional role of the young British adult. The teenager was born.

Deference to one's elders and betters, for so long a hallmark of British society, began to give way to youthful irreverence. The theatrical review, a much-loved form of entertainment embodied by artists such as Noel Coward, Joyce Grenfell and Flanders and Swann, was swept away almost overnight by the student-led satire boom in 1960.

The mass of state-educated youngsters followed close behind. In November 1963, when the Beatles topped the bill at the Royal Variety Performance, John Lennon looked out at the various royals, impresarios and showbiz grandees in the audience and said mockingly, 'You people in the cheap seats clap your hands. All the rest of you, just rattle your jewellery.'

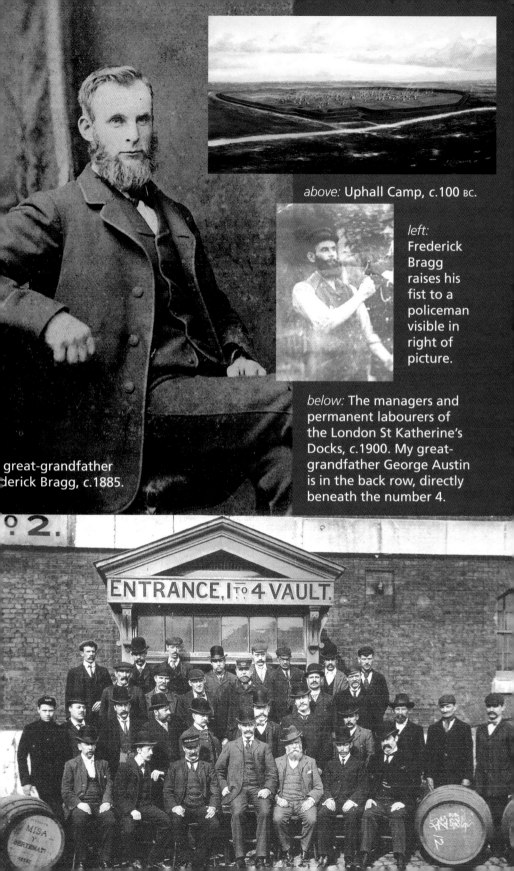

above: Uphall Camp, c.100 BC.

left: Frederick Bragg raises his fist to a policeman visible in right of picture.

below: The managers and permanent labourers of the London St Katherine's Docks, c.1900. My great-grandfather George Austin is in the back row, directly beneath the number 4.

great-grandfather derick Bragg, c.1885.

ENTRANCE, 1 TO 4 VAULT.

William Bragg marries May Austin, April 1918. My great-aunt Hannah sits next to her brother William. George Austin is seated far right.

My grandfather William Bragg, around the time he started keeping his diary, 1911/12.

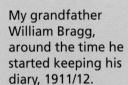

right: My mother Marie (standing) and her younger sister beside a street shrine during a Catholic holy day parade in Cable Street. Note the Italian tricolore hanging in the background.

above: My father Dennis, second from right, with the crew of his M3 Grant CDL tank in India, 1946/7. The searchlight beam was exposed through the narrow vertical slit visible on the turret between the machine gun and the dummy 37mm cannon.

right: Me, fast asleep on the carpet, with proud parents, 1959.

left: William Bragg and my mother Marie at the Festival of Britain, Southbank, London 1951.

Looking forward to the arrival of my own reel-to-reel tape machine, 1969.

Heads-down, no-nonsense boogie. Wiggy (left), Robert Handley on drums (centre) and myself (right) playing in my parents' back room, August 1976.

Suited and booted. Wiggy and me as office juniors, June 1976.

above: Reading my bible, July 1976.

above: Still in thrall to the Rolling Stones. With band mates, standing second left, March 1977.

ortly after
ing seen
e Clash for
first time,
gust 1977.

right background: I'm somewhere in this picture, just beneath the Gays Against the Nazis banner. Rock Against Racism Carnival Against the Nazis, Victoria Park, Hackney, April 1978. PHOTO SYD SHELTON

At the end of 1977, having fully embraced punk.

On stage at the Marquee with Riff Raff, September 1977.

below: **The Clash on stage, Rock Against Racism Carnival Against the Nazis, Victoria Park, Hackney, April 1978.**
PHOTO SYD SHELTON

SMASH
RACE

om Robinson exhorts the crowd, Rock Against
acism Carnival Against the Nazis, Victoria Park,
ackney, April 1978. PHOTO SYD SHELTON

Paul Simonon of The Clash on stage at the Rock Against Racism Carnival Against the Nazis, Victoria Park, Hackney, April 1978. PHOTO SYD SHELTON

That same year, E. P. Thompson published *The Making of the English Working Class*, a classic work which gave a newly emergent view of history that directly challenged the Whig Interpretation.

Thompson wrote from a Marxist perspective, and his version of history was as partisan as that of Macaulay. Whig historians held that progress was the result of an enlightened aristocracy ruling in the best interests of the people. Marxists countered with the belief that the structure of society is dictated by the economic circumstances of those involved and that genuine progress can only be achieved by equalizing those circumstances through class struggle.

Macaulay had relied on being able to marshal the grand sweep of history, illuminated by the actions of those who had emerged as the winners – wealthy, conservative English aristocrats. In contrast, Thompson gave voice to those who had been considered the losers – Luddites, Chartists, radicals – and showed how the great reforms that the Whig historians glorified had often been made in response to pressure from below. Thompson argued that the experiences of the working class were relevant to a proper understanding of British history, and that their achievements were as worthy of consideration as those of their betters – the squire, the warrior, the aristocrat and the monarch.

This was social history – cosmopolitan by nature – and it matched the spirit of the times. As red-brick universities began to fill with students from ordinary backgrounds, the teaching of history was forced to become more democratic. Those academics who followed in Thompson's footsteps sought to hold historical figures to account, looking again at the justification they had given for their treatment of the weak and the poor both at home and in the Empire, unearthing new evidence that came from the victim's perspective.

The democratization of history was a worrying development for those in power. Searching questions raised by social historians about the past behaviour of the ruling classes threatened to undermine the authority of the present leadership, whose response was to fall back on tradition, seeking shelter within the ambiguities of our unwritten constitution.

Historically, the British establishment has resisted calls for a written constitution, knowing that any such document would ultimately be used against them. Aimed at protecting the citizen from abuses of state power, a constitution is a set of rules by which the people agree to be governed. Without one, British law has relied on precedent as its guiding principle, resolving current disputes by referring to how previous generations have acted.

Constantly deferring to the past has produced an establishment which holds that what went before is decidedly preferable to the present state of affairs and unquestionably better than whatever the future may bring. In such a climate, any attempts to deviate from approved behaviour can be dismissed not by recourse to rational debate, but purely in the name of tradition.

Over the past twenty or so years, this insistence on traditional British values has opposed any moves to create a national culture that better reflects our pluralistic society. Language has been at the frontline of this battle, with traditionalists defending their right to use what they consider to be traditionally correct terms such as sambo, paki, nig-nog, queer and spastic. Opponents have argued that behind the language of traditional correctness there lurks an attempt to keep people in their place. Using derogatory terms towards the marginalized in society – minority ethnic communities, gays, the disabled – implies that the user does not want such people to become part of the community. However, traditionalists have countered with a freedom-of-speech argument, claiming that their right to be offensive overrides their duty to show respect to their fellow citizens, on the grounds that 'these bloody people don't deserve it anyway because they're not normal'.[2]

However, the true focus of this battle for hearts and minds has been the teaching of history. Following their country's independence from Britain in 1947, Indian schoolchildren were given new history textbooks that reassessed the contribution of the British Raj, giving greater emphasis to the Hindu-Muslim culture of the Mughals that existed before colonization. When, in 1998, the BJP came to power, a hard-line nationalist party promoting a doctrine of 'Hinduness', it pulped the country's post-imperial history textbooks and provided schoolchildren with a new narrative, which portrayed Muslims as a divisive force in a history which focussed on the greatness of the majoritarian Hindu culture.[3]

In 2002, ultra-conservative Japanese historians produced a textbook which sought to downplay Japan's aggressive behaviour towards its Asian neighbours during the 1930s and 1940s. Its authors' purpose was to 'correct history' by removing any references which might make Japanese schoolchildren uncomfortable about their nationality.[4]

Attempts to control the past have also gone on in this country. A Conservative Party spokesman recently called for history to be made compulsory in schools, saying that young people will not 'value any authority figures if they are not told the inspiring tales of the national heroes of our past'.[5]

The manner by which history and tradition exert their subtle authority on our society can be seen in the British bobby's uniform, which has remained basically unchanged for over a century, the high Victorian helmet with its imposing badge marking the policeman out as an arbiter of the ancient liberties of our forefathers. Likewise, the eighteenth-century periwigs worn by high-court judges and barristers. The archaic garments worn by members and staff of the House of Lords serve to remind us that they represent a far older polity than their democratically elected colleagues in the House of Commons. The wearing of traditional ermine robes gives their Lordships an air of authority that belies their inherent lack of legitimacy.

However, history and tradition can only enforce authority and communicate a sense of superiority if their inspiring tales and colourful heroes are unquestioningly accepted. Hence the focus on school textbooks, particularly those aimed at pre-teens, and the insistence by traditionalists on a return to the teaching of the Whig Interpretation as the single, linear narrative source of our national history.

George Courtauld, described in the *Daily Telegraph* as a forty-year-old head-hunter from Essex, was frustrated at the way his sons were being taught British history. Appalled that 'the younger generation was woefully ignorant of the fascinating heritage of the British Isles', he drew up a chart of what he felt constituted proper history – 'about seven A4 pages' – and pinned it to the loo door for his sons to study whilst on the toilet.[6]

When friends began asking him for photocopies for their children, he realized that there was a market for a book that contained 'the bare bones of our magnificent history'. Unable to find a publisher – 'Everyone seemed concerned about the Britishness of it all' – Courtauld decided to publish the book himself. He managed to get it into the shops in time for Christmas 2004, where it became a publishing phenomenon, going on to sell over two hundred thousand copies.

Only sixty-four pages long, *The Pocket Book of Patriotism* seeks to live up to its title by setting out those things that should make us proud to be British: in short, it is a contemporary take on the Whig Interpretation of History. As might be expected, it delights in its traditional correctness. The title page quotes Shakespeare's Henry V before Agincourt: 'This story shall the good man teach his son'. At least H. E. Marshall had the decency to dedicate *Our Island Story* to boys *and* girls.

So what does this Boy's Own story comprise? The bulk of the book is made up of a list of events, beginning with the erection of Stonehenge in 2200 BC and ending with England's 2003 victory in the rugby world cup. This chronology is divided – in traditionally correct style – into two equal parts, 'Britain' and 'Abroad', and interspersed with fitting quotes. The last of these is Harold Macmillan's 1960 observation that the wind of change is blowing through the African continent, giving the unfortunate impression that, as far as the traditionalist is concerned, no Briton born in the twentieth century had anything worthwhile to say.

There are several pages of longer quotes, including the Ten Commandments, the Lord's Prayer, clauses 39 and 40 from Magna Carta, some bits of Shakespeare, Elizabeth I at Tilbury, Charles I on the scaffold, a touch of Milton by way of response, and three of Churchill's finest orations from the summer of 1940. There follow half a dozen patriotic songs and, just for luck, a slice of Ye Olde England that the traditionally correct love to champion: a table of imperial weights and measures. All in all, pretty harmless stuff.

The only truly contentious point is the inclusion of 'The British Empire and imperial territories in 1920 and the year in which they came under British control'.

Why didn't Courtauld print something a little more contemporary, like a list of all the countries in the Commonwealth – fifty-three sovereign states modelled on our own, including India, the world's largest democracy. Or more helpful might have been an up-to-date list of the British overseas territories: Anguilla, Bermuda, British Virgin Islands, Cayman Islands, the Falklands, Gibraltar, Monserrat, St Helena, Tristan da Cunha, Pitcairn, South Georgia and South Sandwich – all still proudly flying the Union Jack. Instead, the eighty-eight colonies that passed through the hands of the British Empire during its three-hundred-year existence are presented like so many moth-eaten trophies from long-forgotten shooting parties, each mounted with the date on which it was bagged:

Aden	1839
Alberta	1788
Anglo-Egyptian Sudan	1899
Antigua	1632
Bahamas	1666
Barbados	1605
Basutoland	1868

And so on until

Zululand	1887

It's a pity that Courtauld felt the need to include this list, because it casts a shadow over the achievements which he highlights in the chronology. While so many of those accomplishments were positive, the British Empire is, at best, morally questionable, and not just because of the brutality it meted out to those under its rule.

What's questionable about British imperialism? Well, ask yourself this – how would you feel if your country was ruled from afar and you were expected to adopt the language, customs, religion and politics of an alien culture if you hoped to prosper? If you saw the resources of your country exploited for vast profit by merchants wearing weird clothes, speaking a foreign language and eating strange-smelling food? It's enough to make a Eurosceptic weep.

But what of the beneficial aspects of British rule? Niall Ferguson, in his bestselling book *Empire: How Britain Made the Modern World*, lists the positive achievements of British imperialism. But just ask yourself who truly benefited from the following:

- the Anglicization of North America and Australia
- the internationalization of the English language
- the enduring influence of the Protestant version of Christianity
- the survival of parliamentary institutions, which far worse empires were poised to extinguish in the 1940s.

Ferguson includes one further benefit which is hard to argue was solely the work of the British:

- the triumph of capitalism as the optimal system of economic organization.

All European nations were propagating the capitalist ethos, and, given the continued flow of resources from the southern to the northern hemisphere, it is clear who has gained the most from the triumph of capitalism.

The fact is that Britain benefited greatly – and, as the list above shows, continues to benefit – from the Empire. We have much to be thankful for, not least our present multicultural society. Yet those who seek to glorify it should be reminded of the unavoidable truth at its heart: whichever way you seek to justify it, imperialism is nothing more than the imposition of foreign rule on a subject people.

The traditionally correct brigade will seek to convince us that the British Empire was our nation's greatest achievement, and so long as we look no further than Courtauld's list of former territories, we might just believe them. But the chances are that, sooner or later, someone whose parents came from what we used to refer to as Punjab or British Somaliland will point out that, for them, the British Empire meant subjugation, exploitation and, ultimately, humiliation. Some of the children of Empire are now to be found sitting in our school classrooms, and although they are mostly happy to be here, they are no less proud of their heritage than we are of ours. In fact, they are often better informed about the reality that lies behind the neat rows of dates on Courtauld's list:

Aden	captured from the Sultan 1839
Alberta	appropriated by a private company 1788
Anglo-Egyptian Sudan	conquered 1899
Antigua	appropriated from native population 1632
Bahamas	given to Sir Robert Heath by Charles I 1629

| Barbados | appropriated from native population 1605 |
| Basutoland | annexed without consent 1871 |

And so it goes on: claiming, capturing, conquering, and – let's be honest with ourselves – stealing territory all the way to Zululand.

I'm not asking people to be ashamed of the British Empire, just honest with themselves about its creation and purpose. Ultimately, it was driven not by a civilizing mission, but by a nation of shopkeepers seeking cheap raw materials and markets to exploit.

If we are to have a true understanding of our history, then surely all the facts must be considered, good and bad? Unfortunately, this approach causes conservative commentators to complain loudly in traditionally correct terms about a liberal conspiracy against the notion of teaching history that risks making people proud.[7] They would, it seems, prefer our schoolchildren to be taught little about the British Empire other than the fact that it once held sway over a quarter of the world's surface. Anyone attempting to draw attention to how so much of the map came to be coloured pink is liable to be met with charges of self-loathing.

But isn't it a form of self-delusion to drill into our schoolchildren a sense of pride about holding dominion over palm and pine, whilst at the same time trying to suppress any discussion as to how this was achieved? The implication seems to be that we can only truly be great if we ignore the unpalatable aspects of our past. It all smacks of a lack of confidence, a fear that Britain, for all its great achievements, will not be able to withstand honest appraisal, preferring instead to dumb down our history in order to achieve the desired result – a chest-swelling sense of national pride. Unfortunately, evidence suggests that force-feeding schoolchildren with an over-blown idea of their nation's importance can have negative consequences.

In 2000, English hooligans rioting in Brussels during the European Football Championships told the Belgian police who arrested them that their aggressive behaviour should be excused because England had liberated Belgium during the Second World War.[8] 'We're English and proud of it,' said one hooligan when asked to justify the mindless violence unleashed on the Belgian capital.

I'm sure that traditionalists are as ashamed as I am to hear such pathetic excuses for criminal behaviour, but who instilled these yobs with a pride that can only be manifested through belligerence? Who gave these 'patriots' their simplistic version of history, in which our nation played such a grand part that they feel it excuses their loutish behaviour over fifty years later?

And this doesn't just impact on those unfortunate enough to encounter such barbarians on the rampage. The antics of these pride-fuelled hooligans have a detrimental effect on attempts to nurture our sense of national identity. Try to make a case for a positive sense of English identity and you will be met with opposition from otherwise fair-minded people who are dis-gusted by the behaviour of a violent minority of football fans who are 'English and proud of it'. They've seen the boorish behaviour on TV and want no part of it.

In expressing the sense of pride that some demand our schools instil in them, these louts don't make us feel better about ourselves as a people. Quite the opposite – they make us ashamed to be English.

7

Lions and Unicorns

I first came across *The Pocket Book of Patriotism* in the humour section of a large high-street bookshop. The staff had filed it with all the other quirky books that appear around Christmas time, each one hoping to become the surprise seasonal publishing hit.

Over the past few years, the competition for this lucrative accolade has taken on a rather sour tone. Once the field was typified by books that relied on the wit and eccentricity for which the English are renowned. Titles such as *Do Penguins Have Knees?*, *Nice Cup of Tea and a Sit Down* ('The authors do a great service by marshalling legions of biscuits, new and old, and providing a superb critique of the major varieties') and *Never Hit a Jellyfish with a Spade: How to Survive Life's Smaller Challenges* are still to be found, but their gentle irony is in danger of being elbowed out of the way by an altogether nastier strain of stocking-filler.

It's hard to tell whether the publication of *Is It Just Me or Is Everything Shit? The Encyclopedia of Modern Life* marked the low point of post-modernism or the elevation of the pub bore to new heights. That *The Pocket Book of Patriotism* should have to share shelf space with such a title is somewhat ironic, given that the majority of books written on the subject of Englishness and/or Britishness in the past decade could easily have been subtitled *Is It Just Me or Is Everything Shit?*

Vernon Coleman, author of *Why Everything Is Going To Get Worse Before It Gets Better*, followed up that cheery tome with *England, Our England*, which revealed that we are all going to hell in a hand-cart because of our membership of the EU. A. A. Gill entitled his entertaining book on England and the English *The Angry Island*, and lost no time in pointing out that we have good reason to be angry because Everything Is Shit. Roger Scruton's beautifully written *England, an Elegy* was let down by its curmudgeonly insistence that being English is somehow 'forbidden'. By whom exactly?

However, the high priest of pessimism is Peter Hitchens, columnist for the *Mail on Sunday*, whose 1999 book *The Abolition of Britain* is a masterpiece of the genre. It opens with a marvellous chapter in which Hitchens imagines travelling back in time to the day of Winston Churchill's funeral in November 1965. His loving description of a London where the colour brown dominates 'every aspect of human life, from food to furniture', the air 'reeks of cabbage and hot grease' and pubs are unwelcoming places serving 'tepid beer' is so ghastly that one reviewer was moved to ask who in their right mind would want to go back there?

In comparing the London of forty years ago to that of the present, specifically on the day of Princess Diana's funeral, Hitchens sought to illustrate what we have lost. Much as I disagree with his analysis, I couldn't help thinking how wonderful it would be to go back to the London of late 1965, with the possibility of seeing the Beatles or the Stones live, the chance to buy tickets for the World Cup finals that England was about to stage, and the 98 per cent tax rate applied to top earners.

I doubt that Hitchens would share my enthusiasms. He has a well-rehearsed disdain for the Englishness that manifests itself in our national football team. 'I hope the England football team is rapidly knocked out of the World Cup. I really do. And please don't call this group of people "England" . . .', he wrote in 2002.[1]

And whatever you do, don't get him started about the Beatles and the Stones.

His tirade against the modern world seems to have been inspired by a comment that Tony Blair made during the 1997 election campaign, with which Hitchens opens *The Abolition of Britain*:

> I am a modern man. I am part of the rock and roll generation –
> the Beatles, colour TV, that's the generation I come from.

For most people, such a statement would put Blair back in the sixties with boiled cabbage and tepid beer. For Hitchens, however, things could not have been worse if Blair had announced 'David Icke was right. I am actually a shape-shifting reptile come to take over the country.'

Blair's election in 1997 seems to have inspired the steady flow of books decrying modern Britain that have appeared over the past decade. The honour of being first on to the shelves, however, goes to Hitchens, and he presciently identifies the root of the problem on the second page of his book:

Many of those born, raised and educated in surroundings normally associated with Tory thinking and values no longer actually share those values. Few people under the age of fifty now possess what could be described as a Conservative imagination.

If that was true in 1997, it is even more so today. Perhaps that is why Hitchens found the Labour leader's 'rock and roll' comment so chilling. By declaring himself to be of the colour TV generation, Blair was identifying with the vast majority of the population. In that instant, Hitchens must have realized how far removed his traditional values were from those of the average Briton's.

Hitchens, writing in 1998, sensed that the Conservative mindset had lost its grip some fifty years before. It may be significant that before 1948 Britons were expected to pay for their health care and education. Anyone born after that date would have enjoyed the benefits of the Welfare State.

Universal provision immediately had a positive impact on the health of the nation, but its levelling effect on British culture took some time to bear fruit. Most children born after 1940 – the post-war generation – would have been healthier and better educated than their parents. Within months of these original products of the Welfare State leaving school in 1954, the first rock 'n' roll records appeared in the British charts. For those who took up the offer of free further education, a few more years were to pass before they too would exert their influence on the cultural life of the nation. By 1960, they had created a student-led political-satire boom which ridiculed the British establishment in a manner that no previous generation had dared to.

British popular culture of the 1960s was largely funded by the Welfare State, in that the young people produced by its collective provision went on to create and participate in what was known as the Permissive Society, whose emergence was a clear challenge to the traditional mores of Hitchens's 'Conservative imagination'.

The general election of October 1964 was the first in which the post-war generation was able to vote in significant numbers. The Labour government which they put into power proceeded to introduce legislation which reflected their values – the first major social reforms since the 1930s. Abortion was legalized, the death penalty abolished, strict divorce laws were eased, the right of the Lord Chamberlain to censor the content of theatrical plays was abolished and homosexual acts between consenting adults were decriminalized. Most of these reforms were achieved under the stewardship of the then home secretary, Roy Jenkins, who recognized that society had changed in the twenty years since the war. Labour's reforms, radical though they were, merely served to bring the law into line with the mainstream values of the day.

Hitchens condemns every one of Jenkins's reforms, comparing the destructive power of the cultural revolution he unleashed to that of Mao Zedong. Underlying the hyperbole is a genuinely felt longing to return to the moral and social climate of the 1950s. Hitchens expects the Conservative Party to share his view and to do its best to promote the traditional values of previous generations. However, parties that seek to turn back the clock rarely prove successful. The great sea-changes that have occurred in post-war Britain have been wrought by governments who offered a break with the past: Labour in 1945, 1964 and 1997, and the Tories in 1979.

Although Margaret Thatcher was a staunch traditionalist, the election of a woman prime minister was seen by liberals as a positive example of how progressive British society had become. As it turned out, she was not a feminist, but that did not mean that she was not offering something new. Her avowed intent to break with the post-war consensus was attractive to her supporters, who saw it as a modern, forward-looking idea.

Thatcher was the last prime minister of the pre-war generation. Born in 1925, she had spent a life in politics opposed to the collectivist ideals of the Welfare State. Both culturally and morally, she and her ministers represented the parents against whom the post-war generation were determined to rebel. The Thatcherites' antipathy to the cultural revolution of the 1960s was well known. One of Thatcher's closest colleagues, Norman Tebbit, left no one in any doubt regarding the disdain that his generation felt for the era:

'The word "conservative" is used by the BBC as a portmanteau word of abuse for anyone whose views differ from the insufferable, smug, sanctimonious, naïve, guilt-ridden, wet, pink orthodoxy of that sunset home for third-rate minds of that third-rate decade, the 1960s.'[2]

Yet despite their best efforts, the Tories were unable to dismantle the Welfare State, and by the end of their time in power could not even rely on the Church of England to be conservative; to the outrage of traditionalists, Anglicans began ordaining women priests in 1994.

Nor could the Tories trust their own MPs to live by the 1950s morality that they espoused. John Major's 'Back to

Basics' campaign was widely seen as an attempt to set the moral tone of the nation by reasserting traditional values. The campaign backfired when several Tory ministers were forced to resign due to infidelity and corruption. It later transpired that Major himself had been having an extra-marital affair with a fellow Tory MP.

This alone, however, does not account for the staggering defeat that Tony Blair inflicted on the Tories at the next election. New Labour won a huge majority in 1997 because it was new, not because it was Labour. The party ditched many of its own traditional values, even going so far as to match Tory spending plans. Stalwart Labour supporters were aghast, but the public were intrigued. Tony Blair offered them something they had never experienced – a prime minister unencumbered by tradition.

In that sense, Blair was different not only from the Tories but from his own predecessors. Neil Kinnock was a product of the post-war baby boom, just like Tony Blair. He too loved pop music and could play the guitar. Despite this, Kinnock's background in the Welsh Valleys and strong links to the unions led the public to see him as a traditional Labour leader. They wanted a break with the past.

The perceived wisdom is that Blair won by taking his party to the centre of British politics. In fact, Blair has governed from the right of centre, cosying up to big business, taking us into an illegal war, allying himself with the neo-conservatives in the USA and doing things that Thatcher never dared attempt, such as gifting the private sector vast swathes of education and health care. Most significantly, he has defined himself against the past, being generally hostile to the traditions of the Left.

The notion of Blair as a centrist only makes sense when seen against the backdrop of the ideological divisions of the 1980s. By the nineties, the British people were tired of these battles and ready for something fresh. The bi-polar nature of British politics, which had served Labour and the Conservatives well for over sixty years, was becoming stale. Although the fledgling Social Democratic Party had failed to break the mould, it had highlighted an appetite for change. When the Tories were unable to renew themselves following the regicide of Mrs Thatcher, Labour modernizers seized the initiative.

In response, the Conservative Party stuck with its traditional agenda, replacing the defeated John Major with a young right-winger, William Hague. When Hague became only the second Conservative leader of the twentieth century to fail to become prime minister, the Tories sought to remedy the situation by replacing him with another leader from the right of the party, Iain Duncan Smith, a former officer in the Scots Guards. A good old-fashioned hanger and flogger, he was perhaps the most woeful Tory leader of the modern era.

A third election defeat at the hands of New Labour seems to have brought the Conservatives to their senses. In David Cameron, they now have a leader who comes from the colour TV generation. He has already laid down a claim to be more modern than Beatles fan Blair, declaring his favourite album to be *The Queen Is Dead* by The Smiths.

However, his instinct to head for the fabled centre ground may not bring the benefits that the Tories hope for. Politics have been conducted New Labour's way for a decade now. Their style is already familiar. The public may be looking for something new. Fortunately for Cameron, there are plenty of people within his own party ready to offer him advice about the way forward.

Geoffrey Wheatcroft ends his splendid dissection of the failure of the Conservative imagination, *The Strange Death of Tory England*, with a suggestion that the party should compile its next manifesto from the work of George Orwell. Happily, it is not *1984* that Wheatcroft has in mind but a study of the English character that Orwell penned in 1940, from which Wheatcroft drew the following nostrums:

> An essential part of our common national culture is 'the privateness of English life', which centres around 'things which even when they are communal are not official'. 'The power-worship, which has infected the English intelligentsia, has never infected the common people ... England is perhaps the only great country whose intellectuals are ashamed of their own nationality ... the totalitarian idea that there is no such thing as law, there is only power, has never taken root.'

'Short of learning from Orwell,' Wheatcroft concludes, 'the Tories may find themselves at a final dead end'.[3]

Those quotes come from a polemic which Orwell wrote during the Second World War, shortly after the catastrophic retreat from Dunkirk. Entitled *The Lion and the Unicorn: Socialism and the English Genius*, the stated purpose of this short volume was to reconcile patriotism with intelligence. Orwell's left-wing politics had made him a committed internationalist – he fought on the Republican side in the Spanish Civil War – and a staunch anti-imperialist. However, he had a distrust of certain intellectuals whose antipathy towards everything English, he believed, betrayed a cultural divide between themselves and the ordinary working people as great as the class divisions maintained by the gentry. 'The Bloomsbury high-brow, with his mechanical snigger,' he wrote in *The Lion and the Unicorn*, 'is as out of date as the cavalry colonel.'

The Tories have always had a soft spot for Orwell. Born in India during the Raj, he went to Eton and served in the Imperial Police in Burma – just their sort of chap. His essays on cricket, the correct way to make a cup of tea and the decline of the English murder have endeared him to traditionalists and his opposition to the metric system finds favour among Eurosceptics. Orwell's politics were left-wing but his tastes were conservative, a paradox which helped him to pen the greatest book on Englishness ever written.

The Lion and the Unicorn came at the end of the inter-war period, during which a new genre of publishing had gained huge popularity. 'Topography' is not a subject heading that you find in many modern bookshops, but any second-hand dealer will have such a section, largely made up of books written in the 1920s and 1930s about 'the character' of Britain.

H. V. Morton was the most popular of these authors. He travelled around Britain in his bull-nose Morris between the wars and churned out book after book about this little island we live on: in 1927 he set off *In Search of England*, followed *The Call of England* in 1928, a year later was *In Search of Scotland* and spent 1932 *In Search of Wales*. Like some indigenous anthropologist, he explored the darkest reaches of the interior, poking his bull-nose into every sheltered nook and dusty cranny, delighting in the traditional and the homely. The arts of husbandry enchanted him. He stood in awe beneath gothic arch and ancient bower. He found places that the modern world had not yet touched. And he couldn't see a castle wall or sleepy village without evoking the ghosts of the past.

He was writing for the generation that had sacrificed so

much in the Great War, who spent the quiet moments of the day with their own ghosts and memories. Morton's books helped fill the void. His flowery prose offered a sense of comfort, suggesting that it had all somehow been worth it. Eternal England endured, undiminished by the savagery of the Western Front.

The books sold in their hundreds of thousands, spawning a multitude of imitators. Batsford Books excelled at such works during the 1930s, publishing for the mass market. Titles such as *The Heart of England*, *The Countryman's England* and *The Legacy of England* were graced with full-colour jackets that were destined to become iconic. Brian Cook's illustrations for the Batsford British Heritage series utilized the Jean Berte method of printing, with much more brilliant inks than those commonly seen in British publishing. Cook's illustrations took advantage of this to use vibrant swathes of colour, applied as shade rather than detail. A building might appear as a yellow block capped with an orange roof, blue windows and a pink door, a tree just a dark-green blob. It sounds almost infantile, but Cook's superb draughtsmanship ensured that his shapes were instantly familiar. Long shadows predominate and figures are few. Here a ploughman crosses the horizon, his team in full harness. On another jacket, some fishermen lay up a smack.

It is Cook's landscape art that captures the essence of Eternal England. The greensward rises and falls like a gentle swell. Spinneys colour the view, giving meaning to the distance until they merge into the inevitable darkling-blue hills. Towering cumulo-nimbus clouds drift by to explain the startling contrasts of light and shade. In the foreground, the roofs of a hamlet snuggle around the outline of a church tower in the Norman style. The viewer looks down on all this from atop some imaginary crest, a lone figure in the landscape, high on the exquisite sense of solitude, dizzy in the warm silence of a summer's evening. As if inviting us to come back to reality after our sojourn in this earthly paradise, Cook always depicts his landscapes in the Golden Hour, as the sun begins to set and the pubs open.

But does such a pastoral pastiche still have any resonance today, save amongst those souls who scour second-hand book-shops looking for Cook's distinctive jackets? Does anyone still use such images to define something eternal, unspoken and deeply English?

On the very last page of the third and final volume of his 2002 *History of Britain*, Simon Schama struggles with the central dilemma of his project: is this history really British or is it English?

> Some called such a place of hopes and blessing 'Jerusalem'
> and some of us, obstinately, think we can still call it Britain.

He chooses to illustrate this 'place of hopes and blessings' with an uncaptioned photograph of a scene that is touchingly familiar: a landscape viewed from on high, the roofs of a village poking through the treetops, a patchwork quilt of fields bathed in the sunlight of a summer's evening, the long shadows shading the greens and browns, the land rising here and there and, in the distance, those blue remembered hills – it is pure Brian Cook.

It could be Lowland Scotland, although the hills are never quite that far away, and it could, at a pinch, be some gentle vale in the Welsh Borders. Yet it is the sheer ordinariness of the scene, the lack of breathtaking features, the regularity of the pasture, and the comforting domed crowns and spreading branches of the deciduous trees that mark it out as the broad, sunlit uplands of Eternal England.

Conservative politicians have always been fond of this bucolic imagery. Stanley Baldwin, when leading the Tories in the 1920s, made a speech in which he extolled

> The sounds of England, the tinkle of the hammer on the anvil in the country smithy, the corncrake on a dewy morning, the sound of the scythe against the whetstone, the sight of a plough team coming over the brow of a hill, the sight that has been England since England was a land.[4]

Almost seventy years later, Baldwin's successor was still romanticizing the past. In 1993, John Major listed those essential British characteristics that membership of the European Union could never alter:

> Fifty years on from now, Britain will still be the country of long shadows on county cricket grounds, warm beer, invincible green suburbs, dog lovers and – as George Orwell said – old maids bicycling to Holy Communion through the morning mist.[5]

The Orwell quotation comes from *The Lion and the Unicorn: Socialism and the English Genius*. We think of the word 'genius' now as meaning exceptional intellectual power in an individual. In Orwell's day it had another meaning. A pre-war dictionary gives its prime definition as 'a tutelary deity or spirit, supposed to preside over the destinies of an individual, place or nation'. Orwell saw the genius of England in its people.

Writing for ordinary working people rather than intellectuals and academics, Orwell chose to pepper his argument with images that were commonplace in the Britain of his day, the better to illustrate his point. When he wished to describe the diversity of England, he wrote of

> The clatter of clogs in the Lancashire mill towns, the to-and-fro of the lorries on the Great North Road, the queues outside Labour Exchanges, the rattle of pintables in the Soho pubs, the old maids biking to Holy Communion through the mists of an autumn morning.

Only the last of these images sits well with Major's cosy sentimentality. The din of the clogs, the roar of the lorries, the noise of the metropolitan pub where people are playing bagatelle – all are full of life. And in Orwell's day these were quite contemporary scenes. Having painted his determinedly modern picture of the English character, Orwell colours his English landscape with something which might have been taken from Stanley Baldwin's palate, an image from Eternal England: cycling through the morning mist. The contrast is startling. The old maids are clearly oblivious to the hustle and bustle of the mill towns and the Great North Road and the Soho pubs, living lives seemingly at odds with the modern world. Time has passed them by. They are a metaphor for a world that is no longer attractive, if indeed it ever was.

Ironically, it was this image, seemingly chosen by Orwell because it was already out of date in 1940, that John Major chose to evoke the Britain he believed would exist in 2040. But then, the Conservative reading of Orwell has always been highly selective, and never more so than when quoting from

The Lion and the Unicorn, as Geoffrey Wheatcroft's carefully chosen passages bear out.

Did Wheatcroft not feel a shiver of recognition when he read Orwell's description of the English as 'a family in which the young are generally thwarted and most of the power is in the hands of irresponsible uncles and bedridden aunts . . . a family with the wrong members in control'? Did he not feel a twinge of shame when he read Orwell's assertion that 'The lady in the Rolls-Royce car is more damaging to morale than a fleet of Goering's bombing planes'? Most importantly, did he not feel stirred to read the final paragraph of the book, a passage that stands shoulder to shoulder with Churchill's finest oratory as a passionate, progressive call to arms:

> The heirs of Nelson and of Cromwell are not in the House of Lords. They are in the fields and the streets, in the factories and the armed forces, in the four-ale bar and the suburban back garden; and at present they are still kept under by a generation of ghosts . . . Nothing ever stands still. We must add to our heritage or lose it, we must grow greater or grow less, we must go forward or backward. I believe in England, and I believe that we will go forward.

Apparently not.

Instead, Wheatcroft chooses only to hear Orwell when he draws attention to the insularity and anti-intellectualism that has marred Conservativism for over a century. In that sense, he seems to see *The Lion and the Unicorn* as a way back to the traditions of England so long depended upon by the Tories; the deference to and insistence upon 'common sense' against the reason of intellectuals; the opposition to the idea of society, dressed up as a longing for 'privateness'; most important of all, patriotism once again divorced from intelligence.

Wheatcroft has misunderstood Orwell's message. The spirit of Stanley Baldwin has drawn him to Orwell's characterization of English civilization as

> somehow bound up with solid breakfasts and gloomy Sundays, smoky towns and winding roads, green fields and red pillar boxes. It has a flavour all of its own.

Yet he has failed to read the crucial passage which follows that description, in which the true secret of eternal Englishness is revealed:

> Moreover it is continuous, it stretches into the future and the past, there is something in it that persists, as in a living creature. What can the England of 1940 have in common with the England of 1840? But then what do you have in common with the child of five whose photograph your mother keeps on the mantelpiece? Nothing, except that you happen to be the same person.

Whenever I read this quote, I think of walking my dog over the hill opposite our house. I cross a medieval field system, pass a 1940s pillbox and, on reaching the top of the hill, come upon the Bronze Age burial mound that gives the place its name – Bind Barrow Hill. All these things are part of the present – I encounter them every day, me and my dog sharing the space with the men who guarded our coastline against Hitler, with the feudal farming folk and with the Bronze Age people who lived here before England existed.

There are many barrows in this part of the country, some dating back to Neolithic times. They are the plainest of ancient monuments – little more than a low mound on the horizon – yet their survival today should be of great comfort to those who fear that the past will be 'ploughed out' by modern society.

The barrows are still here because the people who came after had a respect for the past, even while they were building the future. The Celts built their hillforts around Neolithic sites. Alfred the Great translated sacred Latin texts into contemporary English. Even those arch modernizers, the Romans, diverted their roads around the ancient monuments they encountered.

Today, when the pace of change is perhaps greater than it has ever been, the temptation to retreat in the face of complex societal problems to a perceived 'Golden Age' is great. The future is uncertain, as the traditionalists are wont to remind us, and the past comforting. However, if we hope to avoid living in a society in which heritage is more important than creativity, we must learn to respect the past but live in the present, and concern ourselves with creating a better future for everyone.

8

Rock Against Racism

I see the first one before I have left the village. As I wait for the oncoming traffic to pass through the bottleneck at Donkey Lane, a car sweeps by flying the English flag from its front window. A red cross on a white background, no more than fifteen by ten inches, fluttering furiously as the car passes. It so surprises me that I forget to acknowledge the driver.

What did they look like? Male? Female? Fascist? What? If their physical appearance gave any clue as to the message the flag was intended to send, I missed it. I drive on, going over in my mind the different contexts that the flag of St George could have in a Dorset village in June 2004.

The most obvious is that it is being flown in support of our national football team, who are about to take part in the European Championships in Portugal – although their opening match against France is over a week away.

Alternatively, the flag could be part of the celebrations to mark tomorrow's sixtieth anniversary of D-Day. There are plenty of flags and bunting in the village to commemorate the event. A massive Stars and Stripes flies outside the British

Legion, in honour of the hundreds of young American GIs who camped around the village in the summer of 1944, who went on to be some of the first troops ashore at Bloody Omaha.

More ominously, the flag could have a political meaning. The elections for the European Parliament are only a few days away. Recent months have seen the emergence of two overtly nationalistic political parties: the UK Independence Party, a fiercely Europhobic group, and the British National Party, who have little to offer voters but anti-immigrant rhetoric.

Although both have made extensive use of the Union Jack in all their literature, neither party has made any headway in Wales or Scotland. For all their unionist pretensions, 95 per cent of their support comes from nationalists living in England. It is not unknown for BNP supporters to hijack the flag of St George as a symbol of their racist views.

On the Dorchester road, near the Neolithic monument known as the Nine Stones Circle, another car passes flying another small English flag from its window. I study the passengers – a family group: two adults and two children – and to my relief none look remotely neo-Nazi. On the road to Blandford Forum, several more flag-flyers pass and a pattern emerges. They all seem to be cars carrying kids. I conclude that the flags are being flown in support of the England football team, rather than the BNP.

It's because of the BNP that I'm driving across the county on this bright summer's morning towards Shaftesbury, a sleepy market town on the Dorset/Wiltshire border. Built on the site of a Saxon *burh*, a defended hill town, Shaftesbury sits seven hundred feet above the Blackmore Vale, south of Salisbury Plain. On a clear day, Glastonbury Tor is visible to the west.

The town's fame rests on the evocative prospect of Gold Hill, a steep cobbled street lined with sixteenth- and seventeenth-century cottages, whose thatched roofs descend in steps down the hill. This image became lodged in the public consciousness in the 1970s when it became the setting for the Hovis television advertisement in which a small boy, dressed in Victorian clothes, struggles to push his delivery bicycle up the hill, while the nostalgic voice-over speaks of the delights of Hovis brown bread and 'real butter' to the theme from Dvorak's New World Symphony.

Thomas Hardy was close to the mark when he described the town as one of England's quaintest spots in *Jude the Obscure*. The bygone age has not quite left Shaftesbury. It is the last place you would expect to be the setting for an anti-fascist rally. Yet that is why I have come here this morning.

For the purposes of the forthcoming European election, Shaftesbury is in the South-West region. Before the elections, the BNP had declared its intention to make the South-West a 'multicultural-free zone'. Blatantly seeking to inflame and then exploit tensions between racial groups and communities, the BNP distributed a leaflet to all households in the area, attacking asylum-seekers. This is fertile ground for them, given that most people believe that Britain takes in around 27 per cent of the world's asylum-seekers. The true figure is 2 per cent.[1]

If the BNP were hoping that the ignorance and prejudice revealed in those figures would ensure that their fear-mongering would go unchallenged in Shaftesbury, then they had chosen the wrong place. A letter appeared in a local magazine from Zara McQueen, describing the anger that she, as a Jewish woman, felt when she found the offending leaflet pushed through her letterbox: 'How dare the BNP pretend that it is a decent and respectable party when at the end of the day many of its members hold the same views as the Nazis.'[2]

Concerned that the town was being targeted by racists, Zara decided to organize a protest march. 'Mother-of-two takes stand against BNP,' announced the local *Daily Echo* on 3 June. The article stated that Zara was Jewish and quoted her as saying that she believed the BNP leaflet demonized Muslims. A spokesman for the BNP claimed to have 'loads of support in Shaftesbury', although, as the *Echo* pointed out, he was unable to give any numbers 'and admitted he did not know where Shaftesbury was'.

However foolish such comments may make them appear, the mere presence of the BNP in an area often leads to an increase in racial tension. Shaftesbury was to be no exception. Following the appearance of this article, Zara received an anonymous phone call threatening to burn her house down and calling her 'Jewish scum'.

If this has made her nervous, she doesn't show it when we meet in the car-park in Angel Lane, where the march which she has organized is assembling. Around two hundred people have gathered here – families with small children, pensioners, students, civic leaders – all concerned to show that their town is willing to make a stand against the racists.

Placards are handed out – '*Say No to the BNP*', '*The BNP is a Racist Party*', '*Racism is a Weapon of Mass Destruction*' – and, accompanied by a solitary policeman, the march begins to wind its way up the narrow High Street. It is Saturday morning and the town is full of shoppers, some of whom stop to applaud and offer encouragement, while others go about their business.

A young guy in jeans and T-shirt, walking backwards up the

High Street a hundred yards or so ahead of us, is the only counter-demonstrator. How does he let us know that he is a BNP supporter? By waving a couple of those little plastic England flags that have suddenly appeared flying from car windows.

The fifteen-minute march takes us to Park Walk, where a small rally is held. Representatives of all of the mainstream political parties speak, along with leaders of various faith groups. When my turn comes, I make the point that the BNP go to great lengths to present themselves as a respectable party, yet they are led by a man who is prepared to make excuses for the conduct of the Nazis. By casting doubt on the facts of the Holocaust, BNP leader Nick Griffin is speaking up in defence of a regime that tried to invade our country, a fact that would seem to undermine his claims to be a patriot.

On hearing that Griffin is a Holocaust denier, a tall, thin, elderly man steps from the crowd to speak movingly of his experiences as an ambulance driver who, as Allied forces moved into Germany in 1945, witnessed the aftermath of the Holocaust first hand. He describes the smell of Belsen – 'We didn't have to ask directions', seeing the piles of shoes beside the crematoria, and a twelve-year-old Romanian girl who had been incarcerated in Auschwitz and weighed just over two stone when he found her.

His spontaneous intervention brings proceedings to an end, as no one can better illuminate the reason why we are all here. As the crowd disperses, several young people walk over to shake him by the hand and thank him for his contribution.

Driving back to West Dorset, stopping for petrol near Blandford Forum, I find the source of the sudden explosion of Englishness. On the forecourt is a tub full of plastic St George's flags with special attachments for displaying from car windows, selling at £1.99 each.

A thought crosses my mind: what if I'd bought these flags, all of them, on the way to Shaftesbury and distributed them among my fellow marchers? What would that lonely counter-demonstrator have done if he had seen two hundred people coming towards him, half of them holding anti-BNP placards, the other half carrying their English flags? Would he still have been able to express his opposition by waving his own English flag or would we have forced him to find some other method to display his racist beliefs? A Nazi salute, perhaps?

The BNP are the most successful far-right party in British politics since the 1970s, when the National Front, formed from the disparate neo-Nazi groupings that had crept away from the ruins of Sir Oswald Mosley's British Union of Fascists, was briefly the fourth-largest party in British politics. With strong-holds in Wolverhampton, Leicester and East London, the National Front's main campaigning tool was a series of high-profile shows of strength. Hundreds of fascists would march provocatively through immigrant neighbourhoods, carrying a forest of Union Jack flags in a conscious echo of Hitler's Nuremburg rallies. National Front graffiti became a regular sight, the two consonants combining to form a prickly symbol as distinctive as a swastika.

The summer of 1976 was the warmest for a hundred years. In London, the temperature reached thirty degrees for sixteen consecutive days, still the longest spell on record. Hosepipe bans were in force across the country as drought conditions set in. And if the days were hot, the nights were stifling, with sleep hard to come by in the airless night.

The oppressive nature of the heatwave was mirrored by the

atmosphere on the streets. Community relations were strained after the National Front won over 100,000 votes in the Greater London Council elections. Towards the end of the summer, over the August bank-holiday weekend, things came to a head.

At Reading, an hour west of London, an audience of twenty thousand had gathered for a three-day music festival headlined by American heavy-metal hero Ted Nugent. On the first day, Friday 27 August, the bill featured artists from the Virgin Records roster, including black Jamaican reggae acts U Roy and the Mighty Diamonds.

Disturbingly, both their performances were met with a barrage of flying beer cans and racist abuse from the audience. The *Melody Maker*, under the headline 'READING'S REGGAE BACKLASH', reported that the Mighty Diamonds were forced to leave the stage 'after banners bearing unmistakeably worded advice had been held high and a thunder of boos had greeted their harmless musical activities'.[3]

The following night, in North London, fans of the Sex Pistols danced onstage with the band at the Screen on the Green cinema in Islington, wearing brown shirts and Nazi swastika armbands. This gig, which would subsequently acquire legendary status, was the Pistols' first major headline show. Their road manager, Nils Stevenson, memorably described the event in his diary:

> The Pistols are starting to attract an interesting collection of freaks who show up on mass tonight. The bill comprises the Buzzcocks, The Clash and Pistols, plus Malcolm's [McLaren] favourite film, *Scorpio Rising*. I can't help thinking most of the punters would have preferred a more mainstream 'stockings-and-swastika' movie like *Cabaret*.[4]

Punk in its infancy was suffused with fascistic imagery. The Pistols crowd took their cue from David Bowie, who appeared to give a fascist salute from the back of an open-topped Mercedes limousine on his return from exile in Berlin in May 1976. The Jam regularly performed in front of a huge Union Jack, which, in the political climate of the time, had unavoidable associations with the National Front. Members of The Clash had, only a few months previously, been in a band which went under the unfortunate moniker of The London SS.

The day after the Screen on the Green gig, Sunday 29 August, saw the beginning of the Notting Hill Carnival, a two-day event in which the capital's black community took to the streets of West London in celebration of their Caribbean heritage. The previous carnival, in 1975, had been marred by trouble between black youths and the police, and as a result it was decided that the police presence should increase from 200 officers to nearly 1,600.

Resentment at this heavy-handed approach simmered throughout the weekend, and late on Monday afternoon, after most of the public had left, large numbers of black youths gathered on the streets of Ladbroke Grove, seemingly determined to confront the police. When officers moved in to make arrests, a riot broke out that left 456 injured and sixty people under arrest.

Although tagged a 'race riot' by the media, this was not a recurrence of the interracial violence that had been stirred up by white racists in the Notting Hill area in the late fifties. This was something that had never been seen in Britain before: black youth in revolt. The young people of Britain, it seemed, were taking sides, and on that August bank-holiday weekend, all the signs suggested that the division would be along racial lines.

The Screen on the Green gig had been the first public appearance of The Clash, a four-piece punk band from West London. Two days later, guitarist Joe Strummer and bass player Paul Simonon found themselves caught up in the violence at the carnival, an experience that would have a seminal influence not just on the music of The Clash, but on the whole punk movement and its political stance.

Strummer, being several years older than the rest of the band, had some experience of the late-sixties/early-seventies counter-cultural underground. He was painfully aware that the radical edge of rock music had been severely dulled by the excesses of the jet-setting lifestyle that many rock stars had succumbed to in the mid-seventies. The only music that he believed to be still capable of carrying a political message was Jamaican reggae. The pop-orientated singles that were hugely popular in Britain in the sixties were superseded in the early seventies by heavier rhythms as reggae went underground, taking lyrical inspiration from the Rastafarian movement, which advocated pan-Africanism and a return to Africa.

Bob Marley, singing revolutionary songs such as 'Get Up, Stand Up' and 'Rebel Music', was reggae's first megastar. In May 1976, his album *Rastaman Vibration* reached number fifteen in the British charts, bringing into the mainstream a Rasta culture which held the smoking of marijuana to be sacred.

For black British youths, whose main complaint against the police was that they were constantly stopping and searching them on suspicion of being in possession of drugs, Marley's stance was inspirational.

As far as Joe Strummer was concerned, smoking dope and being radical went together, so Marley and the Rasta artists who followed in his wake caught his attention. Max Romeo's 'War Ina Babylon', Junior Murvin's 'Police And Thieves' and Culture's 'Two Seven Clash' – which some claim gave The Clash their name – were all dancehall hits that summer and popular with Joe and his fellow band members.

It was the opportunity to hear the latest songs from Jamaica that had drawn them to the Notting Hill Carnival on that Bank Holiday Monday afternoon. As the mood turned from celebration to confrontation, Strummer and Simonon were at first exhilarated by the experience of being shoulder to shoulder with angry black youths as they took on the police. As the riot ensued, however, the two white punks found themselves the focus of that anger, cornered in an alley by a gang of black youths who ordered them to turn out their pockets. Finding only bricks and bottles, the gang realized that these two white boys were somehow on their side, fighting the clamp-down on the streets of West London, and they moved on without further aggravation.[5]

The significance of this event, which would ultimately help to shape my own political outlook, would take some time to manifest itself.

I was eighteen years old that bank-holiday weekend, living with my parents in East London, working as a messenger for a merchant bank. I was oblivious to the fact that punk rock was busy being born in my city, and any hipness that I could lay claim to came largely from reading the *New Musical Express*, a weekly broadsheet which covered the contemporary music scene.

In the mid-seventies, the *NME* had pulled ahead of its rivals *Melody Maker*, *Sounds* and *Disc* by recruiting writers who had cut their teeth on the underground press. As a result, *NME* writers were less inclined to accept rock music at face value. They had attitude and were not afraid to take a stand on the radical issues of the day.

Given its track record, the *NME* should have been a prime candidate to champion the new punk rock. Neil Spencer gave the Pistols their first review in February 1976, having seen them at the Marquee supporting Eddie and the Hot Rods. It was a positive write-up and Spencer was prescient enough to recognize the first great punk-rock statement of aims. Breaking with convention, he included the quote in his review: ' "We're not into music," one of the Pistols confided afterwards. "We're into chaos." '[6]

The review had the effect of legitimizing the Pistols in the eyes of their peers and should really have been followed up with a full-page feature, but instead it was rival paper *Sounds* that became punk's cheerleaders, giving the Sex Pistols a two-page spread in April 1976. Journalist Caroline Coon led the charge in the *Melody Maker*, writing a seminal article on the 'new punk rock' in July.

By contrast, the *NME* was slow off the mark. Former underground journalist Mick Farren wrote a polemical piece in June, entitled 'The *Titanic* Sails at Dawn', in which he argued forcefully that the music industry was artistically bankrupt. The article was a thinly veiled call to arms, which finished by declaring:

> Putting the Beatles back together isn't going to be the salvation of rock and roll. Four kids playing to their own contemporaries in a dirty cellar might.

Yet despite the fact that the Pistols had been playing in and around London for eight months and had featured regularly in a rival publication, Farren never mentions them. The revolution that he calls for is happening on his doorstep, yet he gives the impression of being totally unaware of its existence.

Dressed in leather jacket and shades topped with an afro hair-do, Farren held a view common among *NME* staffers, that new ideas could only come from one place – New York City. To them, punk was an American phenomenon, emanating from CBGB's on the Lower East Side. If there was to be any future for rock, it belonged to musicians working from a template provided by the cultest of cult bands, the Velvet Underground.

The *NME* was of course right to champion the music coming out of the East Coast of America. Artists like The Ramones, the Modern Lovers and Television provided a vital contrast to the soporific sounds of West Coast rock that dominated the American charts in the mid-seventies.

The Eagles, a faceless band of session men, led the way, selling millions of albums of soft country rock, followed closely by Englishman Peter Frampton, whose 1975 *Frampton Comes Alive!*, recorded in concert at the Winterland in San Francisco, remains the biggest-selling live album of all time. The same year, Fleetwood Mac released their hugely successful eponymous album, which captured the world-weariness that seemed to dog those who made Los Angeles their home. The West Coast sound was highly seductive and I was not immune to its charms, although by August 1976 my infatuation with Linda Ronstadt was coming to an end. I didn't even bother to buy the album that she had released that month, *Hasten Down The Wind*.

The main focus of my adulation that summer had been the

Rolling Stones, whose songs became a staple of the fledgling band that had formed in my mum's back room in Barking. With Wiggy, the kid next door who had taught me how to play guitar, on lead guitar and Robert Handley, who lived further along Park Avenue, on drums, we had been jamming for over a year, occasionally joined on keyboards by Steven Rice, a school friend from Rainham.

Together, we went to see the Stones perform twice that year, first at Earls Court and then at the Knebworth Festival on 21 August. Our other great achievement had been to attend the massive concert that The Who gave at Charlton football ground in South London.

Much as I loved these two bands, it was clear that the distance between them and their fans was growing, both socially, as rock stars became millionaires, and literally, as the concert venues moved from 5,000-seat cinemas to 50,000-capacity stadiums and festivals. At Knebworth, we weren't able to get any closer than about half a mile from the stage, and as they didn't have giant TV screens back then, the musicians were nothing more than tiny figures in the distance.

I had been playing guitar for a couple of years and I desperately wanted to become a rock star, but had no idea how to bridge the huge gap between my reality and that of the Rolling Stones. The first hint as to how it might be accomplished appeared in the *NME* in the same week that I went to see the Stones at Knebworth: a review of a record by a bunch of young guys from Essex, playing maximum R 'n' B.

'Proof positive that Britain is the home of punk rock', began Bob Edmands's headline review of Eddie and the Hot Rods' *Live At The Marquee* EP. What Edmands was referring to was not the nascent scene that was forming around the Sex Pistols, but a retro trend that took its cues from the garage bands of the 1960s.

The NME Book of Rock, the first rock encyclopedia, published in 1973, has an entry for Punk Rock, explaining that the term was coined to describe the numerous local white rock bands that sprang up all over America in the wake of the Beatles/Stones-led British invasion – 'punk' originally being American slang for a young person with no respect for authority. Citing bands such as The Kingsmen, ? and the Mysterians, and the Shadows of Knight, the DIY aspect of late-seventies punk is foreshadowed in the observation that the mid-sixties 'was a time when seemingly anybody and everybody could be a rock 'n' roll star by simply growing their hair long and picking up a guitar'.

This was the ethos that had inspired four New York kids to form a punk-rock group in 1974. The Ramones fetishized the throwaway nature of sixties punk rock, responding to the over-long epics favoured by prog rock bands such as Pink Floyd and Yes by recording wilfully dumb songs played at breakneck speed, often lasting less than a couple of minutes.

The Ramones' debut album was released in America in May 1976, around the same time as The Flamin' Groovies' album *Shake Some Action*, which sought to re-cast the sound of the early sixties British invasion. By the time the two bands played a gig celebrating the bicentenary of US independence at the London Roundhouse on 4 July 1976, the phrase 'punk rock', dusted off by American journalists and recycled as a term for this retro tendency, had begun appearing in the English music press.

Journalists looking for native retro-punk-rockers were drawn to Eddie and the Hot Rods, a band from Southend in

Essex. For the previous twelve months, they had been making a name for themselves on the London pub rock circuit, playing covers of sixties punk-rock classics such as Sam the Sham's 'Woolly Bully' and ? and the Mysterians' '96 Tears', along with self-written songs with titles such as 'Teenage Depression' – all, like The Ramones, played at a frantic pace.

The Hot Rods quickly became the epitome of British punk, so much so that when the first copy of what was to become the punk bible, the fanzine *Sniffin' Glue*, appeared in August 1976, it featured the band's frontman, Barry Masters, on the cover. For me and my band-mates, thrashing out old Stones and Faces songs in the back room, Eddie and the Hot Rods' *Live At The Marquee* was a revelation. Their playing was driven by an urgency that had long since deserted our stadium-frequenting heroes. The effect on our sensibilities was immediate.

Within a month of its release, when we got together at our rehearsal studio on the wrong side of the A13, the stand-out track from *Live At The Marquee*, a 100mph version of Bob Seger's 'Get Out of Denver', was already in our repertoire, fitting neatly alongside standards such as 'Substitute', 'Brown Sugar' and 'Route 66'.

The reason why Eddie and the Hot Rods appealed both to me and to the journalists at the *NME* was that, like The Ramones and the Flamin' Groovies, their music had its roots in the formalities of rhythm and blues, the musical form that had fuelled popular music since the 1950s. Although these retro-punks were taking things back to basics, they had respect for the rock 'n' roll tradition and took their musicianship seriously – witness the military precision with which The Ramones started and ended their songs.

And that was perhaps why the *NME* were so reluctant to give any coverage to the Sex Pistols. Here were a band who seemed determined to trash the tradition, who clearly had no musical ability and no respect for anyone or anything. What made neo-punk bands like the Pistols and The Clash so threatening to the underground establishment that held sway at the *NME* was the fact that the messages they gave out – 'Destroy', 'No Future', 'Hate and War' – heralded a violent break with the past. 1976 was to be Year Zero.

The *NME* was missing in action on that pivotal August bank-holiday weekend. A dispute with the print unions meant that the issue carrying the Hot Rods review was the last for several weeks. The paper finally reappeared on 11 September, just as the seventies achieved its apotheosis as a decade – 'Dancing Queen' by Abba reached number one, and sales of loon pants and cheesecloth shirts hit an all-time high.

Yet the men clad from head to toe in denim in the ad for Tommy's Jean Store in Northampton would soon have the smiles wiped from their bearded faces. The seeds of their destruction were being sown: the *NME* had finally devoted an article to the Sex Pistols.

The full-page review of their Screen on the Green gig opens with a quote from Alex Harvey:

Someone's got to come along and say to all of us 'All your ideas about rock and roll, all your ideas about sound, all your ideas about guitars, all your ideas about this and that are a load of wank. This is where it is! . . . Someone's got to come out and say 'Fuck You'.

Well, declares journalist Charles Shaar Murray, taking a

deep breath, there's good news and bad news: someone has finally come out and said 'Fuck You' – and they mean it. But rather than being the breath of fresh air that we had desperately hoped for, they are the musical equivalent of being spat in the face and booted in the cobblers. And they are wearing swastikas as fashion accessories.

> The current vogue for Punkophilia and Aggro Chic has created the atmosphere in which a group like the Sex Pistols could get started and find an audience and – dig it – it is entirely too late to start complaining because they behave like real Nasty Kids and not the stylised abstraction of Nasty Kiddery which we have been demanding and applauding from sensitive, well educated, late-twenties pop superstars.

Dig it indeed.

The malevolence that Murray detected at the Screen on the Green was also present elsewhere: that week's *NME* carried a report of the racist abuse meted out to the reggae acts at the Reading Festival:

> The atmosphere degenerates into something more like a National Front demo. This is not straightforward disapproval, but a malevolent, damn right sinister display.
>
>   The slogans chanted [at the Mighty Diamonds] are offensively obscene and much the same as those favoured by the NF.

But if the radicals seemed to be on the run in that week's *NME*, the fight back was just beginning. On the letters page, a missive appeared from a reader who had been incensed by reports of racist remarks made by guitar god Eric Clapton in early August.

Clapton had a special place in the *NME* star system. As recently as the previous June, his 1971 single 'Layla' had come top in a readers' poll of the top hundred singles of all time ('Bohemian Rhapsody' came forty-sixth). Clapton's ability to interpret black musical styles was underlined by his chart success with Bob Marley's 'I Shot The Sheriff', which went to number one in America in July 1974, marking a renaissance in his fortunes.

All the more disturbing, then, that Clapton should suddenly choose to make a racist outburst. According to Michael Schumacher, in his biography of Clapton, *Crossroads*, the guitarist began his set at the Birmingham Odeon on 5 August 1976 by asking if there were any foreigners in the audience, encouraging them to put up their hands. Once they had identified themselves, Clapton declared, 'I think we should all vote for Enoch.'

Enoch Powell was a Conservative MP whose name had become a byword for racism. He gained notoriety in 1968 by making a speech in which he condemned immigration. Quoting a constituent of his, he claimed that 'In this country, in fifteen or twenty years' time, the black man will have the whip hand over the white man.' Having used such inflammatory language, he was much more careful when articulating his solution: 'stopping, or virtually stopping, further inflow, and . . . promoting maximum outflow'. In short: end immigration, start repatriation. Powell finished the speech with a bleak vision of racial confrontation on the streets of Britain: 'As I look ahead, I am filled with foreboding. Like the Roman, I seem to see "the Tiber foaming with much blood".'

What became known, notoriously, as the 'Rivers of Blood' speech was delivered to an audience of Conservative activists at the Midland Hotel in Birmingham, Powell's home town, a city with a reputation for racial intolerance. Clapton would have been aware of this and may even have waited until he got to Birmingham to make such remarks, in the hope of a sympathetic reaction.

Clapton was fortunate that neither *NME* nor *Melody Maker* sent anyone along to review the show. The week before, his huge outdoor gig at Crystal Palace Bowl had received glowing reports in both papers, and perhaps they felt that he had already had enough coverage for one tour.

However, *Sounds* did have someone there and they related Clapton's outburst in the 14 August issue, under the headline 'SUPPORT ENOCH SAYS "MP" CLAPTON'.

The review of the gig on page forty-seven relayed the whole sordid episode, describing how Clapton

> ... shambled on and then began warning us all about 'foreigners' and the need to vote for Enoch Powell, whom Eric then described as a prophet ... Following some confusion caused by Eric with his announcements, the band then launched into a second number ... More time was then spent on warning us of the danger of the country 'being a colony within ten years' and of how 'Eric was thinking of retiring to become an MP for a constituency in Surrey'.

The shockwaves from Clapton's racist comments took a few weeks to ripple through the anti-racist community. The response was to be the catalyst that returned rock to its radical roots.

Red Saunders's irate letter appeared in all three of the major rock papers:

> When we read about Eric Clapton's Birmingham concert when he urged support for Enoch Powell, we nearly puked. Come on Eric . . . you've been taking too much of that *Daily Express* stuff and you don't know how to handle it. Own up. Half your music is black. You're rock music's biggest colonist. You're a good musician but where would you be without the blues and R 'n' B?
>
> You've got to fight the racist poison otherwise you degenerate into the sewer with the rats and all the money men who ripped off rock culture with their cheque books and plastic crap. We want to organize a rank and file movement against racist poison in music. We urge support for Rock against Racism.
>
> PS. Who shot the Sheriff, Eric? It sure as hell wasn't you!

A contact address for the campaign was provided and within days it was inundated with letters of support. Rock Against Racism had been born, and would eventually grow to be a mass movement, inspiring a generation into political activism.

Of course, the letter to *NME* wasn't a bolt from the blue. Rock Against Racism was the brainchild of the Socialist Workers Party, a small, far-left group who had made a name for themselves confronting the National Front on the streets. For all their Trotskyist intellectualizing, the organizers of RAR hit upon a simple method of undermining the NF's message: they organized gigs at which white punk-rockers performed on the same bill as black reggae bands. That may seem the obvious thing to have done now, but in light of the reception given to reggae acts by the white audience at the Reading Festival, RAR was taking an unprecedented step on the road to multiculturalism.

Rock Against Racism had only managed to stage one small gig in London's East End in late 1976 before British punk shed its retro connotations and became a nationwide phenomenon. The Sex Pistols, as ever, provided the cutting edge, swearing on teatime telly. The result – front-page outrage in all the tabloids – catapulted them into the national consciousness.

The Pistols were true iconoclasts, destroying everything they touched, including the careers of the retro-punk bands. Eddie and the Hot Rods suddenly seemed tame by comparison; the Flamin' Groovies little more than an American bar band. Only The Ramones endured, by staying true to their original template of brief, high-velocity songs which, fortunately for them, were ideal music to pogo to.

Yet although I was mightily impressed with the Pistols' foul-mouthed antics, it was going to take more than a few swear words to shift me from my belief in rock 'n' roll. As far as I was concerned, the Stones, The Faces and The Who were the greatest bands on the planet. Seeing the Stones live had under-lined that fact, despite their 1976 album, *Black and Blue*, being a somewhat disappointing affair. The reason I had wanted to see the Stones had more to do with *Rolled Gold*, a double-album compilation of their best tracks from the sixties, which came out in late 1975.

My attention was caught by the first two sides of this collection, which dealt with material recorded between 1963 and 1966. These were the songs that had inspired the original punks in America, and, like them, me and my mates could think of nothing better to do in the long hot summer nights than get together and play these songs as loud as we bloody well could. As 1977 dawned, we still wanted to be the Rolling Stones.

This failure to recognize that our world had changed was not confined to back-room boogie boys in Barking. *Zigzag*, then the only monthly devoted to rock music, was an A4-sized magazine which still nurtured some of the hippy ideals. Its February 1977 issue featured Rolling Stone Keith Richards on the cover and trailed articles about Jackson Browne, Ry Cooder, Joni Mitchell and arch-hippy Steve Hillage.

Over the next few months, the content of the magazine underwent a radical shift, to the extent that the July issue had Johnny Thunders on the cover and offered features on The Damned, Richard Hell, The Clash, Generation X and the MC5. The back-page advert for a Jesse Winchester album looked rather incongruous, suggesting that the ads department had not yet managed to get their clients to understand that a cultural revolution was under way.

To be honest, I was suspicious of punk. There was a contrivance about the way the Pistols had been created – put together by Malcolm McLaren, a well-known haberdasher, for his own purposes. Shouldn't a band that were going to revolutionize music be driven by their own vision? Hadn't the main outcome of the swearing-on-TV incident been a sudden increase in sales of McLaren's clothing lines?

A whiff of this artifice attached itself to The Clash, too, since their manager, Bernie Rhodes, was McLaren's business partner and worked alongside him in their Kings Road clothes shop, Sex. Would it just be a matter of time, I wondered, before Rotten, Strummer, *et al* were exposed as a bunch of

185

middle-class university graduates, like Roxy Music? Was punk just another art-school prank?

It was this scepticism that kept me from heading out to West London to see the Pistols or The Clash live. I was intrigued by what I read in the music press, but, frankly, I doubted their authenticity.

Around the time that *Zigzag* were undergoing their conversion, I finally found a punk band that made sense to me. The Jam took their cue not from the New York Dolls but from The Who, rejecting the safety-pin chic of the Pistols in favour of the sharp mohair suits, white shirts and skinny black ties of *Ready Steady Go!* Where The Ramones had plundered America's punk-rock past for their look, these guys took their inspiration from that most enduring of all British youth cults: The Jam were Mods.

The original Mod look had been a way of transcending the social boundaries that were still very much in force during the early sixties. Much has been written on Mod narcissism, but while there was great rivalry between peers over who had the hippest threads, records and drugs, the real competition lay elsewhere. If you could look better than your boss, then you could convince yourself that you *were* better than him – and you might even be able to pull his daughter.

Where previously the working class had been proud of its insularity, Mod was an expression of working-class pride achieved through cosmopolitan taste – French clothes, Italian scooters, American jeans, Jamaican ska – anything that set you apart from the drab reality of post-war Britain.

The Mod look had achieved iconic status before Paul Weller tapped into it as a means of Anglicizing punk. And there had been something of it in the air that spring. My band mates and

I had already been to see the archetypal Mod band, the Small Faces, on their reunion tour that March.

Photos of The Jam printed in the music papers immediately set them apart from the Pistols. Whereas the latter's ripped clothes and spiked hair only added to the sense that they were fabricated, The Jam looked sharp. Their clothing was classic but not contrived, giving them an air of working-class authenticity. And where the Pistols' anger was a product of their boredom, The Jam's was possessed with the intensity of the impatient. This is the modern world and if you don't like it, well, get out of the way.

The jarring guitars and clipped, angry phrasing of their first single, 'In The City', provided a perfect soundtrack to the moment. At last, *my* generation – not Pete Townsend's – were going to have their say.

My fellow band mates and I finally got to a Jam gig, at the Nashville Rooms, a pub next to West Kensington Tube station, in April 1977. Seeing the band in such cramped conditions – the Nashville was full to its five-hundred capacity – was electrifying. They played their instruments with furious intent, leaping in the air to fire off power chords like thunderbolts. It was quite different from the energy that Eddie and the Hot Rods had harnessed. The Jam weren't telling us to 'Get Out Of Denver' – they knew where it was at: it was tonight. 'In The City'. London. England.

This was English electric lightning and I was immediately hooked. But then, what was not to like about The Jam?

For all their fire and skill, they were basically a retro-punk band in a neo-punk package, perhaps the first of what would later become known as the 'New Wave'. Their Mod sensibility had a strong resonance for an ex-wannabe suedehead like myself. And they definitely weren't graduates. In fact, only a few months before, they had been knocking out Stones and Who songs to fish-supper audiences in working men's clubs, only one step up from me and my mates playing in our back rooms.

When Weller announced that the band's next gig would be at the Rainbow Theatre in Finsbury Park supporting The Clash, we decided to go along as fans of The Jam, hoping to see them blow away these neo-punk poseurs by the sheer power of their Mod authenticity. The stakes were high. A review of The Clash's debut album by Pete Silverton in *Sounds* had outraged us by stating, 'If you don't like The Clash, you don't like rock 'n' roll. It really is as simple as that.' How could The Clash be rock 'n' roll? They were punks. Defilers of the Temple. Apostates.

Joe Strummer would later say that the 9 May 1977 show at the Rainbow was the moment he held most dear from his time in The Clash. 'That was the night that punk really broke out of the clubs ... it really felt like we were in the right place doing the right thing at the right time.'

The Sex Pistols had tried to take punk out of the London club scene by booking a nationwide tour in late 1976, with The Clash as the support band, but in the wake of their behaviour on TV, almost all of the dates were cancelled. While the Pistols continued to be dogged by controversy, it was left to The Clash to make the running.

The White Riot Tour was set up to promote The Clash's eponymous debut album, which had been released in early April. That night at the Rainbow, they were supported by The Jam, The Buzzcocks, the Subway Sect and the Prefects, a Birmingham band memorably described as 'this hermetic, sarcastic group' by Jon Savage in his masterful book on punk, *England's Dreaming*.

Savage also described the Rainbow gig as being part of 'the last great punk tour', which may have been true if you were a member of the Sex Pistols' clique, but for those of us in the audience at the Rainbow, this was only the beginning – the moment when punk was wrestled from the control of Malcolm McLaren and carried off into the night by an exultant mob.

My memory of the first three bands is dim – I see them playing fast, monotonous songs in black and white. Our heroes The Jam gave it their all, but were unable to fill the space as convincingly as they had at the Nashville just a few weeks before. Their energy seemed dissipated on the vast stage at the Rainbow, their impact dulled.

Then came The Clash, who, by contrast, were about to hit their first peak. Performing in front of a huge image of a line of charging police, taken at the Notting Hill Carnival riot the previous year, the band showed how far they had come since that eventful weekend. They opened their set with 'London's Burning' and the place exploded. When they left the stage an hour or so later, over two hundred seats had been trashed in what some papers described as a 'riot'.

Seat 37 in row K remained intact, but its occupant would never be the same again. What I witnessed that night dispelled all of my lingering doubts about punk. The Clash used the same guitars and amps as the Stones, they threw the same shapes, they even had the same feel to their music, albeit considerably speeded up. Pete Silverton was right, goddammit, The Clash *were* rock 'n' roll.

But unlike the Stones, these guys weren't middle-aged

millionaires; they were our age – late teens, early twenties – and possessed the articulate intensity of youth, that powerful mixture of naivety and passion which each generation strives to harness.

Just a year before, I had worshipped the Rolling Stones at Earls Court – and had smiled indulgently when I'd seen the pictures of them partying with Princess Margaret after the show. Now The Clash were drawing a demarcation line between the generations and I was cheering them on as they loudly proclaimed that the Rolling Stones had no place in punk's Year Zero.

That night, Joe Strummer and I came away from the Rainbow with the same sense of excitement – both of us intoxicated with the conviction that we were in the right place doing the right thing at the right time.

Although they had come a long way since playing at the Screen on the Green in August 1976, The Clash's first album was, for the most part, a product of their experiences on that bank-holiday weekend. 'White Riot', the song which became their theme tune and debut single, described the Notting Hill Carnival riot and called on white youths to take to the streets to vent their anger alongside their black contemporaries. 'Garageland' was written in response to Charles Shaar Murray's scathing dismissal of the band in his review of the Screen on the Green gig. The Clash, he wrote, 'are the kind of garage band that should be speedily returned to the garage, preferably with the motor running'. The spirit of the album was encapsulated by the image that adorned the back cover: a picture taken during the Carnival riot, of the police charging in the shadow of the Westway.

All these influences came together on 'Police And Thieves', their cover of the massive reggae hit from the previous summer.

White men playing reggae have always tended to suffer from having too much respect for the material, whereas Jamaican musicians often take huge liberties with the form when playing it themselves. The Clash made few concessions to the original, performing it over a straight 4/4 beat which gave the song an urgency that Junior Murvin's languid version lacked. It was the first attempt by any band to extend the parameters of punk and was an impressive success. Here was The Clash's multi-racial rhetoric made flesh, a coming together of punk and reggae in which both retained their dignity. On an album full of powerfully polemical songs, 'Police And Thieves' stood out as the most radical cut.

The Clash's album could not have come at a more crucial time. Just a few days before the Rainbow concert, the National Front had taken 8.8 per cent of the votes in local elections for the Greater London Council, coming third in thirty-five of the ninety-two seats that had been contested. The NF had doubled its support since the 1974 election, in some areas winning 20 per cent of the vote. 'WE'LL SOON WIN EAST END SEATS SAY FRONT LEADERS' read the headlines in the *London Evening News* on 7 May.

That same issue of the *News* carried a story by pop correspondent John Blake, headlined 'ROCK'S SWASTIKA REVOLUTION', which reported how punk's penchant for flirting with Nazi imagery had attracted the attentions of the NF:

> The zealots of the National Front haven't been slow to realize that the punks would make up a very handy pre-packed army if only their loyalty could be enlisted. Consequently the Front have been extremely active among audiences – and with the bands themselves.

Below a photograph of the Pistols, a tag line claimed, 'The punk cult is swinging to the Right . . . even the National Front seek their support.'

The message encapsulated by the Clash's 'Police And Thieves' – that black and white youths share common cultural and political ground – made them prime candidates to take part in a Rock Against Racism gig. However, the movement was still in its infancy, organizing gigs that drew small but enthusiastic audiences, their reach hampered by the fact that RAR, controlled by the Socialist Workers Party, was fiercely partisan.

Many on the traditional Left were suspicious of the SWP's motives for getting involved with rock music, as they were renowned for their eagerness to jump on any passing bandwagon in the hope of furthering their own agenda. Having said that, the SWP were the only party that had any grasp of the importance of popular culture and how it could be harnessed to form a mass movement.

Frustrated by their failure to galvanize broader opposition to the National Front, the SWP initiated the Anti-Nazi League, under whose banner they invited mainstream political figures to join with them in a popular front against fascism. The ANL was set up in November 1977 and involved high-profile figures such as anti-apartheid activist Peter Hain and Labour MP Neil Kinnock, both of whom sat on its steering committee alongside trade unionists and SWP activists.

One of the first things the ANL did was to organize a massive rally in Trafalgar Square followed by a march through the East End of London, which would culminate in a free open-air Rock Against Racism concert in Victoria Park, Hackney. The date set for the Carnival Against The Nazis was Sunday 30 April 1978.

In the year since seeing The Clash at the Rainbow, I had cut my hair, traded in my fake baseball jacket for a fake leather jacket, left home and quit my job to play in a band. The five of us who had witnessed The Clash that night – Wiggy, Robert Handley, Steven Rice, Kevin Beech and myself – formed a group called Riff Raff. In the months that followed, we played at the legendary Marquee Club, where the Rolling Stones had started out, the Nashville, where we had seen The Jam, and several of the old pub rock venues around London which had now started to cater for punk rock. We had also landed a recording contract with Chiswick Records, cutting a four-track EP entitled 'I Wanna Be A Cosmonaut'. In short, my life had utterly changed. I had become a punk-rocker.

The Clash had been the catalyst. Seeing them at the Rainbow had solved the conundrum that had been troubling me since adolescence: how was a kid from Barking, who wasn't pretty and couldn't sing very well and had no idea how the music industry worked, going to make it as a rock star? Up until that moment, my best guess had been to conform to the prevailing fashions of the day: dress like rock-star-next-door Peter Frampton ('The Face of '76', according to *Sounds*), write songs about girls and summer and hope that someone noticed me.

It took The Clash to show me the way.

Conformity won't get you noticed, punk – confrontation is the quickest way to get people's attention. You're not pretty? So what? Show the world you don't care by putting a safety pin through your cheek to make yourself even more unsightly. Can't sing? Who cares? It's what you are singing *about* that matters. Don't understand the workings of the music industry? Well don't worry, we're going to turn that world upside-down.

And, hey, don't wait for someone to come along and do it all for you. Do it yourself.

This DIY ethic was the central tenet of punk. It cut us free from complacency and consumerism, empowering us to create. And it came with its own manifesto:

> The music industry will no longer dictate what records get released – You will decide because you will make them!

> The music papers will no longer dictate what is good or bad – You will decide because you will write your own fanzines!

> Fashion designers will no longer dictate what you wear – You will decide because you will develop your own style!

> Old farts will no longer patronize you with their hippy ideals – You will decide what is right and what is wrong, because you are the future!

By taking control of the means of production of all the things that were important to us, we were going to change the world.

More than any other band, The Clash seemed to embody these ideals, although, in a sense, they were merely doing what all good artists do – mirroring the concerns of their audience. But we didn't want to be mirrored, we wanted to be led, and where The Clash went we followed. When two weeks before the ANL/RAR Carnival Against The Nazis they were added to the bill, we knew we had to be there too.

My political sympathies at the time chimed with the ideals of RAR. When my band mates and I had gone into the studio to make a demo tape in March 1977, one of the four tracks we recorded was a cod reggae song that I had written called 'Rivers Of Blood', which sought, sincerely yet somewhat clumsily, to refute Enoch Powell's vision of a race war on the streets of Britain.

There is an important difference, however, between writing about the struggle and standing up to be counted. Attending the Carnival Against The Nazis was the first political act I ever undertook and it was, in its way, as significant as seeing The Clash at the Rainbow.

The organizers had been expecting a crowd of around twenty thousand – the number of Rock Against Racism badges they'd sold in the previous twelve months – but when we arrived in Trafalgar Square it was clear that the turnout was massive. While the National Front marched beneath their ranks of Union Jacks, we gathered amid union banners, yellow Anti-Nazi League roundels and punk pink RAR stars. We walked the six miles to Victoria Park in high spirits. Ten thousand whistles had been handed out and we all took turns on the megaphone to lead chants of 'The National Front is a fascist front! Smash the National Front.'

En route to the East End, the march wound its way through the City, where, only months before, I'd been working as a messenger for a merchant bank; Cheapside, past the record shop where I used to kill time listening to the latest releases on Stiff Records; across Princes Street, home of the bank I'd worked for; up Threadneedle Street, past the Bank of England and then along broad Bishopsgate towards Shoreditch and the East End.

There had been talk of trouble – the last big anti-NF demo had turned into a riot when a crowd of five thousand anti-fascists had refused to allow the NF to march through

Lewisham in August 1977 – but we never encountered any opposition, apart from one little old man in a flat cap, standing, beer in hand, outside a pub near the top of Brick Lane, giving the Nazi salute to the passing marchers. Perhaps he was the last of Oswald Mosley's blackshirts, reduced to making a futile gesture in the face of this massive show of strength by the anti-fascist movement.

When we finally reached Hackney, it became clear that the event had vastly exceeded expectations. An estimated hundred thousand people had converged on Victoria Park – one person for every vote that the NF had won in the London council elections the year before.

The Clash were not top of the bill that day, their late addition forcing them to perform mid-afternoon. They delivered a short sharp set of favourites from their first album, along with a few new songs like 'Tommy Gun'. From the reaction of the crowd, it was clear that most of us had come to see them play. Whatever followed would surely be an anticlimax. But the crowd did not disperse, staying to hear sets from joint headliners Steel Pulse and the Tom Robinson Band. Both had been staunch supporters of RAR during its first year, appearing at several gigs.

Steel Pulse were British reggae rockers from Birmingham whose current hit was their chilling anti-racist anthem 'Ku Klux Klan'. The Tom Robinson Band were led by a singer who stood out even in those days of stand-out personalities. The first 'out' gay pop singer who didn't dress like an alien, Tom Robinson oozed normality, not even bothering to cut his curly shoulder-length locks to meet the strict regulations that punk had imposed on hairstyles. He looked as affable as your best mate and dressed like him too. His homosexuality was not made palatable by being hidden behind a veil of androgyny, nor was it lightened by camp. Tom was gay and out and angry.

And incredibly brave. Homosexuality was a taboo subject, even for the punk audience. In 1978 you could easily get your head kicked in if someone thought you were a 'queer'. Having had a top-five hit in late 1977 with the anthemic '2-4-6-8 Motorway', a song extolling the overwhelmingly straight activity of truck-driving, Robinson followed it up with 'Sing If You're Glad To Be Gay', a bitter, ironically titled song which expressed to a straight audience how badly gays were treated by society in general and by the police in particular.

When the Tom Robinson Band sang that song at Victoria Park, a strange thing happened. All of the men who were standing near me and my friends began singing along with gusto and kissing each other passionately on the lips. Turning around, we were aghast to find that we had been standing beneath a huge banner that proclaimed 'Gays Against the Nazis'. Somewhat embarrassed, we shuffled away as politely as we could.

Having grown up in Barking, I'd never encountered an 'out' gay man before. I wasn't so much shocked as puzzled. What were these gays doing at a Rock Against Racism gig? Surely the day was all about black people, wasn't it?

Eventually, the penny dropped: just as Hitler didn't only target the Jews, the fascists were against anyone who was in any way different. Blacks, Asians, gays, lefties, punks – we were all inferior as far as the NF was concerned. From that day on, I knew what I needed to do if I wanted to oppose the forces of conservatism – be as different from them as possible, celebrate that difference and stand together in solidarity with whoever they targeted.

That first ANL/RAR carnival was a watershed, setting the tone for the decade to come. Those of us who were there that day would go on to support the Two Tone movement, the miners, CND, anti-apartheid, Nicaragua, Red Wedge, the GLC, Live Aid. It was the moment when my generation took sides.

It was also The Clash's greatest moment. Although they undoubtedly did better gigs, the context of their performance that day seemed to fulfil the hopes that they had raised. The Clash sealed their mythical status as rock's greatest rebels that Sunday afternoon, nailing their ragged colours to the mast of political pop for ever. However, the pressure of trying to live up to the expectations of their audience would prove to be their undoing.

In the heady days of punk, I truly believed that The Clash were going to change the world – which was foolish of me, because they were only a rock 'n' roll band. Unfortunately for them, The Clash believed this as well – which was foolish of them, too. The contradictions of trying to live up to their own ideals while becoming huge rock stars ultimately tore the band apart.

That they didn't bring civilization to its knees by playing loud and fast polemical songs does not detract from the lasting effect they had on the lives of those of us who were willing them to succeed. When my turn came to take actions which lived up to the political sentiments of my songs, the lessons I had learned from The Clash's mistakes were invaluable.

Their failure to engage fully with politics was central to my decision to work closely with the Labour Party in the hope of defeating the Tories in the 1987 election. The sad realization that The Clash were much better at posing than they were at politics forced me to overcome any fears of being seen as 'uncool' and take the flak I attracted for founding the Labour-supporting collective of musicians and artists known as Red Wedge.

The Clash's failure to change the world helped me to keep my own role in perspective. I realized early on in my career that responsibility for changing the world lies not with the performer but with the audience. To suggest otherwise would be the worst kind of charlatanism, excusing the audience from any responsibility for making the world a better place.

What a performer *can* do, however, is bring people together for a specific cause, to raise money or consciousness, to focus support and facilitate an expression of solidarity. Which is precisely what The Clash did in Victoria Park for Rock Against Racism. Before I saw the hundred thousand like-minded souls gathered that day, I was reluctant to oppose the casual racism I'd heard at work. The realization that I was not the only person who hated what the NF stood for gave me the courage to speak out against the racists and homophobes.

The Clash taught me a valuable lesson that day, which I have in the back of my mind every time I write a song or step out on to a stage: although you can't change the world by singing songs and doing gigs, the things you say and the actions you take can change the perspective of members of the audience. The Clash brought me to RAR, Tom Robinson introduced me to the politics of sexuality, and those brave gay men with their big pink banner made me realize that we were all on the same side. And although the world was just the same as it had always been as I travelled home on the Tube that evening, my view of it had been changed for ever.

9

The Old Country

All children of migrants grow up surrounded by reminders of the old country. The words they hear, the food they eat, the tales they are told all speak of another place, where the sun always shone and nobody had to lock their doors, an altogether preferable environment to the one they now find themselves in. Whenever older relatives get together, they slip back seamlessly to conversations from long ago and whole genealogies unfold as the names of distant relatives tumble from the family tree. Having never met any of these people, the youngsters can only sit and listen, until the names of these family members become familiar to them, their stories capable of stirring the emotions whilst simultaneously remaining quite unfathomable, like the words of 'Auld Lang Syne'. It is possible to see what the old country looked like through photographs, but the sounds and the smells and the space have all gone.

The old country that my parents came from was called the Second World War. I was born little more than a dozen years after it ended, and I grew up in the house where my father had lived all his life. The War poked out from old suitcases tucked under beds and rattled around in the back of sideboard drawers. It peeked out from behind peeling wallpaper and gathered dust in Grandma's bureau. It was under the piles of bikes and karts in the shed. You could see it, touch it, and even, in the case of an old rubber gas mask, wear it. Each artefact came with a story, a memory that could be unlocked with the magic phrase 'What's this for, Dad?'

The treasure trove for such items was the attic. Our family had lived in that house – or the one next door – since just after it was built around the turn of the century, and the attic became the repository of our past. Whenever my father had cause to go up there, I would stand at the bottom of the ladder, waiting to hand him whatever it was that he was depositing, or catch whichever thing he had gone up to retrieve. My reward was to be allowed to climb the ladder, whilst my father held it in place, and peer into the darkness at the top of the house. Clinging on to the top rung, my torch illuminating jumbled piles of ancient artefacts, I felt like Howard Carter peeping into the tomb of Tutankhamen. What treasures lay here beneath the dust of ages?

It was a strange place to come from, the Second World War. There was terrible suffering and privation there. Nobody knew what tomorrow might bring and yet, somehow, the simpler life seemed easier to endure than the mind-numbing drudgery of the years that followed. They had done incredible things in the War, stuff we could only see in movies. Their life experiences had been much more heightened than ours, and people talked longingly of the sense of community they had found. But no one wanted to go back and live there again.

Each Christmas, we would get together at my Nan's house and gather round the piano while she played songs from the

Old Country. Furniture would be pushed back, space made and dancing done. We would 'Roll Out The Barrel', we 'dillied and dallied, dallied and dillied', despite being explicitly told not to do so by 'My Old Man'. Everybody would join in with gusto, even we children, who had no idea what the archaic words meant that we were singing. Some sounded like the blood-curdling rituals of a Cockney death cult: 'Under the table you must go, ee-i, ee-i, ee-i-o, if I catch you bending, I'll saw your legs right off!' This was the place my people came from.

Gradually, contemporary music replaced the old songs and no one sang any more. The insularity of our parents' culture couldn't match the diversity we were enjoying in post-war England, and in the 1970s we tended to look beyond our own community for stimulation. Nobody talked much about the Old Country any more.

The years passed and the elders passed on, my father Dennis among them, aged fifty-two, in 1976. The artefacts started to go missing from their hiding places as the kitchen was refurbished, wardrobes thrown out, the outhouse demolished and the extension built. I wouldn't know where to look for that stuff now, except perhaps at a boot sale. Or in a museum.

Then my brother calls to tell me that Mum's roof is leaking, that we have to get someone to fix the tiles. 'How bad is it?' I ask. 'You can see the sky from the attic.' 'You've been in the attic? What's up there?' I ask. 'Old stuff,' he says. 'Lots of old stuff.' I smile. Of course. The one place that hasn't been refitted and cleared out. The repository of memories.

If the Old Country still existed anywhere, it would be up there.

The two-bedroom, bay-windowed terraced house in Barking which I grew up in was built around 1904 and members of my family have lived there ever since. My great-grandfather George Austin lived in the house next door – where my father was born – and my grandparents and parents shared our house until my grandmother died in 1963. As a result of this long period of single occupancy, the attic has never been emptied during a removal; no one has ever sorted through its contents deciding what's worth keeping and what should be thrown away. Things have just accumulated up there, each generation laying down another stratum, like geological sediment, one on top of the other.

The stuff nearest the trapdoor comes from the past few decades: old stereo equipment, vinyl singles, electric curling tongs. The further you venture in, however, the older the deposits become. Cardboard boxes full of dusty paper-chain Christmas decorations give way to leather suitcases lined with yellowing newsprint from the *Daily Sketch*. Lift a box and you instantly travel back in time. Beneath my brother's 1970s Scalextric set is a case containing our father's 1930s Meccano. It is like some great cultural palimpsest.

Some objects bring childhood memories instantly flowing back. Here is the Stella VHF radio set that was our main source of entertainment before the television arrived in 1964. The woven fabric facade recalls Sunday lunchtimes listening to *Round the Horne* and *The Jimmy Clitheroe Show*, the radio competing with the shrill hiss of the pressure cooker as the succulent smell of roast dinner filled the air. And though we never drifted far from the BBC, the radio console hinted at another world beyond the cosy confines of the Home Service: Hilversum, Rheims, Luxembourg, Eireann.

Old doors and bed headboards laid across the joists provide a means of moving amongst the dusty piles. Clearly not every item has been kept for sentimental value. Some have been put in this place because it was once felt that 'they might come in handy some day': an old roll of faded lino; a deckchair, its coloured fabric turned to black; what appears to be the windowframe from our outside toilet that we knocked down in the early 1970s.

But careful inspection reveals items of genuine interest. There are objects from my father's 1930s childhood: several wooden fishing reels, a copy of *Allcock's Anglers' Guide* dated 1935, two lengths of line and a Metropolitan Policeman's whistle. A tin marked 'Pascalls Saturday Assortment – a sporting variety of wrapped sweets' holds a number of fishing weights. An ancient leather football lies deflated next to what look like a couple of rounders bats and a dusty copy of the programme for the historical pageant which marked Barking's charter celebrations in 1931.

Then, an item from the Old Country: in a disused water tank atop a pile of old magazines sits a gas mask, still in its canvas carry bag. And here, in a small leather suitcase, lies my father's battledress uniform. The round-bottomed, waist-length baggy blouson and straight-cut trousers look new, the worsted serge fabric proving its durability after sixty years confined in the attic. The insignia on the tunic retain their colours too: the red/yellow shoulder strip of the Royal Armoured Corps, the white Mk1 tank symbol of the Royal Tank Regiment, the herringbone Lance Corporal stripes and the India star. The label inside states that this is the 1940 pattern battledress, 1943 issue.

Dad joined the Army in late 1942, having left school aged fifteen three years earlier. Five days before he left home for the very first time, he gathered together all his important documents in an envelope on which he wrote 'Odds and Ends 1/11/42'. The contents hold clues as to what he had been doing since war broke out.

A purple ticket offering a free meal at the AFS and ARP canteen implies that he may have been active in the civil-defence services during the Blitz. Each local authority had been charged with setting up an Auxiliary Fire Service and an Air Raid Precautions scheme. A letter from the town hall inform-ing him that his time in the Control Room Messenger Service is coming to an end confirms that he did serve with the ARP.

Control-room messengers were youths aged fifteen to eighteen, often members of the Boy Scouts or Boys' Brigade, who volunteered for the task of keeping lines of communication open after air raids. Even a few bombs dropped in a minor raid would have the effect of disrupting services; telephone lines were particularly vulnerable, cut by flying debris or snapped when their poles were blown down. Equipped with a bicycle, the control-room messenger could reach heavily hit areas that might be inaccessible to vehicles, weaving his way through the rubble-strewn streets, able to dismount and carry his bike over greater obstacles.

Amongst the documents is a small, stiffened card printed with the names of thirty-three different locations in the borough, each with its own designated number. These are the ARP posts, the front line in the battle against the bombers. From here an ARP warden, one sixth of whom were women, would be first out into the streets after the raid was over, assessing the damage and reporting as quickly as possible to the control room, from where support services would be despatched.

Dad's job was to help get that message through. Number one on the list of ARP posts is Northbury Junior School, where I

was taught country dancing. Once, on our way into a Parents'
Evening, he showed me where, as a teenage messenger, he had
been blown through the open swing doors of the main entrance
by the blast of a bomb that had landed on the nearby railway.

A receipt for the sum of half a crown records that my father
joined the 1st Cadet Battalion of the Kings Royal Rifle Corps
on 1 October 1941. A xeroxed sheet lays out the special orders
for the cadets, who were affiliated to the 2nd County of
London battalion of the Home Guard. A hand-drawn diagram
on a scrap of paper details the various facets of the barrel
group and body group of a .303 Lewis machine gun, a relic of
the First World War with which some Home Guard battalions
were armed. The weight, rate of fire, muzzle velocity and range
are all noted.

A copy of the National Service Act's Explanatory Note has
the date of my father's registration for conscription written in
his own hand: 15 August 1942, exactly six months after his
eighteenth birthday. A form calls him to his medical on 15
September. The Ministry of Labour offers him the chance to
apply for work as a miner instead of joining the services: the
reply form is still attached. The document that bears the latest
date is the envelope itself – 1 November 1942; five days later
he enlisted.

My grandfather, William Bragg, had responded to the outbreak of war by dusting off his old six by four-inch notebook
diary that he had begun as a teenager in 1911. He was little
more than halfway through its pages when his entries abruptly
ended on 25 February 1918, with a note that the Bolshevik
government had accepted peace terms with the Germans.
Twenty-one years later, he simply turned over the page and
began again:

Sept 3rd 1939 Sunday – England declare War on Germany.

This time, however, there was no celebratory ride through the streets of London to cheer the coming of war with the crowds outside Buckingham Palace. Any illusions about what the conflict might bring were shattered almost immediately:

At 11.15 am air raid siren blows for first raid.

The bombers never came that Sunday morning, nor the next day when my grandfather records that the sirens sounded at two forty-five a.m., nor the day after, when the warning lasted from six forty-five to nine a.m. However, the people of Barking were right to be anxious. The Luftwaffe had identified 'Zielgebiete' – target areas – for attack in the London area. One of these was centred on the Beckton gasworks and the Northern Outfall Sewerage plant at Barking Creek.[1]

Initially, though, the war seems far away in Grandfather's diary. Warsaw surrenders. Scapa Flow is bombed. The 'RFA', as he refers to the Royal Air Force, flies over Berlin. The Graf Spee is scuttled off the River Plate. He even finds time to think of other things beyond the conflict, recording the deaths of 4,500 people in a Turkish earthquake in December 1939.

As 1940 begins, things start to get closer to home. On Monday 8 January, rationing begins:

Sugar 12oz; bacon and ham 4oz; butter 4oz.

A month later, an entry records the first German bomber to be shot down over England. Then on 10 May, the tone suddenly changes as the war lurches west:

Germany invades Holland, Belgium and Luxemburg.

If the British had held any hopes of avoiding the onslaught of Hitler's blitzkrieg, they finally dissolved that Friday afternoon. Neville Chamberlain's government had failed to keep the Nazis out of Czechoslovakia, Poland and Norway. Could they be trusted to keep them out of Britain? The same entry provides an answer to that question:

Mr Chamberlain resigns PM succeeded by Winston Churchill.

A national government was formed, determined to fight, but still the news was bad. The British Expeditionary Force, advancing into Belgium to meet the invading Germans, found themselves cut off from the south and were forced to retreat towards the coast. On 29 May, it was announced that the BEF was evacuating Dunkirk and an appeal was made for any vessel capable of crossing the Channel to come to their assistance.

The desperation of such a request would have been clear to anyone who heard it. Small boats capable of ferrying men would not be able to bring back tanks or field guns. This was not a strategic withdrawal. The Army had been routed. The nation held its breath. After six days, Grandfather was able to record:

BEF evacuated from Dunkirk 350,000. Loss about 30,000.

There follows a lull in the diary entries, implying that Grandfather was now too busy preparing for the expected onslaught to write. He returns to his diary to record the grave news of the fall of France on 16 June. Now all of Britain's

European allies had been defeated. Two days later, Churchill told the House of Commons that the battle for Britain was about to begin: 'Let us now brace ourselves to our duties, and so bear ourselves that, if the British Empire and its Commonwealth last for a thousand years, men will still say "This was their finest hour".'

German air-force bases were now just across the Channel in northern France, within striking distance of London. Throughout July 1940, they were probing Britain's defences.

In Barking Park, a battery of eight 4.5-inch heavy anti-aircraft guns were sited, mounted in thick concrete emplacements, aimed at German bombers following the route of the Thames into London. During the enforced black-outs of the Blitz, the flash as the guns were fired would illuminate the rooms of the houses along Park Avenue like lightning striking overhead.

On 8 August, the Luftwaffe began their attack in earnest. The next few pages of my grandfather's diary read like a scorecard for the Battle of Britain.

Thurs 8 Aug 60 German planes down in a day. 16 British lost.

Sun 11 Aug 60 German planes down and 23 English. Total number of planes down since June 18 is 387.

Tues 13 Aug 78 German planes down. 191 in three days.

These numbers reflect the fact that the figures for German losses were hugely inflated by the press for morale-boosting purposes. The actual numbers shot down for the days concerned were much lower.

Similar entries appeared throughout August. Sometimes the fighting over Barking was so intense that Grandfather and Dad would watch the dogfights from our back garden, cheering the RAF on. Then suddenly, on 7 September, the Luftwaffe change tactics. The diary entry begins 'London's worst air raid'. The factory where William Bragg works is gutted and he records that bombs destroyed a small house in Tanner Street just a few blocks away from the family home. The Blitz has begun.

The focus of the diary now switches from the air battle to the number of raids and the damage done. Such was the intensity that a night without an attack became noteworthy:

Sunday 5th Oct No night raid, full nights sleep bed at 11.30. Alert sounded at 5.30 in the morning.

The following Thursday, Grandfather notes that St Paul's Cathedral has been hit and the high altar damaged. Then, on 15 October, the war comes to Park Avenue.

Mr Vernon's three houses bombed. Lodger killed in Mr Carlton's house.

The war-time bomb-damage records show how close the house came to being hit. Whilst ours was slightly damaged, the next three houses along the street were category C – seriously damaged. The next three houses along from them were all category A: the bomb had totally demolished them. All six properties were knocked down and rebuilt after the war.

My father was fond of pointing out to me and my brother the differences in style of those six houses, compared to the rest of the street, because it gave him the chance to tell us once again the grisly tale of the lodger in Mr Carlton's house.

Apparently, the lodger lived in the attic and wasn't fond of sleeping in the damp, cold air-raid shelter. Nodding towards the terraced row opposite our own, Dad would solemnly inform us that, after the raid, his remains were found in the attic of the house across the road.

My grandfather, grandmother and father were in the air-raid shelter at the bottom of our garden when the row of houses was hit, and the shelter did its job, protecting them from the blast and the debris. However, while they sought cover from high-explosive bombs, their empty house was in danger of being destroyed, perhaps without them realizing, by a much smaller device.

The 'fire bomb' – just eighteen inches long and a couple of pounds in weight – was filled with highly combustible chemicals such as thermite or magnesium, designed to ignite on impact and start a fire. A single fire bomb which crashed through roofing tiles and lodged in the attic was capable of burning a house to the ground.

The average cluster contained seventy-two bombs and by dropping them at night, when commercial properties were empty and most people were taking shelter, the Luftwaffe created a huge workload for the already stretched fire service. The bombs fell everywhere, raining into the streets, hitting the ground with a metallic clang followed by a fizzing noise as the chemicals burned, giving off a cold white light.

On 29 December 1940, tens of thousands of incendiaries were dropped on the City of London, causing over 1,400 fires, creating what came to be known as the Second Great Fire of London. Shocked at the extent of the damage, Grandfather makes his longest diary entry of the war:

London's worst night raid. Guildhall burnt down, MacQueen's, Den's firm gutted; fires everywhere. Thousands of incendiary bombs dropped. An air battle over London by RAF. Four famous churches [hit]: St Stephen's Coleman St, St Vedast's Foster Lane, St Mary's Aldermanbury, St Brides Fleet St and St Lawrence Guildhall Church, St Thomas Hospital, Trinity House on Tower Hill, PLA offices and All Hallows Church, home of Toc H, Whitechapel Church.

In all, nineteen churches, sixteen of them built by Christopher Wren in the wake of the original Great Fire of London, were destroyed that night. At one point, St Paul's itself was in danger of being lost, surrounded by a sea of flame. However, most of the damage was done to offices and warehouses, which, it being a Sunday, were empty. Despite the devastation in the City, only 163 people were killed.

The menace of the fire bomb had to be addressed. Two days later, Herbert Morrison, the Minister for Home Security, announced the formation of the Fire Guard, calling for volunteer street parties to be formed to combat individual fire-bomb incidents, while leaving the emergency services free to tackle more serious fires. Posters appeared depicting a swastika emblazoned 'Fire Bomb Fritz'. The caption declared, 'Britain shall not burn!'

Given the opportunity to come out from the shelter at the bottom of the garden and actively defend our street from the forces of fascism as a citizen volunteer, my grandfather answered the call.

Fire guards were organized into parties of three and reported to their posts at the sounding of the air-raid alarm. Each team was equipped with a stirrup-pump and bucket, some sand mats with which to damp down the incendiaries, and, by way of a uniform, a steel helmet and an arm band to identify the wearer as a fire guard. Each member of the team had a specific job – one to operate the pump, one to use the hose and one to replenish the water. A note alerting my grandfather to attend fire-guard training identifies him as the hose man.

The stirrup-pump, a vertical hand pump steadied by a foot-plate – hence the name – could, when placed in a bucket of water, produce either a thirty-foot jet of water or, by adjusting the nozzle, a fifteen-foot spray. The latter was recommended for dealing with fire bombs. The spray did not extinguish the device, but the hydrogen and oxygen in the water caused the chemical to consume itself more intensely, fizzing out in the space of a minute rather than the ten to fifteen minutes that the bomb was designed to burn for. The nozzle could then be adjusted to produce a jet of water to deal with any fires the bomb may have started.

My grandfather notes in his diary that he undertook his first fire-watch duty on the night of 23 January 1941. On Wednesday 19 March, he records that he and my father had their most hair-raising night of the Blitz.

Worst experience in air raid with fire bombs with Den.

Father and son, both now volunteers for the Civil Defence, were caught in the first major raid of the Luftwaffe's Spring Offensive. The logbook for ARP post number eight, which was situated in the boathouse in Barking Park, just fifty yards from the family home, offers some insight into the danger they encountered.

The alert sounded at eight fourteen p.m. and fifteen minutes later fire bombs began falling. At nine p.m., the logbook states that explosive incendiaries were dropped in Barking Park and Longbridge Road. These were particularly nasty devices aimed at killing those who were sent to deal with them. They would burn normally for a short while, long enough to be detected, then suddenly explode, showering anyone trying to extinguish them with molten magnesium. I have an image of my grandfather and father desperately trying to deal with these devices while the bombers droned overhead and the anti-aircraft guns in the park roared back their defiance, their bright firing flashes illuminating the blackout like a ferocious lightning storm.

Three hundred bombers attacked London that night, aiming for the London Docks. 1,881 fires were started and the casualty rate was the highest of the Blitz so far, with 631 people losing their lives in the East End. Grandfather had been right to record it as his worst experience.[2]

Eventually, the threat of incendiary bombs became too great for the volunteer fire guards to cope with, and in August 1941 compulsory enrolment was introduced. A newspaper cutting kept by my grandfather, dated 11 August, assures volunteers like himself that they will not have their arrangements changed under the new system. Anxious not to undermine the morale and camaraderie of the service, the government has asked local authorities not to break up existing teams.

My grandfather kept a number of newspaper cuttings from the War, from battle reports and maps of the fighting to practical stuff like how to fit beds into an Anderson shelter and the maximum retail price of fish. These ended up in the Victorian portable desk that became a family heirloom, along with a number of other documents that my grandfather felt were worth preserving.

The envelope containing my father's pre-enlistment papers is there, along with a copy of the Home Guard Training Manual 'Joining Up? A Handy Guide for Every Recruit' and a book called *Unarmed Combat*, which proclaims on the cover 'Your Answer to Invasion – Ju-jitsu' and contains some 'capital moves' and 'devastating blows' to use against the Nazi invaders.

Clearly, there was no way that my grandfather, in his late forties when war broke out, was going to use ju-jitsu against German paratroopers. These books belonged to my father and all date from before his enlistment. The only document amongst the important papers of the war years that I can be sure was purchased by my grandfather and placed there by him is a slim sixty-one-page booklet published in December 1942, the month after my father joined up. 'The Beveridge Report in Brief' was published by HM Stationery Office and cost 3d. and its presence here was significant. Grandfather's diary ended in 1945 and my father's training manuals were of interest only as historical artefacts. The Beveridge Report, however, would go on to have a direct effect on my life.

10

The Great Charter

In December 2005, traditionalist British newspapers reacted with outrage to the news that there were plans to re-make the 1954 movie *The Dam Busters*. In a *Daily Telegraph* column headlined 'TORIES NEED TO WOO BIGGIN HILL, NOT NOTTING HILL', Simon Heffer attacked the new Tory modernizers before moving on to mock the decision of former German Chancellor Gerhard Schroeder – or 'the recently deposed Reichskanzler of Germany', as Heffer referred to him – to learn English at a college in Wales.

> I just hope that when he finally returns to the Reich no one waves him goodbye with the traditional 'For you, Herr Schröder, the eisteddfod is over.'

You'd think that someone with such a deep sensitivity for European history would welcome a new film that portrayed one of the most daring exploits of the War, but no: 'DAM BUSTERS RE-MAKE DESERVES TO BOMB' was his next strapline.[1]

A few days later, the *Daily Mail* joined the spat with a

full-page article by historian Andrew Roberts. *The Dam Busters*, he declared, could not be re-made because

> the original movie was by far the finest war movie of all time, but also because the Britain that created it has long been replaced by a different kind of country entirely.[2]

The Dam Busters is a dramatization of Operation Chastise, an attempt by the RAF to disrupt Nazi war production by breaching three dams in the heavily industrialized Ruhr region of Germany. The film follows the development of the 'bouncing bomb', designed to skim across the water and detonate next to the dam itself. To achieve this, the bomb had to be released just sixty feet above the water surface at a precise speed of 250mph. Of the nineteen aircraft from 617 Squadron, only eleven returned from the May 1943 raid, and although two of the dams were successfully breached, causing widespread flooding and loss of life, the disruption to war production was minimal.

The film glosses over the outcome of the raid, concentrating instead on the ingenuity of Barnes Wallis, who developed the bomb, and the incredible skill and bravery of the Lancaster bomber crews who carried out the attack, led by Group Captain Guy Gibson. The film ends with Wallis stating that had he known that fifty-six men would not come back from the raid, he would not have developed the bomb. Gibson disagrees, claiming that had those men been aware that they would not be coming back they would still have undertaken the mission.

Roberts considers this scene to be central to understanding not just the War, but the nature of Britishness itself:

Gibson was speaking the truth: those involved in the Dam Buster raids were putting their lives before their country – and for patriotic reasons and comradeship rather than military discipline, which makes the film a central document in understanding what it once meant to be British.

While I agree that *The Dam Busters* is undoubtedly a classic British yarn, it is possible to find films that offer a better insight into what it meant to be British during the Second World War. The day after Roberts's piece appeared, my eye was caught by a full-page advert in a monthly music and film magazine, promoting the Best DVDs of 2005. The first DVD of the band Franz Ferdinand was featured, as were The Prodigy and the wonderful Death Cab for Cutie. '*Interrogation*: a film by Rysard Bugajski' was there, along with a documentary on the Moog synthesizer. However, at the very centre of the array, surrounded by so many hip and groovy products, was 'The Humphrey Jennings Collection'. Anyone reading the name might assume that they were a band of earnest young men with cardigans and short back and sides, making angular music for the twenty-first century. However, the black-and-white cover shot, of a weary London Blitz fireman, would suggest otherwise.

Described by Lindsay Anderson as 'the only real poet that British cinema has produced', Humphrey Jennings began making documentaries with the pioneering GPO Film Unit in the 1930s. In 1937, he was a co-founder of the Mass-Observation movement, who conducted interviews, sent out questionnaires and asked volunteers to keep diaries with a view to understanding more about the everyday experiences and views of the British people.

At the outbreak of war, he and his colleagues were seconded to the Ministry for Information and tasked with producing morale-boosting films. Jennings's efforts were highly impressionistic, stretching the rules of documentary film-making. The DVD contains his three classics: *Listen to Britain*, *Fires Were Started* and *Diary for Timothy*.

Listen to Britain, made in 1941, contains no dialogue at all, consisting of a montage of the sights and sounds of Britain during wartime. It opens with a shot of a field of corn gently moving in the breeze, the silence of which is gradually drowned out by two approaching Spitfires. For the next nineteen minutes, the film moves seamlessly from one image to another, juxtaposing domestic, military and social scenes, all, in the manner of Orwell's litany in *The Lion and the Unicorn*, overwhelmingly ordinary: solid breakfasts and gloomy Sundays, smoky towns and winding roads, green fields and red pillar boxes.

The film captures the spirit of the time perfectly, yet the Ministry of Information, fearing that the lack of dialogue might be too avant-garde for the British public, commissioned a superfluous introduction which sought to explain what was about to be shown.

Dating from 1943, *Fires Were Started* uses a genuine London Fire Service crew to portray twenty-four hours in the lives of Blitz firemen. Jennings never used professional actors, preferring to give the people a starring role in their own stories. For the first time in British cinema, the working class were portrayed with dignity, instead of the comedic stereotypes of the inter-war years. The sheer ordinariness of the participants brings *The Lion and the Unicorn* to mind again, with Orwell's 'crowds with their mild knobby faces, their bad teeth and gentle manners'.

Jennings's last wartime documentary, *A Diary for Timothy*,

was to be his masterpiece, combining all the best aspects of his earlier work. Taking the form of a letter to a child born on the fifth anniversary of the start of the war, 3 September 1944, the film seeks to explain the events of the first six months of his life. Thirty-nine minutes in length, its narrative written by E. M. Forster and spoken by Michael Redgrave, it was released shortly after the war ended.

The film opens with Timothy's birth and the tone is set from the start; the narrator tells him how lucky he is to be born in Oxford. 'If you'd been born in wartime Holland or Poland or a Liverpool or Glasgow slum, this would be a very different picture. All the same, you're in danger, Tim, for around you is being fought the worst war ever known.'

Against images of soldiers marching, bombed streets and a baby being weighed, the narrator begins to explain how this dire situation came about. As he says 'You see, Tim, this was total war,' the camera cuts not to fleets of aircraft or ships, but to big chunks of coal, moving across the screen on a conveyer belt, like tanks rushing into battle.

The story highlights the experiences of four main characters: a Welsh miner, a farmer, a train-driver and, lastly, an injured fighter pilot recuperating after crashing his plane in combat. All are busy doing their bit, but as autumn turns to winter, the news from the front is all bad.

The Battle of Arnhem raises the hope of the war being over by Christmas, only to end in defeat and disappointment. V2 terror weapons continue to cause heavy casualties. Then, in December, just as the Allied armies in the west are about to enter Germany, news comes through of Hitler's counter-attack through the Ardennes Forest, in what became known as the Battle of the Bulge.

A palpable gloom descends as a war-weary population realize that the fighting will drag on into 1945. The narrator touches on the sense that, although the war is clearly coming to an end, there may yet be more suffering to endure, observing that 'the bad is so mixed with the good, you never know what's coming'.

The events of 1944 draw to a close with Timothy's first Christmas: 'The day all children want to be happy on' says the narrator. 'But it's a day we all ought to be at home. And so many of us aren't. And never will be.' The portrayal of Christmas Day itself is masterfully handled. As 'O Come, All Ye Faithful' is sung in the distance, the action moves from the farmer's house to the Welsh mining village to the scullery of the London train-driver's home, as each raises a glass in a simple toast to 'absent friends'.

It's hard not to be moved by the thought of what must have passed through the minds of the audience when the film was first shown in 1946. It is one of the most touching moments in British cinema, made all the more poignant by the fact that these are not actors on a movie set but real people in their own homes.

Then, as the year turns, things begin to look up at last. Word comes that the Red Army have broken through German lines in southern Poland. The BBC plays the Soviet national anthem. The V2 attacks cease. A sense of momentum builds over scenes of the RAF pilot beginning to recuperate. The Russians move into Germany. A group of English schoolchildren give a concert beneath a huge hammer and sickle banner in front of the slogan 'Greetings to the Red Army and the glorious fighting forces of the United Nations'.

Then a radio announces that British and American forces

have crossed the Rhine. Victory is at hand. Over a closing shot of baby Timothy, the narrator lays down a challenge to him and the rest of the post-war generation:

> 'Up to now, we've done all the talking, but before long, you'll sit up and take notice. What are you going to say about it? And what are you going to do? You heard what the miner was saying – unemployment after the war and then another war and then more unemployment. Will it be like that again? Are you going to have greed for money or power ousting decency from the world as they have in the past? Or are you going to make the world a different place, you and the other babies?'

Jennings went on to make other films, but none had the power of his wartime documentaries. The conflict had transfigured the British people and Jennings captured that transfiguration.

This is why I have to disagree with Andrew Roberts when he says that *The Dam Busters* could never be re-made because it captures a Britain we'll never see again. Of course you could make *The Dam Busters* again. A bit of CGI might even make it more exciting. With luck and attention to detail, it may even retain the spirit of the original.

A re-make of *A Diary for Timothy*, however, would be impossible, and not just because Britain doesn't look like that any more. No amount of computer wizardry could summon up the hopes and fears expressed in Jennings's film. Here is the Britain that we'll never see again, the true measure of what we have lost. Whatever myths were later dreamed up at Pinewood and Shepperton and Ealing, Jennings's *Diary* serves to remind us that the true spirit of the Blitz, of Dunkirk, of the fire-watchers and the real dam busters, was one of collectivism.

This spirit had not been created by design; it was a product of the war. Unlike the unemployment of the thirties, the bombs dropped on Britain fell upon rich and poor alike. Out in the countryside, those who opened their spacious homes to evacuees from the cities were appalled to see at first hand the poverty endured by the working class. Social distinctions began to break down as everybody was forced to 'muck in'. For the first time, the British people realized what could be achieved if they worked together for the common good.

Orwell had recognized in *The Lion and the Unicorn* that if Britain hoped to win the War, radical changes would be needed. This was not a struggle between rival imperial powers, as in 1914–18. The forces of fascism could only be met and defeated by the forces of egalitarianism.

> It is only by revolution that the native genius of the English can be set free. Revolution does not mean red flags and street fighting, it means a fundamental shift of power.

The first hint of how this shift might be achieved came in July 1941, when Churchill met with American President Franklin Roosevelt aboard a warship off the coast of Canada. At the end of the conference, the two leaders produced a joint statement which set out 'certain common principles in the national policies of their respective countries on which they base their hopes for a better future for the world'.

Since the beginning of the War, there had been a clamour in Britain for the government to present a clear vision of what fruits victory would bring. Everybody knew what they were fighting against; now they wanted to know what they were fighting for. Churchill, however, looked no further than the winning of the War, leading some to fear that, just as after the Great War, when many had longed to return to things as they were before 1914, he imagined the same would be true at the end of this conflict.

After the awful years of the Depression, however, few wanted to go back to the pre-war status quo. What was needed was a vision of a new and better world to counter Hitler's chilling promise of a new order. Churchill resisted any such forward thinking, telling the War Cabinet in January 1941 that 'precise aims would be compromising, whereas vague principles would disappoint'.[3]

Six months later, at his meeting with Roosevelt, he was unable to avoid a specific statement of war aims if he hoped to convince America to join forces. The American president needed something concrete to prove to his opponents in Washington that America was not getting involved in another imperial conflict. The Atlantic Charter, as the declaration became known, set out for the first time a vision of how the world would be when fascism was defeated. Among the principles enshrined in the statement were self-determination, free trade, territorial integrity, freedom of movement, improved labour standards, economic advancement, social security for all and freedom from fear and want.

The realities of war had forced the British government to disregard the vested interests which had held sway during peacetime and implement socialistic solutions to the problems of supply and demand. The Atlantic Charter gave the green light to those who wished to continue this kind of socialism – a central organization of the nation's resources – beyond the end of the War.

Labour ministers in the coalition government responded to

the promise of the Charter by asking how the many piecemeal measures of delivering welfare to the unemployed could be drawn together into a single system to provide universal provision. Since the early years of the twentieth century, British politicians had struggled to provide some welfare for citizens. The 1906 Liberal government introduced old-age pensions, health insurance and unemployment exchanges, but these measures were limited, relied on means testing and felt, to many, little different from the poor relief of the nineteenth century.

Arthur Greenwood, the minister in charge of reconstruction, appointed William Beveridge, a former director of the London School of Economics, to chair a committee of civil servants to look at how the unemployed could best be provided with support while they sought work. Beveridge, who had long been campaigning for welfare reform, took the bit between his teeth with such enthusiasm that when the report was published in December 1942, it contained a disclaimer from the government, stating that the views expressed were Beveridge's alone.

Perhaps it was the language of the preamble, with its echoes of *The Lion and the Unicorn*, that put them off.

Any proposals for the future, while they should use to the full the experience gathered in the past, should not be restricted by consideration of sectional interests established in the obtaining of that experience. Now, when the war is abolishing landmarks of every kind, is the opportunity for using experience in a clear field. A revolutionary moment in the world's history is a time for revolutions, not for patching.

The organisation of social insurance should be treated as one part only of a comprehensive policy of social progress. Social insurance fully developed may provide income security; it is an

attack on Want. But Want is only one of five giants on the road
of reconstruction and in some ways the easiest to attack. The
others are Disease, Ignorance, Squalor and Idleness.[4]

If the politicians were hoping to distance themselves from
such ideas, they were wrong-footed when the report became an
immediate success, selling 635,000 copies. Its publication came
at a time when, although defeat was unlikely, victory seemed
far away, and its proposals, which represented a radical break
with the past, were received by the British people as the first
glimmer of light at the end of the tunnel.

By stating that his report was aimed at conquering only one
of the five giants, Want, Beveridge had put the four other giants
on the agenda. The positive response to his report meant that
issues such as health and education could now be addressed,
safe in the knowledge that the public supported reform.

At the outbreak of war, the threat of aerial bombardment
had caused the government to open the hospitals to all, regardless of their ability to pay. Initially, the Emergency Hospital
Service was open only to civilian and military casualties, but as
the war dragged on, the list of those eligible grew considerably.

However, bringing both private and public hospitals into the
scheme highlighted the inequalities in health provision across
both geographical and social divides. In early 1944, the
government produced a white paper outlining a National
Health Service that would be free to all at point of need – paid
for not by contribution but directly from taxation. The giant of
Disease was to be confronted.

Next on the agenda came the giant of Ignorance. Evacuation
had revealed flaws in education that could only be resolved by
a complete overhaul of the system. The 1944 Education Act

provided free education for all children up to school-leaving age, which was set at fifteen. The Act made further education an option for the first time for working-class teenagers. Clause 41 placed a statutory obligation on every local authority to provide facilities for full- and part-time education for persons over compulsory school age. John Lennon, born in 1940, was one of the first to benefit from this provision. Having failed at grammar school, Lennon was accepted into the Liverpool College of Art in September 1957. There he was able to follow his growing interest in music and girls.

The art-school movement had flourished in the Victorian period, offering a haven for those whose talents were more artistic than academic. The colleges had tended to attract the kind of upper-middle-class eccentric youths that had flourished in England during the years before the Second World War. The provisions of the 1944 Education Act opened the doors for talented young people from the lower classes. Keith Richards attended Sidcup Art College, where an early version of the Rolling Stones played a concert. Pete Townsend of The Who, Ian McLagan of the Small Faces, Ray Davies of the Kinks, Eric Clapton and Syd Barrett all attended colleges of art in London.

The creative atmosphere of the art schools played an important part in the emergence of the sixties counter-culture in England. Not only the musicians, but the film-makers, writers, painters and graphic designers who made London swing during that decade were products of the 1944 Education Act, and clause 41 in particular.

Should anyone doubt that his vision was tied to the conduct and outcome of the War, Beveridge explicitly connected his report to the war aims set out by Churchill and Roosevelt in the Atlantic Charter:

[These proposals] are concerned not with increasing the wealth of the British people, but with distributing whatever wealth available to them in total, as to deal first with first things, with essential physical needs. They are the sign of the belief that the object of government in peace and in war is not the glory of rulers or races, but the happiness of the common man. That is a belief which, through all differences in forms of government, unites not only the democracies whose leaders first put their hands to the Atlantic Charter, but those democracies and all their Allies. It unites the United Nations and divides them from their enemies.

Freedom from Want cannot be forced on a democracy or given to a democracy. It must be won by them. Winning it needs courage and faith and sense of national unity: courage to face facts and difficulties and overcome them; faith in our future and the ideals of fair-play and freedom for which, century after century, our forefathers were prepared to die; a sense of national unity overriding the interests of any class or section.[5]

These closing words place the Beveridge Report in the tradition of the struggle for rights that has gone on in England since Magna Carta. If the Great Charter of English Liberties, as the revolutionaries of the seventeenth century called it, can be said to be the first manifestation of the sense of fair play that we pride ourselves as being central to our notion of what it means to be English, then the Beveridge Report was that principle made flesh.

However, Beveridge is different from Magna Carta in one important respect: Britain is unique among modern nations in that it has no historical document that begins 'We, the People', no single declaration of universal rights. The Beveridge Report, with its vision of universal provision, fills that role, the first agreement in our history to be struck between the rulers and the people.

And like the Beveridge Report, Magna Carta was not designed to be a constitutional document. As signed by King John at Runnymede in 1215, it was a peace treaty between the king and his rebellious barons. The original text ranged widely across their grievances, specifying the exclusion from office of certain allies of the king, securing the return of hostages to the Welsh and Scots courts, and even attempting to set rudimentary trading standards:

> Let there be one measure for wine throughout the kingdom and one measure for ale, and one measure for corn, namely 'the London quarter', and one width for cloths whether dyed, russet or halberget, namely two ells within the selvedges. Let it be the same with weights as with measures.[6]

Royal finances were also high on the agenda. King John's insistence on 'scutage', or shield-money, from his nobles instead of service at arms amounted to a tax on the barons, one which John levied eleven times in sixteen years to finance his wars in France. Those unable to pay up risked having their lands confiscated or even imprisonment. It was fear of this arbitrary nature of the king's power that led the barons to rebel, calling for a promise from him in writing to recognize their rights.

John was convinced that ancient custom was on his side; the barons' attempts to curtail his royal prerogative were unprecedented in medieval Europe. Yet the rebels were determined to secure a charter of their liberties, even if it meant a radical break with the past. In the short term, they were unsuccessful. John had no intention of adhering to Magna Carta, viewing it simply as a way of buying time. His insincerity led to bitter civil war, which continued after his death in October 1216.

His heir, Henry III, was a boy of eight when he became king, and during the resultant regency, it made sense to govern by council. In such an atmosphere, the reintroduction of Magna Carta by the king's advisers acted both as a gesture of conciliation to the rebel barons and a stable framework for the regency.

In 1225, towards the end of Henry's minority, a revised text was produced – less a peace treaty, more a charter of rights, which in time would come to be viewed as the definitive version. The central principles of Magna Carta – of government by consent and equality under the law – have shaped the character of the English people ever since, as they have sought to define themselves in opposition to arbitrary power.

Other important rights such as habeas corpus, protection from indefinite detention without a legal hearing, only became linked with Magna Carta during the seventeenth century. In 1626, Charles I imposed a forced loan, which his royal prerogative powers allowed him to levy without the consent of Parliament, on his wealthy subjects. When five knights of the realm were imprisoned without charge for refusing to pay up, their counsel, John Selden, claimed this was an exercise of arbitrary power, evoking the right not to be imprisoned without due legal process enshrined in Magna Carta.

The courts, however, ruled in the king's favour, suggesting that the knights' only recourse was to petition the king. Members of the House of Commons now took up the knights' cause, presenting the Petition of Right in 1628, which sought to curtail the royal prerogative powers by extending the guarantee of due process to all:

> And whereas also by the statute called 'The Great Charter of the Liberties of England,' it is declared and enacted, that no freeman may be taken or imprisoned or be dissiezed of his freehold or liberties, or his free customs, or be outlawed or exiled, or in any manner destroyed, but by the lawful judgment of his peers, or by the law of the land.
>
> And in the eight-and-twentieth year of the reign of King Edward III, it was declared and enacted by authority of parliament, that no man, of what estate or condition that he be, should be put out of his land or tenements, nor taken, nor imprisoned, nor disinherited nor put to death without being brought to answer by due process of law.[7]

The king's reception of the petition was lukewarm. He attempted to undermine its legitimacy by refusing to give it his assent. Eventually, he was forced to relent. The Commons had used Magna Carta to draw a line in the sand with regard to the absolute power of kings.

Angered by the Commons' assertion of its rights, Charles dissolved Parliament, instigating a long period of personal rule during which he resorted to obscure and long-forgotten laws to raise taxes without consent. When his right to do so was questioned, the justices of the Kings Bench belittled the authority of Parliament, dismissing it as nothing more than a forum by which peers and Commons made their grievances known to the king and humbly asked for redress. One judge observed, 'I never read nor heard that Lex was Rex [law was king] but it is common and most true that Rex is Lex [the king is the law].'⁸

Charles was able to fund his expenses during peacetime through these legally dubious taxes, but could not afford to go to war. When the Scottish Presbyterians rebelled against his attempt to impose the Anglican prayer book on them, their defeat of Charles in the Bishops' War meant that he was forced to recall Parliament. An important point had been proved: for practical reasons, the king could not rule without the consent of his people.

The House of Commons moved swiftly to ensure that the personal rule of the monarch could no longer be imposed upon the nation. It was these reforms that led ultimately to a civil war that was fought on the issue of rule by consent.

Charles lost the Civil War, surrendering to parliamentary forces in May 1646. He proved impossible to negotiate with and in January 1649 Parliament decided to put Magna Carta to its ultimate test. Based on the principle that no man is above the law, they put the king on trial for treason.

This was the most radical break with the past in English history. Previously, treason had been a crime committed by rebels against the monarch. Parliament now defined it as a crime by the king against his own people. In the past, monarchs had been removed barbarously, either in battle or by cold-blooded murder. Now, for the first time, a king would be held to account by the people, his fate decided not by sword or by intrigue, but by English law.

The king was found guilty of causing the deaths of an estimated one in ten Englishmen. The court did not go so far as to strip him of his title, which would have meant a commoner's death, the lingering butchery that was suffered by those who were hung, drawn and quartered. Instead, he was allowed to die in a manner felt befitting for royalty – a swift, surgical beheading.[9]

On that cold January morning in 1649, the English sent a signal to the world that they believed, above all, in government by consent. The king was executed, the deed not hidden behind the walls of the Tower, but carried out before a crowd in Whitehall. In this very public display, the promise of Magna Carta was upheld for all to see.

It is from this dramatic act that our modern liberties derive. Never mind that the Commonwealth of England, a republic in all but name, failed to outlive Oliver Cromwell. The terms under which Charles II was restored to the throne in 1660 were the same as those offered to his father. The constitutional reforms of the Commonwealth were not repealed. When the Stuart Restoration failed in 1688, the precedent of 1649 convinced Parliament to avoid a return to tyranny by stage managing the 'Glorious Revolution', a consolidation of parliamentary power neither glorious nor revolutionary in its nature.

In effect, Parliament deposed the Catholic king, James II, engineering his replacement by his Protestant daughter Mary and her husband William of Orange. Before they were allowed to become king and queen, Parliament presented them with a deal-breaking agreement which sought to limit still further the powers of the Crown. The Bill of Rights, like Magna Carta and the Petition of Right before it, was a deal struck between the monarchy and the ruling class.

The effect of these reforms on the vast majority of the English people was slight. Magna Carta had secured the rights of the barons, the Petition of Right had done the same for knights of the realm. During the Commonwealth republic, this was extended to members of Parliament and the 1689 Bill of Rights had the effect of drawing the gentry into the equation. Not only did women have no say in who sat in Parliament, the labourers toiling in the fields, the craftsmen producing the nation's wealth and the soldiers building the British Empire were still without a vote; all were denied a mechanism for holding those in power to account.

The struggle through which the ancient liberties of England would be extended to every citizen would continue for another two centuries. Drawing on the traditions of the Levellers and Diggers, eighteenth-century radicals sought to put democracy on the agenda.

Foremost among them was Thomas Paine. Born in Thetford, Suffolk in 1737, Paine was the son of a Quaker, who rose from humble beginnings to become an excise man, his first political essay being a call for better pay and working conditions for his profession. In 1774, Paine met Benjamin Franklin in London, who persuaded him to emigrate to America, where he became a journalist.

He arrived in Philadelphia shortly after the first Continental Congress had been convened in September 1774, where representatives of the colonies had decided to boycott British imports in retaliation for the imposition of unfair taxation and customs duties. Once again, the traditional English principles of fairness and rule by consent were being marshalled against an abuse of absolute power. The British government responded by blockading the New England ports and sending troops to disarm colonist militias, sparking the outbreak of war.

When the second Continental Congress met in May 1775, there was still not a majority amongst the colonies for independence. In January 1776, Paine produced a pamphlet entitled 'Common Sense', which made the case for abandoning the hereditary rule of the British monarchy in favour of a more representative government. The 120,000 copies that were distributed amongst a population of less than three million colonists were to prove highly influential, convincing many, including George Washington, of the case for independence. One by one, each of the colonies instructed their delegates to vote in favour of separation and on 4 July 1776, the Declaration of Independence was adopted.

'Common Sense', the most widely read argument for republicanism to be written by an Englishman since Cromwell's Commonwealth republic of the 1650s, had echoes of the Good Old Cause in its declaration that in America, Lex is Rex: 'The Law is King'.

Paine's next work, *Rights of Man*, was so controversial that he was put on trial for sedition in his absence by the British government, who feared that the radicalism of revolutionary France might cross the Channel. What made Paine so dangerous was his ability to articulate the concept of universal human rights and his advocacy of wealth redistribution from the rich to the poor. He argued strongly that

> the laws which are enacted by government control men only as individuals, but the nation, through its constitution, controls the whole government, and has a natural ability to do so. The final controlling power, therefore, and the original constituting power are one and the same power.[10]

Dismissing the 1689 English Bill of Rights as 'but a bargain, which the parts of the government made with each other to divide powers, profits and privileges', Paine was equally scornful of the reliance on tradition and custom rather than reason and rights:

> The doctrine of precedents, drawn from times and circumstances antecedent to those events, has been the studied practice of the English government. The generality of those precedents are founded on principles the reverse of what they ought to be; and the greater distance of time they are drawn from, the more they are to be suspected.[11]

Written over 150 years before the Beveridge Report, *Rights of Man* also contained a fully costed proposal for a basic form of national insurance, family allowance, housing, free education and pensions, all funded by progressive taxation.

'This support', Paine made clear, 'is not of the nature of charity, but of right'. In seeking to liberate the British people from subjection to aristocratic power, Paine also hoped to free them from the greater tyranny of poverty.[12]

E. P. Thompson considered *Rights of Man* to be one of the foundation texts of the English working-class movement, setting the course for the social legislation of the twentieth century. He also recognized how Paine's work linked the seventeenth-century politics of the English Commonwealth with the radicals of the early nineteenth century.[13] Paine had a great influence on both the American and French revolutions – he is credited with coining the term 'United States of America' – but failed to bring about change in his own country, dying in New York City in 1809.

By the early nineteenth century, even Parliament saw the need to extend the voting franchise. However, the failure of the

1832 Reform Act to deliver anything like universal suffrage led to the formation of the Chartists, the first genuinely grassroots campaign for democratic reform that Britain had seen.

A second Reform Act, passed in 1867, extended the franchise to male urban householders. Women and the working classes were still not considered responsible enough to vote. A third set of reforms were introduced in 1884–5, extending the 1867 rights to the countryside and so bringing in many agricultural labourers who owned their houses. Even with these reforms, 40 per cent of adult males and all women were left without representation.

In the early twentieth century, the most radical proponents of reform were the Suffragettes, who took direct action in order to win the right to vote. During the First World War, when many women were needed to perform jobs vacated by men who had been called up, the argument against female suffrage became hard to sustain. It was also noted that the majority of those men who had fought in the war were not entitled to vote.

The 1918 Representation of the People Act abolished the property qualifications for men and offered the vote to women over thirty who were either householders, the wives of householders or graduates of a British university. Overnight, the size of the electorate trebled from 7.7 million to 21.4 million. After it became clear that women voters were not a danger to the constitution, a further Act of Parliament in 1928 finally put women on an equal footing with men. Now everyone over the age of twenty-one had a vote.

The right to hold those in power to account had taken over seven hundred years to become the birthright of all English men and women. Only by constantly seeking to push back the boundaries of liberty had the principle of rule by consent been established. Only by breaking with the past had it been achieved.

The huge influx of women voters put social issues firmly on the agenda, providing a boost to the Labour Party, which between the wars emerged as a viable governing party, though it was unable to gain the majority needed to enact its full programme. It took the Second World War finally to convince the British that collective provision was the best way to deliver social justice. The first hint of this change came after Dunkirk, with the widespread realization that we were all in it together. This new mood was finally given voice in the general election of 1945, the first for ten years.

The Labour manifesto contained a faint echo of the English Commonwealth republic of the seventeenth century with its declaration that

> The Labour Party is a Socialist Party, and proud of it. Its ultimate purpose at home is the establishment of the Socialist Commonwealth of Great Britain – free, democratic, efficient, progressive, public-spirited, its material resources organised in the service of the British people.

Standing on the platform of full implementation of Beveridge's plans, Labour scored a resounding victory, stunning the world by throwing Winston Churchill out of office – thus proving that the democratic institutions which they had fought to preserve had survived the War intact and were in perfect working order.

Having struggled for so long for the right to speak, write, publish and vote, the British people were now offered the right to health care, education, housing and social security. Recalling the desperate poverty of the Jarrow marchers rather than the glory of the Allies' march into Germany, they voted by a landslide to continue the collective spirit that had produced our finest hour.

At the heart of that victory was the covenant that the Beveridge Report represented: a modern charter of rights agreed between the rulers and the ruled and ratified by the people in a general election.

11
Britishness *v.* Multiculturalism

It is a broadly accepted fact that, over the past fifty years, Britain has become a classless society. The chairman of the Conservative Party recently welcomed this development, citing it as one of the Labour Party's genuine achievements.[1] This, however, has not been achieved by abolishing class boundaries; their fault lines are still visible at every level of our society. Accent can still betray one's background in an instant. Class consciousness also survives – and not just among the lower orders. Witness the lengths that the Countryside Alliance went to in order to argue that lots of working-class people enjoy fox-hunting too.

The class distinctions – in attitude, language and dress code – are all still there, reflected back at us every day by our national newspapers, from the royal court circular and social register in *The Times* to the topless page-three girls in the down-market *Sun*. What has changed is that such things no longer really matter. The 'classless society' is a misnomer for a society not in which class has disappeared, but in which class is no barrier to achievement. People expect to be judged on their ability, not their background, and tend to judge others by the same criteria. Class distinctions still exist, but are no longer recognized by the majority of people as conferring a hierarchical status. We're pretty blithe about class these days, and our society is more at ease with itself as a result.

The classless society was not achieved by making everyone the same. It came about because the great disparity in wealth that kept the classes apart was undermined by a redistribution of income aimed at creating a fairer society. The effects of such measures were visible in the years following the Second World War. As the working class began to benefit from the collective provision of health care, housing and education, so the inclination to defer to their 'betters', as their parents and grandparents had done, was replaced by a new confidence, exemplified by the Swinging Sixties.

Better wages and living conditions encouraged the working class to adopt the aspirational values of the middle class that had for so long sought to exclude them. Of course this was not achieved without a degree of acquiescence on the part of the upper and middle classes, but the changes were primarily driven by a determination on the part of the working class to assert their right to be judged on their abilities alone. So complete was this transformation that, in the 1980s, many voted for Margaret Thatcher.

It is this confidence, spreading throughout our society, that has demolished the barriers of class. Some have labelled it 'individualism' and sought to package it as an ideology. Its aspirational qualities have led commentators to claim that we are all middle class now. What is true is that many now have the expectation that life will get better, a notion that has been associated historically with the middle class.

Did this process require the assimilation, integration or dissolution of the working class? Quite the opposite. The past fifty years have seen the middle and upper classes adopt the language, attire and interests of the working class in the search for wider acceptance. Why do you think that people will pay more for a pair of brand-new jeans if they have been made to look old and worn? Jeans that are frayed and faded give the wearer an air of having come through hard times, just as a working-class accent gives the speaker an air of authenticity.

Long before white English kids began speaking like Jamaican yardies in order to seem tough, public schoolboys were adopting cockney accents for the same reason. And looking at all the merchant bankers slumming it at Premiership football matches, you have to ask who has assimilated whom.

This process has brought about massive changes. A hundred years ago, the majority of the population were excluded from society: poorly educated, not allowed to vote, kept in place by a rigid class system. Organization and struggle by ordinary working people led to improvements in their standard of living, and as a result, class ceased to be a divisive issue; feelings of social exclusion gave way to a sense of belonging.

Those of us who wish to see race and ethnicity no longer a cause for division and exclusion could learn from studying how Britain was transformed. Like the 'classless society', our struggle to create an inclusive, pluralistic society also labours under a misnomer – that of 'multiculturalism', a term that means different things to different people.

For some, it's all about taste and the enjoyment of things from outside your own community. In this sense, multiculturalism becomes little more than a form of consumerism.

Sadly, not everyone who eats chicken tikka masala is cured of their prejudices.

Others see multiculturalism as an ideology, a view particularly strong among those on the Left. With the decline of Marxism, the struggle to create equality through economic means has been replaced with demands for cultural equality. However, multiculturalism cannot, of itself, deliver an equal society. The Berlin Wall may have crumbled – and good riddance to it and the totalitarianism that raised it – but that does not detract from the fact that genuine equality can only be achieved through social justice.

Then there is the notion that an area can be considered to be successfully multicultural if black and ethnic-minority groups are visibly present. However, this demographic multiculturalism doesn't guarantee a positive atmosphere.

Others use the word pejoratively, a practice rooted in a perception by members of the majority indigenous population that multiculturalism denies their right to express themselves as they see fit.

Even the chair of the Commission for Racial Equality, Trevor Phillips, is unsure exactly what the term implies. He caused a stir recently by rightly suggesting that multiculturalism could have a negative effect if it meant diversity as a route to division rather than cohesion, resulting in ethnically different communities living totally separate lives. His comments were seized on by right-wing commentators, who twisted his view that ethnic fragmentation is a catastrophe into a statement that multiculturalism itself is catastrophic for our society. What the reaction to his speech did highlight was that multiculturalism is a term in need of clearer definition.

Rather than describing a matter of taste, a campaign for

cultural equality, a reverse hierarchy or an excuse for separatism, perhaps we should think of a multicultural society in the same way that we perceive our present classless society, as an evolutionary process which does not necessitate the abolition of cultural differences or the assimilation of one group into another. The multicultural society would be one in which ethnicity, like class, no longer matters.

I'm not seeking to encourage indifference. Apathy and ignorance are the main ingredients of bigotry. The crucial lubricant in this process is respect. Without it, friction will hinder progress and leave ugly scorch marks on our communities. History shows that by refusing to tug their forelocks to their betters, the working class gained confidence in their right to be recognized as part of society. The ethnic minorities are no different.

This transition towards a multicultural society is already under way in parts of the country, most notably London, now recognized as the most multi-ethnic city in Europe. Figures from the 2001 Census reveal that 2.2 million people living in London were born outside England – over 30 per cent of the capital's population. Three hundred different languages are spoken within the M25 and London is host to fifty non-indigenous communities with populations of over one hundred thousand.[2]

Some of these communities have been here for a long time. The Italian community in London was already over ten thousand strong when my great-grandparents were married in St Peter's, Clerkenwell in 1906. Others, from places such as Russia and Albania, are newer arrivals.

A recent survey of multi-ethnic London suggests that the aspirational urge that broke down class barriers is present within the black and ethnic-minority communities:

One principle was confirmed and reconfirmed by every encounter. Vietnamese, Somalis, Congolese, Koreans, Portuguese, Nigerians, Turks and Poles are really just the same as everybody else – they work hard, love their kids and move to the suburbs when they can afford it.[3]

These new Londoners are ready to take their turn on the journey to belonging that resulted in my Italian relatives moving from the narrow streets of Stepney to the leafy suburbs of Romford and beyond.

The high visibility of the black and ethnic-minority communities in London undoubtedly helped the city win the right to host the Olympic Games in 2012. While other cities sent sober-suited bureaucrats to bid for the Games in Singapore, London's official delegation of a hundred people included thirty youngsters from the East End, representing twenty different nationalities between them. Their presence in the hall during the final votes underlined London's credentials as the most diverse city among those bidding.

However, the jubilation when the Games were awarded to London was cut short the next day when the capital suffered its most devastating attack since the Blitz. Four suicide bombers murdered fifty-two people and injured seven hundred more, striking at London's transport system in the middle of the morning rush hour on 7 July 2005.

If the terrorists were hoping to spoil the jubilation that accompanied London's victory, they could not have chosen a more multicultural target. When details of the victims emerged, they were as representative of London's multi-ethnic make-up as were the thirty East London schoolkids who helped us to win the Olympic bid.

Two weeks later, on 21 July, London was again targeted by suicide bombers. Mercifully, none of their bombs exploded. Five men were later arrested and charged with attempted murder.

What both groups had in common was that they claimed to represent Islam and be involved in a jihad against Britain. The 21 July bombers were all born in East Africa and fitted the terrorist stereotype of foreign-born insurgents plotting to destroy our way of life. The four men who carried out the 7 July attacks, however, were Britons, all of whom had either been born or grown up in Yorkshire. The eldest, Mohammad Sidique Khan, had been a well-respected teaching assistant at a local primary school until the day of the bombing.

The sight of Khan attempting to justify his actions in a video clip released after the bombings was chilling. Most disturbing of all was the fact that, although he portrayed himself as a jihadi before the camera, he spoke in the flat tones of a Yorkshireman. He was one of us.

Before the last bodies had been removed from the Underground, some commentators began to question whether multiculturalism, which they claimed had been too tolerant of Muslim extremism, was in some way complicit in these attacks. Minette Marin wrote in the *Sunday Times*:

> Multiculturalism has been deeply demoralizing to all kinds of people in all kinds of ways, undermining their values, undermining a sense of common purpose, above all undermining the confidence of the host country.[4]

Three days later, the *Daily Telegraph* ran a front-page headline stating 'MULTICULTURALISM IS NOT WORKING, SAYS TORY

CHIEF'. Inside, senior Conservative David Davis called for the promotion of 'the common values of nationhood'.

A number of similar articles appeared in the right-wing press, arguing that multiculturalism had failed and that the remedy was a return to British values. What these values were was never explicitly stated, but the implication was clear: multiculturalism is the opposite of 'Britishness'.

Travelling home on the train one evening, a week after the second, unsuccessful, wave of attacks, I found myself sat next to a man struggling to open his *Daily Telegraph*. The paper's decision to retain its traditional broadsheet format was not helping matters in the crowded carriage. When he did finally make himself comfortable, I found it impossible not to look over his shoulder at the article he was reading.

'WHAT DOES IT MEAN TO BE BRITISH?' asked the banner headline above a two-page spread which published and discussed the results of a YouGov poll of 3,505 people, who had been asked a number of questions relating to their sense of being British. When my fellow passenger got off the train at Brockenhurst, leaving his paper behind, I was able to study the results for myself.

The feature was dominated by a photograph of Kelly Holmes, the British middle-distance runner who won two gold medals at the 2004 Athens Olympics, holding the Union Jack moments after her triumph. She was the person most cited when the respondents were asked to name the contemporary Briton that they took most pride in. Holmes, daughter of a Jamaican father and English mother, beat the Queen into second place, while Trinidadian-born broadcaster Trevor McDonald came third. It certainly made me proud to be British, knowing that my fellow citizens had chosen to be represented by a woman of mixed race and a Caribbean immigrant as well as our head of state. And these were not the choices of a bunch of self-loathing lefties: 80 per cent of those asked felt that Britain had been, on balance, a force for good in the world.

The most revealing part of the poll was that in which respondents were given a series of phrases that might be used to define what it means to be British and asked to indicate how important they thought each one was in defining 'Britishness'. The *Telegraph* printed the results based on the number of times a particular phrase or word had been deemed 'very important' by those polled.

Surprisingly, the monarchy was only cited as 'very important' by 39 per cent. The fact that Britain had once had a great empire figured even less, with only 25 per cent commenting on its importance. The House of Commons could only manage 37 per cent, while the Church of England scored a miserable 17 per cent, with only cricket, the motorways and the quality of our restaurants below it. So much for our great institutions.

On the bright side, parliamentary democracy fared rather better, gaining 49 per cent. And the top three offered real food for thought: in third place, with 54 per cent of those polled thinking it was 'very important', came 'the British people's sense of fairness and fair play'; second was 'Britain's defiance of Nazi Germany in 1940', cited by 59 per cent; and the single thing that the majority of people thought was most important in defining who we are was 'the British people's right to say what they think'.[5]

That the Second World War should be up there alongside freedom of speech and insistence on fairness should surprise no one. What was the War about, if not defending a free and fair society? And even after all this time, it is an experience that continues to exert a strong hold over our notion of what it means to be British.

As recently as 2002, Sir Winston Churchill topped the BBC poll of Great Britons, winning over a quarter of the 1,622,248 votes cast and defeating such notables as Brunel, Princess Diana, Shakespeare, Darwin and Newton.

The wording of the option in the *Telegraph*'s poll touched on why the Second World War – and 1940 in particular – is highly significant. It's not the defence of Britain against Nazi Germany that we feel most proud of, it's 'Britain's defiance'. That belief – that we stood alone against the all-conquering might of Nazi Germany, after all our allies had fallen – is central to our sense of who we are.

Churchill embodies that defiance and the speeches he made during the summer of 1940 gave voice to the spirit of resistance against fascism, not just in Britain, but throughout the world. His speech to Parliament following the fall of France, made on 18 June 1940 and subsequently broadcast on the BBC, rings down the ages:

'The whole fury and might of the enemy must very soon be turned on us. Hitler knows that he will have to break us in this island or lose the war. If we can stand up to him, all Europe may be free and the life of the world may move forward into broad, sunlit uplands. But if we fail, then the whole world, including the United States, including all that we have known and cared for, will sink into the abyss of a new Dark Age made more sinister, and perhaps more protracted, by the lights of perverted science. Let us therefore brace ourselves to our duties and so bear ourselves that, if the British Empire and its Commonwealth last for a thousand years, men will say, "This was their finest hour".'

On that same day, a cartoon by Low appeared in the London *Evening Standard* which seemed to sum up the message of Churchill's speech. A lone British Tommy stands on a wave-swept out-crop, defiantly waving his fist at oncoming Luftwaffe bombers. The caption reads 'Very well, alone.'

David Low was perhaps the greatest political cartoonist appearing in the British press during the Second World War and the image he drew on 18 June has entered the mythology of the summer of 1940. A month later, however, *Punch* published a cartoon by Fougasse, the pseudonym of British cartoonist Cyril Bird, which wryly sought to offer a truer perspective on Britain's lone stance against Nazism.

Two Tommies sit on a cliff top, one reading a paper, the other smoking a pipe, gazing across the Channel towards France. One says to the other, 'So our poor old Empire is alone in all the world.' 'Aye, we are,' the other replies. 'The whole five hundred million of us.'

By August, the reality of the situation seems to have got through to Low as well. His cartoon 'Reception Committee' shows a welcoming party of soldiers from New Zealand, Canada, Australia and the UK waiting on the beach for the expected Nazi invaders.

In truth, Britain had been drawing on manpower and resources from her Empire since the beginning of the War. A fully trained Canadian division began arriving in Britain within two months of the outbreak of war and was part of the British Expeditionary Force in France in 1940.

The many nationalities of the pilots who took part in the Battle of Britain give some indication of the breadth of international support that the country was able to call on. There were 141 Polish pilots, of whom 29 were killed in combat, 86

Czechs, 29 Belgians, as well as 103 New Zealanders, 90 Canadians and 29 Australians. Other nations represented include America, France, Ireland, South Africa, Rhodesia and Jamaica. These were the few among the Few, the vanguard of tens of thousands of young men and women from many nations whose presence in our country would begin a process of cultural change that we are still undergoing.

Until 1940, the majority of people in England grew up eating English food, wearing English clothes and listening to English music. The War changed all that. And nothing had a greater effect on monocultural Britain than the setting up in London of the American Forces Network, the first radio station to break the BBC's broadcasting monopoly. Coming on air in July 1943, the aim of AFN was to give US servicemen in Britain a slice of home. Millions of Britons tuned in to hear the latest hits from America, enjoying the informal style of broadcasting in contrast to the stuffy approach of the BBC.

By the end of the War, a multi-racial, multi-ethnic, multi-cultural force had been assembled to fight fascism, with Britain as its focus. Two and a half million people from the Indian sub-continent were fighting on our side, while the total number of Africans who fought for Britain during the Second World War is approximately 372,000.

While the Indians and Africans mostly served on their own continents, thousands of West Indians came to Britain to work in the war effort alongside the British people. Their most significant contribution was in the RAF, where 5,536 served as ground crew and another three hundred flew as aircrew. The majority came from Jamaica and their wartime experiences here helped to shape post-war immigration.[6]

In recent years, historians have focussed on an event in 1948 as marking the beginning of Britain's journey towards a multi-cultural society. On 22 June that year, the SS *Empire Windrush* arrived at Tilbury Docks in Essex, bringing men from the British West Indies who were seeking to escape unemployment back home. The Britain they came to was still struggling to overcome the privations of war. Rationing remained in force and there was a shortage of decent housing in cities which had been hit hard by the Blitz.

Although all the West Indians were British citizens, having been born in a British colony, efforts were made to dissuade them from coming to the mother country. Their progress was reported in the newspapers and mild panic ensued in Whitehall as civil servants fretted about the best way to deal with the 'problem'.

Eventually, it took the intervention of Labour Prime Minister Clement Attlee to ensure that the passengers of the *Empire Windrush* were treated with the due respect afforded British passport holders. In a letter dated 5 July 1948, replying to angry backbenchers who had written to him demanding something be done to dissuade these immigrants, he reminded them that

> It is traditional that British subjects, whether of Dominion or Colonial origin (and of whatever race or colour), should be freely admissible to the United Kingdom. That tradition is not, in my view, to be lightly discarded, particularly at a time when we are importing foreign labour in large numbers.[7]

Efforts were made to find work and accommodation for the *Windrush* passengers and within a decade over twenty thousand West Indians had followed them, finding work in the public sector which had been greatly expanded by Attlee's Labour government.

In the story of post-war immigration, the *Empire Windrush* passengers were pioneers, but it is wrong to portray them as simple Caribbean folk who knew nothing of the country to which they were headed. Papers in the National Archive reveal that a significant minority of the men on the *Windrush* had already been to Britain. Before the ship left Jamaica, the passengers were interviewed by officials from the Colonial Office in an attempt to ascertain what skills, if any, they possessed.

They were also asked if they had any previous experience in the UK. Of those who declared they had, a clear picture emerges:

STEWART, Vincent Roy	3 years with RAF
YIN, Clarence Edward	3 years with RAF as radar operator
FARRER, Alvin Walton	4 years with RAF
PLUMMER, Allan	Served with RAF
BROOKS, Clarence	RAF Air Crew
CASE, Lloyd	Served in RAF as a mechanic
CALLUM, Robert	RAF Bomber Command[8]

In all, almost one third of those interviewed had been to the UK as part of the war effort, most of them in the RAF.

Mike and Trevor Phillips, in their book *Windrush: The Irresistible Rise of Multi-racial Britain*, outlined the motives that drew those who had been in the forces back to Britain.

To the men returning from the war, life in the Caribbean seemed slower, smaller and poorer than it had been before, with even fewer opportunities for advancement or self-expression, and governed by the same oppressive structure of imperialist control. They had been to the centre of the world, bombed it, and watched their friends die in the conflagration. They knew what it felt like to live in London and Leicester and Lancashire. They had seen new and surprising possibilities, and it was now impossible to control their aspirations on a Caribbean colony.[9]

Travelling to Britain had also given the West Indians a new perspective on their own position in society. For the black servicemen, used to seeing white people in the colonies in positions of power and wealth, the realization that some Britons could neither read nor write and lived in abject poverty came as a shock. Up close, the English were not so different from the Jamaicans as they had at first seemed.

It was not the *Empire Windrush* which brought these people to Britain; they had first come in response to Winston Churchill's speech on 18 June 1940, in which the great war leader reached out beyond our own beleaguered island to issue a call to arms to the five hundred million citizens of the British Empire and its Commonwealth.

Our defiance of Nazi Germany, of which we are rightly proud, was not achieved by Britain alone, but by rallying forces from many nations to stand with us against the might of Hitler's forces. The Empire and Commonwealth sent their best to help defend Britain, men and women of different races, classes and creeds, who stood together against fascist tyranny and aggression. In our finest hour, the seeds of our multi-cultural society were sown.

12

The Rules Have Changed

In an article that accompanied the *Daily Telegraph* feature about what it means to be British, Alice Thompson argued that the British 'are a tolerant nation who enjoy diversity but like to stick to the rules'. But what are the rules? Where can you find them, these common values that bind us as a society? Where are they written down? Furthermore, why are these 'our' values and how did we come to acquire them? Is there anything of substance behind our vague notion of Britishness?

For instance, is there a law that guarantees a British citizen the right to say what he or she thinks, the value considered most important to the respondents in the *Telegraph* poll? Certainly we have nothing which expresses our right to freedom of speech as clearly and emphatically as the First Amendment of the US Bill of Rights:

> Congress shall make no law respecting an establishment of religion, or prohibiting the free exercise thereof; or abridging the freedom of speech, or of the press; or the right of the people

peaceably to assemble, and to petition the government for a redress of grievances.

Drawn up by the founding fathers in 1789, this document contains a set of principles which unite a geographically disparate and ethnically diverse nation. At the heart of what it means to be American is a piece of paper – a written constitution. Its contents are not merely an expression of universal values; they are also a fundamental set of principles which Americans use when framing new laws.

The present US administration's attempt to make it illegal for any US citizen to burn the nation's flag offers an insight into how a Bill of Rights should function. Many Americans support President George W. Bush's initiative on this issue, arguing that such an act of disrespect to the symbol of their nation is an affront to the majority of the population. However, opposition to this move comes not only from those who support such behaviour, but also from patriotic citizens who would not wish to desecrate the flag themselves, but who are none the less determined to uphold the freedom of expression such action represents. The judges, whose job it is to interpret the law in accordance with the US Bill of Rights, have consistently ruled that flag-burning is a form of 'symbolic speech', and is therefore protected by the rights guaranteed to all US citizens in the First Amendment.

The emotional attachment of the average American to the Stars and Stripes is evident to anyone who has ever visited the USA. Despite this, US courts have passed down judgments which recognize that the flag is only a symbol of the freedoms guaranteed to all Americans, and that to change the constitution to protect the flag would be to compromise the very values which it represents. As should be the case in a healthy democracy, the principles upon which the nation was founded are more important than its symbols.

American schoolchildren begin to learn about the US Bill of Rights at around the same age that I was being taught the Whig Interpretation of History. Ironically, it is the Whigs whom we have to thank for the creation of our own Bill of Rights.

The determination of the Stuart kings to rule without the consent of Parliament and the people was not curbed by the Civil War and the execution of Charles I in 1649, nor by the eleven years of the English Commonwealth republic. Following the death of Oliver Cromwell, a coup d'état was staged which brought Charles II to the throne and filled Parliament with royalist sympathizers. The restored king worked on his relationship with the newly constituted Parliament – after all, most of the members were men who had supported his father. However, when Charles II died in 1685, the throne passed to his brother, James II, who felt no such loyalties and began, like his father had done, to seek ways to rule without Parliament. Using his royal prerogatives, he filled the army and the judiciary with his placemen and kept troops camped outside London to stifle any opposition.

Parliament bided its time. James was not expected to live long and his daughter, Mary, heir to the throne, and her husband William of Orange were Protestants. However, in June 1688, Parliament's worst fears were realized when James's queen gave birth to a son. The prospect of the continuation of the Catholic Stuart dynasty set off a series of events which led to the first major formalization of the English constitution since Magna Carta.

The Whig aristocracy plotted with William and Mary,

inviting them to 'intervene' in English politics and thereby guarantee a Protestant succession. When William landed with a large army in Devon, he was greeted not as an invader but as a liberator. This show of support for William convinced James to flee to France with his wife and son, leaving a power vacuum.

Determined not to be sidelined by another absolute monarch, Parliament took the opportunity to constrain the powers of the Crown, offering the throne to William and Mary and their successors on condition that they agreed to Parliament's terms as laid out in a document called the Declaration of Rights. William and Mary accepted and, following their joint coronation in 1689, the provisions of the Declaration were passed into English law as 'An Act Declaring the Rights and Liberties of the Subject and Settling the Succession of the Crown', which we know today as the Bill of Rights.

It established in law certain inalienable rights that were deemed to belong to all Englishmen. In reality, it would be several centuries before these rights would be enjoyed by all the citizens of England. The majority of clauses were designed to strengthen the power of Parliament and to protect parliamentarians from the arbitrary power of the Crown.

The 1689 Bill of Rights forbade the sovereign from taxing the people, raising an army or establishing courts without the consent of Parliament. Subjects were free to elect members of Parliament without interference from the Crown, petition the sovereign, and, if Protestant, bear arms. No one charged with an offence was to be fined without trial, or given cruel and unusual punishment or excessive bail. And freedom of speech was guaranteed for the first time, but only in Parliament, where proceedings could not be questioned by any court except Parliament itself.

After forty years, the issues which the king and Parliament had fought over in the Civil War were resolved in favour of the Good Old Cause – parliamentary democracy. The right of the English to be governed by consent was finally established in law.

The English Bill of Rights of 1689 was a defining document in our constitution, becoming the basis for the development of human rights not only in Britain but also in other emerging democracies. The need for an independent judiciary, the right to bear arms and to a fair trial, and protection from cruel and unusual punishment and unfair fines all appeared a hundred years later in the US Bill of Rights, itself an instrument for proscribing abuses of power by the supreme authority in America, the federal government. However, the limited scope of the English Bill of Rights, which was concerned mostly with the relationship between Parliament and the monarchy, prevented it from becoming the embodiment of our values in the way that the Bill of Rights has done for Americans. Instead, it became one of a number of documents which, taken together, are said to form Britain's 'unwritten constitution'.

'Unwritten' is something of a misnomer. Britain has a constitution, it just doesn't involve the citizenry. The 1689 Bill of Rights regulates the relationship between Parliament and the Crown; hence the use of the term 'constitutional monarchy' to describe our form of government. The British constitution is 'unwritten' in the sense that it lacks a single document which codifies and regulates the relationship between government and citizen. This absence of a formal expression of the common values which bind us as people has made it difficult to define the limits of acceptable behaviour, whether by citizen or by government.

Most people assume that 'Britishness' is a mixture of fairness, tolerance and, above all, decency, and are dismayed when they see their fellow Britons – be they politicians or foulmouthed louts – failing to live up to these standards. Acres of newsprint calling for a restoration of 'traditional British values' are not going to make the slightest difference until we have all agreed on what these values are.

Some argue that one of the great strengths of Britishness is our reticence about our values, so much so that to highlight them would seem immodest or phoney; surely one just knows what they are? Such people tend to be secure in their sense of where they belong in society. If we are to convince the people of Barking and Dagenham that the rights of the indigenous majority are protected, while at the same time presenting new would-be citizens with something tangible to work towards – not least what we mean when we say 'decency' – then we have to ensure that traditional British values are based on something more than the assumptions of Middle England.

Our constitution also suffers from being mostly a collection of assumptions. Under British law, the citizen has 'negative rights': you are assumed to be free to do anything which is not forbidden by law. These rights have evolved over time, with each generation making amendments either by royal decree, Act of Parliament or judicial ruling. Thus the legal guarantees of the freedoms that we enjoy are scattered throughout our history, contained in the outcome of obscure judgments and dusty legislation stored in a tower of the Palace of Westminster.

Under such an arrangement, our rights as citizens become a matter for the government of the day, which can expand or restrict our freedoms simply by passing new legislation through Parliament, giving the impression that our rights are granted. However, modern constitutional law recognizes that rights ultimately reside with the individual, that they are inalienable and must be respected. The purpose of a Bill of Rights, therefore, is not to grant freedoms, but rather to protect the freedom of the individual from the power of the state, by providing a set of fundamental rules by which we, the people, agree to be governed. As a legal document, the function of a constitution is to limit the power of government.

In Britain, however, the government has the power to make up the rules as it goes along, simply by passing an Act of Parliament. The weakness of this arrangement is that it inverts the relationship between rulers and ruled – the government limits the power of the constitution. This places a huge amount of power in the hands of politicians. A prime minister with a large majority, a supine House of Commons, powerless select committees, an illegitimate House of Lords and an unwritten constitution has very few constraints on his authority. The term 'elective dictatorship' has been coined to describe this situation, but the image of a prime minister surrounded by a court of special advisers and spin doctors is reminiscent of the absolute monarchy of the Stuart kings.

This similarity has become more apposite since the introduction of the 1998 Human Rights Act, which incorporated the European Convention on Human Rights into British law. Hailed by the government as a great leap forward for civil liberties, the HRA didn't actually give us any rights that we did not already have under the Convention; it simply made it possible to petition our own courts for redress, rather than having to take our case to the European Court in Strasbourg for justice. It was a significant gesture by a Labour government in the first flush of a massive landslide victory, yet now that our judges are putting it to its intended use, it is clear that the prime minister views it as an irksome constraint on his powers, much as Charles I regarded the Petition of Right.

Like the Welfare State, the European Convention on Human Rights was a product of post-war determination to create a better world in which dictatorships could no longer flourish. By promoting universal notions of freedom and democracy, the nations of western Europe hoped not only to snuff out the dying embers of Nazism, but also to counter the threat of the Soviet Union, which had set up puppet regimes in eastern Europe.

In order to achieve this, Britain, along with Belgium, Denmark, France, the Republic of Ireland, Italy, Luxembourg, the Netherlands, Norway and Sweden, signed the Treaty of London on 5 May 1949, which created the Council of Europe, a body which predates the EU and remains separate from it.

The Council's first task was to draft a convention on human rights which would reflect the liberal values for which the Second World War had been fought. Churchill himself was supportive of such a move, stating in a speech at the Albert Hall in April 1949 that 'there would be no hope for the world unless the peoples of Europe unite together to preserve their freedom, their culture and their civilization founded upon Christian ethics'.[1]

British lawyers, led by the Conservative Lord Chancellor, Lord Kilmuir, were responsible for the original draft of the European Convention on Human Rights in 1950. Britain, a founding signatory, was the first nation to ratify the treaty. Initially, it was held that only states could bring cases to the body which administered the Convention, the Court of Human Rights in Strasbourg. However, in 1966 the government gave British citizens the right to bring individual cases to the court.

It soon became clear that the rights available under our domestic law were not as comprehensive as those guaranteed by the European Convention. With the cost of taking a case to Strasbourg becoming increasingly prohibitive, justice was available only to those who could afford it. To overcome this inequality, the Labour Party made a commitment to incorporate the Convention's rights into our domestic law, thus making them available to everyone in the British courts.

The principles enshrined in the Human Rights Act broke with the doctrine of 'negative' rights, introducing to common law the recognition that each citizen has inalienable 'positive' rights as an individual which need to be protected by law. The topsy-turvy British constitution was starting to right itself.

However, there were no celebrations to accompany the Human Rights Act. No great effort was made to inform people that their citizenship had been significantly upgraded. While the Act was welcomed by those it was designed to protect, the new rights and freedoms were vociferously derided as yet more bureaucracy and red tape by those whose bad practices it sought to restrict.

For reasons of expediency, the government had simply bolted the European Convention on to the British legal system, rather than constructing a domestic Bill of Rights. This made it an easy target for Eurosceptic commentators intent on condemning the Human Rights Act as part of a sinister plan to force us into a European superstate. The new rights were further undermined by a series of court cases in which the

Act was used to support the rights of the accused. The tabloids responded with outraged headlines claiming that the Act was more concerned with the rights of criminals than those of their victims.

In common with its predecessors, Magna Carta and the 1689 Bill of Rights, the Human Rights Act has much to say about the treatment of those accused of crimes. Of the demands made by the barons at Runnymede in 1215, those which have survived to this day are the right to a fair trial and prompt justice. At the heart of Magna Carta, arguably the earliest expression of what were to become British values, is a recognition of the rights of suspected criminals.

Because they are designed to govern the relationship between citizen and state, rights inevitably come into play when the state is called upon to dispense punishment on behalf of society. Criminals act with impunity, without any care for the rights of individuals or the community at large. In order for the state to maintain the moral high ground, it has to be seen to act with a degree of humanity when taking punitive action. The prohibition of arbitrary imprisonment known as 'habeas corpus' in British law, the right to a fair trial and the presumption that you are innocent until proven guilty are designed to facilitate the prompt release of those who have been wrongly accused. Without such rules there would be little to protect the innocent from being incarcerated indefinitely without charge or trial.

Once found guilty, criminals are deprived of their liberty for the duration of their sentence, but not of their right to be treated humanely. Images of the abuse of Iraqi detainees in the Abu Ghraib prison in Baghdad were a shocking example of what can happen when jailers are allowed to act without restraint, a stark reminder of why it is important to protect the rights of those held in custody.

While some tabloids might regularly call for suspected criminals to forfeit their human rights, history shows us that in societies which follow such practices – Hitler's Germany and Stalin's Russia, for example – no one is safe: the knock at the door can come at any time, for any reason or none whatsoever. The rules which protect the rights of suspected criminals protect us all.

However, the terrible events of 11 September 2001 have changed the nature of the relationship between the individual and the state. In the immediate aftermath of 9/11, anyone boarding a plane was regarded as a suspect. Suddenly, the airlines wanted to know much more about you – not just your name and where you were going, but details of your background and motivations. This suspicion of intent soon spread beyond the airports into society at large.

In the wake of the attack on America, the British government enacted a series of laws which have seriously eroded the presumption that an individual is innocent until proven guilty. The Police and Criminal Evidence Act has transformed the powers of the police, allowing them to make arrests for minor offences such as dropping litter, or for protesting against the government. Once held, they can fingerprint, photograph and take DNA evidence from you – by force, if necessary – and hold it in a national database for ever, whether or not you are charged. The Terrorism Act gives the police the power to carry out searches which do not have to be founded on reasonable suspicion. Anti-social behaviour orders can be granted on hearsay evidence – that is, gossip and rumour.

Perhaps the clearest sign that our government considers us

all to be suspects is the decision to introduce identity cards. Only once before have British citizens ever had to carry ID cards and that was during the Second World War, when genuine fears of a fifth column of Nazi infiltrators made it sensible to be able to confirm the identity of individuals. That, however, was during a national emergency, when other civil liberties were also suspended for the duration of the War. The introduction of ID cards during peacetime is an altogether different matter.

The government has justified this unprecedented move in the name of security. ID cards, they argue, will protect us from identity theft and illegal immigration, make us safer from terrorists and allow better access to public services. In order to achieve this, the government will require forty-nine pieces of information about each individual, which they will store on a central database known as the National Identity Register. Each ID-card-holder will be given a unique Identity Registration Number, which will allow other arms of the state – including the police, security services, tax authorities, customs and excise, vehicle licensing and the health service – to track individuals through the entire system, making it possible for the state to build a profile of the behaviour of each citizen.

The advantages of such a comprehensive database are clear. Had the police been using a fully integrated national system, Ian Huntley may have been prevented from murdering the Soham schoolgirls, Holly Wells and Jessica Chapman. No parent could possibly complain about an initiative designed to better protect their children. When asked to strike a balance between the security of a child and the rights of a murderer, I would always tip the scales in favour of the victim. I also accept that the child-protection agencies and police must sometimes cast their nets wide in order to apprehend a suspect, under the principle that it is better to err on the side of caution than risk a child being harmed. However, implicit in that principle is an admission of the possibility of error, and if innocent people do fall under suspicion, then they too are victims, not of the criminal, but of the state.

The chance of this happening is increased by a centralized identity database, which allows the government to compile a behavioural profile. Should your behaviour pattern match that of a suspect, you may be drawn into a widely cast net. The implications of this could range from wrongful arrest to simply having it noted on your file that you were once part of an investigation for suspect behaviour.

In 2006, the Criminal Records Bureau revealed that it had mistakenly labelled 2,700 innocent people as paedophiles, pornographers and violent criminals. The Home Office admitted that the errors had arisen in situations where the personal details of innocent individuals were similar to those of people with a conviction. The BBC reported the case of a woman who was refused a job because the Criminal Records Bureau had incorrectly identified her as a convicted shoplifter.[2]

If someone should become the victim of an error by the state, should not the scales of justice be tipped in favour of the rights of that victim? It was in order to establish this principle that the barons demanded that King John sign the Magna Carta.

The introduction of ID cards may well prove to be a necessary evil that does, on balance, protect our security as individuals in a modern globalized society. The question we must ask ourselves is whether the government's acquisition of greater powers in the name of our security must always result in a loss of individual liberties, or whether there is a case to be made for strengthening the rights of the citizen each time the state moves to strengthen its defences. Should a list of fundamental citizens' rights be printed on the back of your ID card?

Following the devastating attacks on the London transport system by British-born Muslim suicide-bombers in July 2005, the prime minister announced a series of measures aimed at weeding out extremism, including prohibitions on freedom of speech, the right to peaceful assembly and habeus corpus. This was necessary, he said, because 'the rules had changed'.[3] It is at times such as these that our 'unwritten' constitution fails us. Without an enshrined set of principles codifying the limits of governmental power, there is little to stop an over-mighty executive from riding roughshod over not just the citizen, but the judiciary, Members of Parliament, the House of Lords and anyone else who stands in its way. Whichever party is in power, the problem remains the same: the prime minister can declare that the rules have changed, because he alone has the power to change them.

In England, there is a long tradition of resistance to unchecked power. If there is a single trait in our character that has historically set us apart from other nations, it is our determination to limit the authority of those who rule over us. The English have defined themselves in terms of their opposition to absolute power in a series of great constitutional moments: first, the arbitrary nature of feudal kingship was limited by Magna Carta; then, in 1534, we threw off the unaccountable power of the Pope with the Act of Supremacy; the Civil War was fought to replace the Divine Right of Kings with the then revolutionary idea of rule by consent, a process that culminated in the 1689 Bill of Rights upon which our present liberties are based.

This process did not stop with the creation of Great Britain.

The greatest constitutional moment of modern times was the product of a mature democracy. The founding of the Welfare State in 1948 changed the relationship between citizen and state by establishing the right to free education, free health care, national insurance, affordable housing and a state pension, funded by progressive taxation. It marked the entrenchment in our everyday lives of that value which the British people take pride in exemplifying: fairness.

The introduction of the Human Rights Act in 1998 was not a constitutional moment, not least because its implementation was so low key. The failure of the Labour government to defend its own legislation has further undermined its content in the eyes of the British people.

Seeking to exploit the prime minister's embarrassment over this issue, Conservative leader David Cameron made a speech recently in which he promised to scrap the Human Rights Act altogether and replace it with a British Bill of Rights. Cameron stated that 'A modern British Bill of Rights needs to define the core values which give us our identity as a free nation'.[4] Yet his lack of substantive detail suggested that his sudden interest in this issue was party political rather than stemming from concern for the rights of ordinary citizens. The question remains whether or not the Conservatives have moved on from the view held by Margaret Thatcher, that individuals owe no responsibility to anyone except themselves and their blood relatives. 'There is no such thing as society,' she said in 1987. 'There are individual men and women and there are families.' Traditionally, the Tories have regarded the rights of others as placing unnecessary restrictions on their own freedom.

Of course, Cameron has the luxury of being in Opposition, which allows him to float ideas about the future direction of the country without having to implement them. It may even be that he fully intends to create a British Bill of Rights if he becomes prime minister. But is it wise for us to wait for someone from within the Palace of Westminster to decide what rights we have, given that all politicians face a conflict of interest on this issue? Can we really entrust them with the task of framing a set of principles designed to limit their own powers? Are we so complacent that we are prepared to let them write the rules by which we agree to be governed? Is any single political party capable of defining the common values that constitute 'Britishness', never mind entrenching them in law?

These issues are being debated now because we are living in an increasingly rights-based society. The many flavours of freedom that were propagated during the latter half of the twentieth century have given way to the realization that, unless we can hold to account those who exercise power over our day-to-day lives, we will never truly be free. Living as we do in a globalized economy which forces us to make difficult choices at a dizzying pace, it is becoming clear that rights, enforceable by law, are the true currency of liberty. A set of common values, enshrined in a single document, would liberate us from vague notions of 'Britishness' and 'multiculturalism' by defining who we are.

What better way of marking the three-hundredth anniversary of the creation of Great Britain in 2007 than by initiating a debate about the fundamental values which define us as a nation, with the aim of creating a formal set of principles by which we consent to be governed in a new Declaration of Rights?

Like all of our great constitutional moments, the moral authority for this must come from below. Individuals could come together in citizens' groups across the country and hold debates with the aim of drawing up their own set of principles upon which they would like to see the new settlement based. At the end of the consultation period, each group could send a delegate to a constitutional convention, which would draw up and democratically ratify a Declaration of Rights. This document, with an accompanying petition of support, could then be presented to Parliament and, like the Beveridge Report before it, be used as a lever to produce reform.

Yet the road to liberty has never been smooth. The suffragettes were maligned, as were the Chartists before them. My great-grandfather Frederick Bragg had to fight to win the eight-hour day at the gasworks, and George Austin ultimately had to put his pension on the line in the 1911 strike to end the humiliation of the call-on at the dock gates.

A new constitutional settlement will not protect us from terrorism, globalization or bad governments. We will still have to accept limits to our freedom, such as ID cards. But those cards could be not merely a means of identification, but a symbol of citizenship, guaranteeing the holder access to our rights.

A campaign for the introduction of a new Bill of Rights would have the effect of binding us together, just as the 1948 settlement united people through the principle of collective provision. An open debate would allow traditionalists to contribute along with modernizers, pragmatists as well as idealists. The formulation of our fundamental rights would not only help to define our common values; it would also highlight the responsibilities that we have to one another, promoting respect for our fellow citizens.

Putting some flesh on to the notion of 'Britishness' might

help to assuage the angst felt by the majority, by recognizing a mainstream culture rooted in the principles of fairness, tolerance and decency that we as a people have traditionally espoused.

13
Born Under Two Flags

In one of the most unpleasant comments on race made by a senior Conservative politician since Enoch Powell's 'Rivers of Blood' speech, Norman Tebbit claimed in 1990 that 'A large proportion of Britain's Asian population fail to pass the cricket test. Which side do they cheer for?' The implication was clear – if you failed to support England against India, Pakistan, Bangladesh or Sri Lanka, then you didn't belong here.

Glossing over the fact that he was not at all concerned where the sporting loyalties of Britain's Australian population lay, he had grossly misunderstood the opportunity afforded to British Asians when a team from the sub-continent takes on England at home. If you've had the word 'Paki' spat at you by the English for as long as you can remember, it is surely difficult to suppress an urge to cheer when a bunch of 'Pakis' turn up and beat the English at their own game.

Tebbit could never have got the same mileage from questioning the loyalty of British Asian football fans. They are still a rare breed, although you might expect a sudden burst of enthusiasm if Pakistan ever faced England in the World Cup.

The possibility that they may one day meet in competition underlines the universal nature of the Beautiful Game. Our cricket team will never play a test series against Germany or Brazil. Our rugby team were crowned 'world champions' after winning a competition which involved a mere twenty nations. One hundred and ninety-four countries entered teams into the 2006 football World Cup, thirty-seven from Asia alone, including Pakistan, who failed to qualify after losing to Kyrgyzstan. You can go anywhere in the world these days – even to the USA – and see kids playing football. Loved by billions, it remains the game of the common man. How many of the England football team were privately educated, like rugby hero Jonny Wilkinson, alumnus of Lord Wandsworth College in Hampshire?

Perhaps that's why the *Daily Mail* was moved to ask, the week before the 2006 World Cup began, 'England flags: patriotic or plain chav?' Highlighting the huge number of English flags to be seen in the poorer parts of London and their relative scarcity in Belgravia, the *Mail* reported that some residents of the more expensive parts of town were worried that displays of support for the England team might be blighting house prices in the area.[1] The implication was clear. These damn 'chavs' – the media's favourite derogatory term for the white working class – have no understanding of the proper use of the flag. We raise it, Middle England seemed to want to remind the lower classes – your job is to salute it.

And it wasn't only the reactionary press that felt threatened by chavs with flags. The left-leaning *Guardian* carried a feature on the subject by Joseph Harker, as full of racial stereotyping as anything seen in the *Daily Mail*:

I've been looking at the drivers of these flag-waving vehicles, and – OK, I admit this isn't exactly scientific – half of them are in white vans, and the rest are white, male, tattooed, pot-bellied 35- to 55-year-olds: exactly the type I've been seeing on TV for the past month complaining about 'our houses going to the asylum seekers', or that 'we're losing control of our country'. I can't tell if these drivers come from Barking and Dagenham, where the BNP gained 11 seats, but that borough is just a short drive from where I live, so who knows?[2]

That's right, Joseph, just as every dark-skinned young man with a beard is probably a terrorist.

There is a simple reason why so many ordinary people have recently turned to the St George's Cross as a means of displaying their support for our national team. It's the only thing we English have that belongs to us alone. Of the thirty-two countries that competed for the 2006 World Cup in Germany, there was only one which didn't have its own parliament or passports or national anthem: England.

Of these three, it is the last which rankles most. It's been years since our Welsh and Scottish neighbours stopped singing the British national anthem, 'God Save The Queen', at sporting events. It didn't take an Act of Parliament, or the United Kingdom to crumble or the monarchy to collapse, to make the change. When the Welsh sing 'Hen Wlad Fy Nhadau' they are sending out a message, and even if the language is unfamiliar, the meaning is clear: 'Hello, we're from Wales and we're very proud of it.' England's continued attachment to the British anthem smacks of a lack of self-confidence, a worry that, without it, we might somehow be a lesser people. The message sent out every time we sing 'God Save The Queen' is one of ambiguity: 'Hello, we're the English, but we're not really sure what that means.'

We used to feel the same about the Union Jack. Look at footage of the 1966 World Cup Final, the holiest event in the canon of the modern English identity; there are more German flags than English ones visible in the crowd. The whole stadium is awash with red, white and blue. Even the mascot of the tournament, World Cup Willy, wore a Union Jack waistcoat.

The transfer of emotions to the flag of St George can be traced back to the 1996 European Football Championships, which were held in England. The organizers came up with a multicoloured football as a symbol of the event and coined the slogan 'Football's Coming Home' in honour of England's invention of the game in the nineteenth century. The host nation was drawn in Group A, which included Scotland, and a match between the two at Wembley on 15 June created a dilemma for the England fans: should they carry their traditional symbol, the Union Jack, or was it inappropriate on this occasion as it also represented the Scots? There is nothing like an ancient rivalry to sharpen the need for a symbolic gesture, and the Scots can always be relied on to rise to the occasion in confrontation with 'the Auld Enemy': along with masses of Scots Saltires there was a smattering of banners bearing the numbers '1314' as a reminder of the year that 'proud Edward's army' of English noblemen was defeated by Robert the Bruce at the Battle of Bannockburn.

It is sometimes said of the Scots that they rely on the English to help them define who they are; on that afternoon at Wembley Stadium, the reverse was true. The presence of so many Scotsmen in the sacred crucible of English pride and desire, for the first time in a generation, served to remind us that we had our own symbol, a white banner crossed with red, and that we were England. The reclamation of the St George's flag began that day – helped, no doubt, by the 2–0 victory over the Scots. Yet even five years later, when our family moved out of London to live by the coast in rural Dorset, the most common place to see the England flag was flying from the top of a church tower.

The sudden appearance of thousands of little England flags fluttering from car windows during the 2004 European Championships did cause some anxiety to those of us who traditionally associated such displays with belligerent xenophobia. However, it soon became apparent that the flag had become the symbol of our liberation from that stereotype. Spontaneously, without any prompting from political parties or national institutions, the English had decided they were going to rehabilitate their flag and its meaning.

And not before time. Nobody ever makes the assumption that a white van with the Welsh dragon on the back bumper must be driven by a racist. Scottish car stickers bearing the word 'Ecosse' could be construed as a dig at the English, but no one gets called a Little Scotlander as a result. Until recently, however, to display the St George Cross on your car was to risk condemnation. Clearly that is no longer the case.

As seen flying from all sorts of vehicles during the summer of 2006, the flag is a symbol of support for our national football team, who reflect England's diverse society. Men who can trace their English ancestry back for generations play alongside the sons of recent immigrants, all of them proud to wear the England shirt. I share that pride, and view the resurgent popularity of the St George's Cross as emblematic of a broadening of the English identity, accessible to anyone who wants to be part of it.

This flag fest has also emboldened those whose loyalties lie elsewhere to join in the celebrations. And why shouldn't they? All Britons are born under two flags and no one thinks it odd if their loyalties are sometimes divided. Whether you feel more comfortable under the flag of your home nation or the Union Jack is a matter of personal preference. England's appearance at the World Cup has given us all licence to step back from our communal identity as British passport holders and dust off the flag that best expresses how we think of ourselves. For my missus, the fact that Trinidad and Tobago were drawn against England gave her a rare opportunity to revel in her Caribbean identity.

Born in Point Fortin, Trinidad, to white British parents, Juliet doesn't look like most people's idea of a Trinny, but her dedication to 'island life' explains in part why we live by the sea. Suddenly transformed into a supporter of the smallest nation ever to qualify for the World Cup, she even convinced our twelve-year-old son, Jack, to support the Soca Warriors against England. When our next-door neighbours ran the flag of St George up their rusty flagpole, we sent off for the T&T flag, which we flew from our balcony.

Juliet and Jack looked up to it in pride, while I was quietly amused by the puzzlement it caused our friends in the village, who were most understanding when I explained that I had no choice in the matter as the majority in our house were supporting the islanders. Although Trinidad and Tobago didn't go on to win the World Cup, our participation in the flag fest had a positive result: everyone now knows that Juliet is from Trinidad, and Jack has gained a new dimension to his identity.

Juliet has since admitted to me that she was a little hesitant about coming out as a Trinny, concerned that by flying the flag of one of England's rivals we might attract the attentions of belligerent boneheads. She needn't have worried; the fact that Juliet's Trinidadian identity came as a surprise to our neighbours is indicative of the fact that, as a white woman growing up in Britain, her Caribbean background has not prevented her from being accepted as British.

As the 2006 World Cup flag fest was getting under way, I got a wry text from a mate of mine, Big Paul, a black Londoner, conscientious roadie, avid Gooner, on tour with a show in the north of England:

Hi Billy, in Sunderland just walked out of a newsagents, lady
in the shop asked me if I wanted to buy a St Georges Cross
flag for today's match England v Jamaica. I think the flag has
been reclaimed from the thugs, Bill.

The implication of the woman's question is as clear as that posed by Norman Tebbit: which side are you on? The irony of Big Paul's comment is that he'd spent many nights on the *England, Half English* tour listening to me tell audiences that we had to reclaim the flag.

Paul was born in England to Jamaican parents. When I texted him back to ask which team he'd be supporting that day, his answer came back quick as a flash: Arsenal. I smiled. This was his way of letting me know that he'd not changed his view on identity since we'd had a long discussion on the subject one night after a show.

C'mon Paul, I'd said to him, you were born in England, you speak English; admit it – you're English. No, he replied, I'm not. What are you, then? His response amazed me: I'm a Londoner and I'm a European. Me too, I said, but what about the bit in the middle? No. He shook his head. I'm not English and I'm not British. It puzzled me that he could make such a distinction. He explained it simply enough: in London, I'm accepted. Nobody questions my right to be there. But what about Europe? I asked. I'm glad to be a citizen of the EU, that's something that was given to me. I didn't have to kick down any doors to get it. So it's about acceptance, then? That's right. When I was growing up, I dreamed of playing football for England just like any other kid, but as you get older you realize that you're just not accepted. Now people want to accept me, I don't care. I don't need a flag to know who I am.

Big Paul and I are connected by a shared identity, but not one symbolized by the St George's flag or the Union Jack. We are both Londoners – even if one of us now lives in Dorset by the sea – and we are Europeans, both happy to be citizens of the EU. The fact that he has never felt accepted by England or Britain has not led Paul to completely reject society as a whole. Instead, he has placed his loyalty in those communities that nurtured him, declaring himself to be an urban internationalist in contrast to the provincial nationalism he encountered when growing up.

Paul's ability to construct his own sense of who he is illustrates that, rather than being a matter of blood and soil, identity is personal, each of us defining who we are, where our loyalties lie, how we relate to society. This only becomes problematical when someone else tries to tell you who you are, based on your colour, religion, accent or surname, seeking to deny your individuality by recourse to stereotype. The right of individuals to be who they want to be, say what they want to say, go where they want to go and believe what they want to believe should be sacrosanct in a democracy, as should the extension of those same rights to every other individual in society. Respect is the key to this equation, and freedom its end result.

We can't force Big Paul to be British if he feels that he has never been accepted as such. We have to respect his own sense of identity, based as it is on his own experiences. The question that we need to be asking those who feel excluded – whether by race, religion, culture or politics – is not 'Are you British?' but rather 'Where do you call home?' If that place is within Britain, then we can begin to construct an inclusive sense of identity based upon the notion of where you are rather than where your parents or grandparents were from.

Establishing space rather than race as our foundation, we can imagine a Britishness which is the sum of every building, field, road, path; every food, custom, belief, culture; every person – in fact, everything that is in Britain today, a Britishness that can only be truly appreciated by understanding how and why these things came to be here. The British identity is well placed to encompass such diversity. Assimilation has not, historically, been a prerequisite for inclusion; the Scots and the Welsh have been able to hold on to their national identities, the latter through seven hundred years of English subjugation. Far from being the antithesis of multiculturalism, Britishness has that very concept at its heart, the Union Jack a visual representation of the coming together of people of different nationalities, ethnicities and faiths to form a modern state.

But how do newcomers fit into our island story? Is there room in this concept of Britishness for those whose ancestors were not here when Magna Carta was written or the Bill of

Rights passed? Does history have anything to offer the excluded?

I am the first in my family line to have been born in a time of universal suffrage. Full participatory democracy was only achieved during my father's lifetime. When my grandfather was called up to join the 28th Middlesex Regiment in November 1915, he and millions like him did not have the right to vote. My great-grandfather had to take industrial action to gain recognition of his right to be treated fairly. And his grandfather was prepared to be ostracized in his own community for his belief in freedom of conscience.

My ancestors were not included in the provisions of Magna Carta or the Bill of Rights. Over the centuries, the struggle for inclusion has been defined time and again in terms of social justice, each successful generation helping those who followed. The non-conformists supported the early trade unionists in their battle for recognition; the trade unions supported the formation of the Labour Party to represent ordinary working people; the Labour Party supported the Suffragettes; women voters were decisive in the landslide that led to the formation of the Welfare State; the children of that bright dawn marched alongside post-war migrants as they fought for their rights in the seventies and eighties.

This process didn't end with the election of New Labour in 1997. Far from it. As someone once said, liberty is always unfinished business. Each wave of newcomers has to negotiate the hostility of the settled population, just as the working people of this country had to endure the opposition of the gentry to their aspirations.

The newcomers don't want to be merely accommodated – they want to be accepted. Willing to take their place at the back of the queue, they seek nothing more than a level playing field which allows them to progress, as those before them have done, from the margins to the centre ground. To do so, they rely upon those British values of fairness, tolerance and decency that we claim to care so much about.

A citizen-led debate about the formulation of a Declaration of Rights would undoubtedly bring such values to the fore, while arguments about the limits of individual freedom would serve to underscore the responsibilities that we owe to each other as members of society. In the process of defining our fundamental rights, we have an opportunity to strengthen the bonds that bind us together by reminding each other that our freedom to do as we please is both circumscribed by and reliant upon the responsible behaviour of everybody else.

The modern cult of consumer individualism has undermined our sense of collective responsibility by focussing our attention on our own short-term needs. As a result, respect has become such a scarce commodity in our society that some, mistakenly equating it with fame, are willing to debase themselves in the hope of gaining it.

Yet respect for the rights of others is the crucial component of individual freedom. Ask anybody who has ever been bullied; when another more powerful individual chooses not to respect your rights as a human being, your freedom of movement, of association, of dress, of expression can all be severely curtailed.

Thus a document which contained a set of universal rights would not only serve the purpose of protecting us as individuals from the more powerful, but also encourage social solidarity across divisions of gender, race, faith and class. Respect for the rights of others, no matter what their background – the traditional British value of fairness – is the foundation of a cohesive society.

The need for such social solidarity is vital in an age of mass migration. Mainstream politicians, cowed by the constant flow of negative headlines about 'bogus asylum-seekers' in the right-wing press, are afraid of the reaction they might get from voters if they stand up for the rights of economic migrants. Yet British businesses actively seek the cheapest labour in an effort to maximize profits.

People complain that they have never been consulted about the changes that have been forced on them, as if vacancies in low-paid jobs could somehow be subject to a democratic mandate before being filled. The unpalatable truth is that our booming economy is built on the exploitation of workers who are desperate enough to accept conditions that few Britons will tolerate.

When people say that immigrants 'do the jobs that no one wants', the picture it paints is of the most disgusting and base forms of employment, too dirty or dangerous for the average citizen. In fact, immigrants do very ordinary jobs; it's the conditions of their employment that no one wants. They work the longest hours for the lowest wages and can be hired and fired at a moment's notice. Those who are illegal live in fear of being betrayed to the authorities, and if they are taken advantage of by unscrupulous employers, they have no mechanism by which to have their complaints taken seriously.

A Declaration of Rights which had at its core our ancient tradition of holding those in power to account would have to concern itself with the workplace, and not just for the benefit of the lowest paid. Any hope of attaining some semblance of a genuine work–life balance for the majority of the population will need to rely on more than the goodwill of employers.

Our history teaches us that workers' rights have an important role to play in the creation of a cohesive society. It was the struggle to obtain a better work–life balance, begun by the gas labourers at Beckton in the 1880s, that led ultimately to the formation of the Welfare State in 1948. The role of my ancestors in this struggle places me firmly in the dissenting vein of the many traditions that make up our national character. However, this label is something of a misnomer. Portrayed as oppositionist and disloyal by those in power, the dissenting tradition has nurtured and extolled the concept of fairness which has become central to our sense of who we are.

It is not a tradition which relies on foreign philosophies or imported ideas; rooted firmly in the demands of Magna Carta and the opposition to Charles I, it is part of the core fabric of our nation. Ruthlessly resisted by the status quo, it has done more than any other tradition to shape our common values, each successive generation seeking to expand on these ideas for the benefit of those excluded by faith, race, gender and economics.

It has done so in the cause of a fairer society, in which the freedom of the individual is underpinned by the collective provision of education, health care, housing and pensions. This principle of fairness, revolutionary at the start of the twentieth century, has come to define us as a nation and it is one of which I am immensely proud.

Defending our rights, campaigning for greater accountability, fighting for social justice, standing up for the traditional value of fairness: these are the things which mark me out as a patriot. Rather than pledge my loyalty to someone else's idea of Britishness, I know my history well enough to appreciate that it is my tradition which has done so much to shape our society by constantly working to broaden the definition of what it means to belong.

As the majority become nervous about perceived threats to their quality of life and standard of living, the challenge we face is stark: do we stay true to our belief in fairness and seek collective solutions to society's problems, or do we leave it to market forces to sort things out in the hope of personal enrichment? Do we extend the right to belong to those in our communities whose parents were born elsewhere, or do we attempt to keep the world at bay by closing our borders and turning on our neighbours? I believe in this country and in those traditional values which served my ancestors so well in the past. Through their constant struggle to be treated fairly they were able to bequeath to me the liberties that I enjoy today. In staying true to my inheritance, I hope to repay the debt I owe them by continuing to play my part in the creation of a fairer society, which we in turn can pass on to our children.

Notes

Introduction

1. Barking and Dagenham Council Assembly meeting, Agenda and Minutes, item 13, 17 May 2006.
2. *Observer*, 28 May 2006, p. 16.
3. 'Citizen Extra', Charter88, April 2006.
4. *Fascism and Zionism*, Suzanna Kokkonen, www.wzo.org.il/en/resources/view.asp?id=585

1. Apollo in Essex

1. www.yre.org.uk/history.html
2. *Mail on Sunday*, 9 April 2006.
3. *Uphall Update*, issue 3, February 1989.
4. *The Victoria County History of Essex*, vol. 5, 1966, p. 184.
5. Dr A. Sherratt, 'Linking Wessex with Three Rivers in Avon', *British Archaeology*, no. 20, www.britarch.ac.uk/ba/ba20/ba20feat.html
6. P. H. Reaney, *Place Names of Essex*, 1969, p. 11.
7. www.bbc.co.uk/cgi-bin/wales/learnwelsh/welsh_dictionary.pl

8. Gerlyver Kernewek-Sawsnek, *Lexicon of the Cornish Language*, www.pauldavies.net/cornish/lexicon.cfm
9. Agence Bretagne Presse, www.agencebretagnepresse.com/dico/dico.cgi
10. Pamela Greenwood, 'Uphall Camp, Ilford – an update', *London Archaeologist*, vol. 9, no. 8, spring 2001, p. 215.
11. *The Victoria County History of Essex*, vol. 5, 1966, p. 185.
12. www.molas.org.uk/projects/ELG/ssilford.asp
13. Nick Merriman, *Prehistoric London*, Museum of London, 1996, p. 40.
14. *London Archaeologist*, vol. 6, no. 4, autumn 1989, p. 96.
15. Barry Cunliffe, *Iron Age Communities in Britain*, 1991, p. 366.
16. 'Four department stores and almost three hundred shops, restaurants and cafés in an amazing 128,295 square metres of prime retail space', 'Lakeside' pdf, *Capital Shopping Centres*, May 2005.
17. Pamela Greenwood, 'Uphall Camp, Ilford – an update', *London Archaeologist*, vol. 9, no. 8, spring 2001, p. 214.
18. www.cronab.demon.co.uk/gua.htm
19. 'The State of the Borough: An Economic, Social and Environmental Audit of Barking and Dagenham', September 2003.
20. Sarah Kyambi, *Beyond Black and White*, IPPR, 2005.
21. 'The State of the Borough: An Economic, Social and Environmental Audit of Barking and Dagenham', September 2003.

2. The People of the Hyphen

1. Bede, *History of the English People*, chapter 12.
2. Ibid, chapter 13.

3. Ibid, chapter 14.
4. Ibid, chapter 15.
5. Home Office, *Life in the United Kingdom*, 2002, p. 19.
6. Bede, *History of the English People*, 1990 Penguin Classics edition, see D. H. Farmer's introduction, p. 24, 'Bede's famous account of the Angles, Saxons and Jutes reflected the political realities of his own time, rather than the archaeological realities to which he had no access.'
7. Procopius, *History of the Wars*, VIII xx 4–8.
8. Michael Lapidge *et al.*, eds, *The Blackwell Encyclopaedia of Anglo-Saxon England*, 1999, p. 194.

3. A Tradition of Dissent

1. R. R. Aspinall, 'The Dock Strike in London 1911', Docklands Museum archive (unpublished), 1985.
2. Thanks to Dave Topping at the Museum of London.
3. *A Short History of the Church and Its Pastors for the Past 150 Years*, Rattlesden Baptist Chapel, 1963.
4. J. H. Y. Briggs, *The English Baptists of the Nineteenth Century*, Baptist Historical Society, 1994.

4. Voices from Across the Ocean

1. Cecil Sharp, *English Folk Songs from the Southern Appalachians*, 1917, paperback edition 1968.
2. www.springthyme.co.uk/ballads/balladtexts/2_ElfinKnight.html

5. To England, Where My Heart Lies

1. Robert Cantwell, *When We Were Good*, 1996, p. 2.
2. Victoria Kingston, *Simon and Garfunkel: The Biography*, 1998, p. 19.

3. Clinton Heylin, *Bob Dylan: The Recording Sessions*, 1995, pp. 13–18.
4. Bob Dylan, *Chronicles: Volume 1*, 2004, p. 113.

6. Singing the History

1. Quentin Hogg, *The Case for Conservatism*, 1947, quoted in Peter Hennessey, *The Prime Minister*, 2000.
2. Some bloke I met in a pub in Whitstable, summer 2003.
3. Maria Misra, *Views of Empire*, BBC Radio 4, 30 May 2006.
4. Kathleen Woods Masalski, *Examining the Japanese History Textbook Controversies*, www.indiana.edu/~japan/Digests/textbook.html
5. Tim Collins, Shadow Education Secretary, quoted in *Daily Telegraph*, 27 January 2005.
6. *Daily Telegraph*, 2 December 2004.
7. Anthony Browne, 'The Left's War on Britishness', *Spectator*, 23 July 2005.
8. *Panorama*, BBC1, 20 June 2000.

7. Lions and Unicorns

1. Peter Hitchens, 'Why I can't wait for it all to be over for England', *Mail on Sunday*, 2 June 2002.
2. *Independent*, 24 February 1990.
3. Geoffrey Wheatcroft, *The Strange Death of Tory England*, 2005, p. 285.
4. Stanley Baldwin, speech to the annual dinner of the Royal Society of St George, 6 May 1924.
5. John Major, speech to the Conservative Group for Europe, 22 April 1993.

8. Rock Against Racism

1. *Answering the Asylum Myths*, SW TUC, 2004.
2. *Blackmore Vale Magazine*, 30 April 2004.
3. *Melody Maker*, 4 September 1976.
4. Nils and Ray Stevenson, *Vacant: A Diary of the Punk Years 1976–1979*, 1999, p. 43.
5. Pat Gilbert, *Passion Is a Fashion: The Real Story of The Clash*, 2004, p. 101.
6. 'Don't look over your shoulder, but the Sex Pistols are coming', *NME*, 21 February 1976.

9. The Old Country

1. Ubersichtskarte der Zielgebiete 1 bis 1V London Luftwaffe 1940, Winston G. Ramsey, *The East End Then and Now*, 1997, p. 334.
2. Winston G. Ramsey, *The Blitz Then and Now*, vol. 2, 1988, p. 488.

10. The Great Charter

1. Simon Heffer, *Daily Telegraph*, 10 December 2005.
2. Andrew Roberts, 'The best Dam film ever made', *Daily Mail*, 14 December 2005.
3. Angus Calder, *The People's War*, 1969, paperback edition 1992, p. 98.
4. The Beveridge Report, OHMS, 1942, paras 7, 8.
5. Ibid, paras 459, 461.
6. Magna Carta, 1215, chapter 35.
7. Petition of Right, 1628, clauses 3, 4.
8. *Magna Carta*, ed. Ralph V. Turner, 2003.
9. Geoffrey Robertson, *The Tyrannicide Brief*, 2005.

10. Thomas Paine, *Rights of Man*, Penguin Classics edition, p. 192.
11. Ibid, pp. 193, 196.
12. Ibid, p. 243.
13. E. P. Thompson, *The Making of the English Working Class*, 1991, p. 99.

11. Britishness *v.* Multiculturalism
1. Francis Maude, *Guardian*, 7 April 2006.
2. 'London: the world in one city', *Guardian*, G2, 21 January 2005.
3. Ibid.
4. *Sunday Times*, 31 July 2005.
5. *Daily Telegraph*, 27 July 2005.
6. Figures from 'Together', Imperial War Museum multi-media resource pack.
7. Public Record Office, CO 876/88.
8. Public Record Office, LAB 8/1499.
9. M. and T. Phillips, *Windrush: The Irresistible Rise of Multi-racial Britain*, 1998, p. 45.

12. The Rules Have Changed
1. Roy Jenkins, *Churchill*, 2001, p. 816.
2. 'Criminal records mix-up uncovered', http://news.bbc.co.uk/1/hi/uk/5001624.stm
3. Prime minister's press conference 5 August 2005, www.number-10.gov.uk/output/Page8.asp
4. http://www.conservatives.com/tile.do?def=news. story.page&obj_id=130572&speeches=1

13. Born Under Two Flags

1. 'England flags: patriotic or plain chav?', *Daily Mail*, 1 June 2006.
2. 'Flutters of anxiety', *Guardian*, 18 May 2006.

Acknowledgements

Writing a book is nothing like writing a song. The moment of inspiration that produces a new song is just that, a moment captured like a photograph. You may have another go to see if you can get a slightly better exposure, but basically it's there in a flash. And that's what I've been doing for a living these past twenty-five years: creating snapshots. In comparison, writing a book is like painting in oils on a twelve-by-twenty-foot canvas. You can spend a week on a single detail, only to lose sight of the overall work. Colour and shade are everything and sometimes ideas have to be completely rethought or even painted over. It's painstaking work which requires a sustained level of concentration to achieve results.

The genesis of this book can be found in my attempts to reconcile my love of folk music with my punk-rock sensibility. There was something very English about the levelling tendencies of the punk movement that struck a deep chord. However, it was not until I began working with my multi-instrumentalist band, the Blokes, that I was able to harness their talent for playing world music to give voice to my own sense of radical

Englishness. Following the release of our album *England, Half English*, I realized that there was much more to be explored on this issue and so the idea of writing a book was born.

My agent, Rachel Calder at Sayle Literary Agency, helped me to formulate my ideas and explained to me how the book trade worked. She found me a wonderful editor in Bill Scott-Kerr, whose enthusiasm for this project has matched my own. I want to thank him and his colleagues at Bantam Press for the encouragement they have given me and the patience they have shown while I learned, on the job, the skills required of an author.

Once I began writing, Camilla Roberts was a most helpful researcher, following leads and seeking out details. Linda Rhodes, the Local Studies Librarian at the Barking and Dagenham Local Studies Centre at Valence House Museum, Dagenham, provided important information on the history of my home town and my ancestors' role in it, as did Jenni Munro-Collins at the Newham Local Studies Library in Stratford. My grasp of the significance of Uphall Camp for the London area was greatly enhanced by a chat with Jon Cotton at the Museum of London. Jane Sidell at the UCL Institute of Archaeology shared with me her knowledge of the Thames and its tributaries during the Iron Age. Michael Leach of the Essex Society for Archaeology and History kindly provided access to the Society's papers on Uphall Camp.

Jeff Place at the Smithsonian Centre for Folk Life and Culture sent me a whole dossier on the Anglo-American folk-music tradition; Malcolm Taylor, Librarian at the Vaughan Williams Library, provided the background for the song 'Scarborough Fair' and others; and Stuart Wheeler, Assistant Librarian, The Archive and Reference Library, The Tank

Museum, Bovington, Dorset, was kind enough to supply me with background details of the movements of my father's regiment in India between 1945 and 1947.

Thanks are due to Patrick Wright for the encouragement he showed when I first contemplated this book, and to Martin Carthy, who never tired of my constant queries about the sixties folk boom. Also to Paul Stinchcombe, who had a huge influence on my understanding of human-rights legislation and constitutional reform. He was just one of a number of people who were kind enough to read chapters, offer thoughts and ask pertinent questions, among them Tanya Ott in Berlin, who crucially brought an outsider's perspective to my arguments about Englishness.

My manager, Peter Jenner, and everyone at Sincere Management were kind enough to give me their encouragement while I put my musical career on hold in order to write this book.

None of this would have been possible without the support of my family, who have had to live with this project for the past couple of years. Writing is a solitary affair and the commitment involved is often at odds with family life. My missus, Juliet, our son Jack and my godson Jamie had no choice but to go through this process with me and I love them all the more for it.

Lastly, I want to thank my father, Dennis, for providing me with a strong sense of history, and my mother, Marie, for instilling in me her fierce sense of independence.